For John Raines,
who inspired so much of this.
In profound gratitude & appreciation,

Philadelphia
January 2008

Bourdieu on Religion

Key Thinkers in the Study of Religion

Edited by Steven Engler, Mount Royal College, Canada

Key Thinkers in the Study of Religion is a series of compact introductions to the life and work of major figures in the study of religion. Each volume provides up-to-date critical evaluations of the place and value of a single scholar's work, in a manner both accessible to students and useful for instructors. Each volume includes a brief biography, analyses of key works, evaluations of criticisms and of overall impact on the field, and discussions of the work of later scholars who have appropriated or extended each key thinker's approach. Critical engagement with each key thinker's major works makes each volume a useful companion for the study of these important sources in the field. Aimed at the undergraduate and introductory graduate classrooms, the series encapsulates and evaluates foundational contributions to the academic study of religion.

This series is sponsored by the North American Association for the Study of Religion (NAASR), an affiliate of the International Association for the History of Religions.

Forthcoming:

Dumont on Religion
Ivan Strenski

Lévi-Strauss on Religion
Paul-François Tremlett

Derrida on Religion
Dawne McCance

Bourdieu on Religion

Imposing Faith and Legitimacy

Terry Rey

LONDON   OAKVILLE

Published by Equinox Publishing Ltd.

UK: Unit 6, The Village, 101 Amies St., London SW11 2JW
USA: DBBC, 28 Main Street, Oakville, CT 06779

www.equinoxpub.com

First published 2007

British Library Cataloguing-in-Publication Data

A catalogue record for this book is available from the British Library.

ISBN   978 1 84553 285 7 (hardback)
ISBN   978 1 84553 286 4 (paperback)

Library of Congress Cataloging-in-Publication Data

Rey, Terry.
  Bourdieu on religion : imposing faith and legitimacy / Terry Rey.
      p. cm. — (Key thinkers in the study of religion)
  Includes bibliographical references and index.
  ISBN-13: 978-1-84553-285-7 (hb)
  ISBN-13: 978-1-84553-286-4 (pb)
1. Bourdieu, Pierre, 1930-2002. 2. Religion and sociology. I. Title.
  BL60.R49 2007
    306.6092—dc22
                              2007020457

Typeset by S.J.I. Services, New Delhi
Printed and bound in Great Britain by Lightning Source UK Ltd, Milton Keynes,
and Lightning Source Inc., La Vergne, TN

Dedicated to

John C. Raines,
mentor, colleague, and friend

Contents

Preface

Provincialism and ethnocentrism come in many forms, not least of which is under an academic, scholarly guise. The social-scientific study of religion is, of course, not immune to such hazards – showing, for instance, in our choice of topics, our implicit cultural assumptions, the bibliography of many of our studies, and/or our range of theoretical toolkits (limited, for instance, to just one discipline, gender, language, school, and/or region of the globe).

Not that such trap was successfully avoided at all times by Pierre Bourdieu – or by Terry Rey, or by myself, for that matter – but maybe those risks are part and parcel of the reasons why Bourdieu has been so conspicuously absent, and for so long, from the reaches of our discipline.

Pierre Bourdieu (1930–2002) is considered in many quarters as one of the most influential thinkers of the second half of the twentieth century. A sociologist, indeed, but no less of an ethnologist, an anthropologist, a linguist, and a philosopher, with a postmodern bent for flouting and cross-pollinating disciplinary traditions, Bourdieu was an heir, among others, of the work of Marx, Engels, Weber, and Durkheim – and not least of their work *on religion*, precisely. Surprisingly, however, his name is often all but unknown for many (most?) US specialists in the social-scientific study of religions.

Whatever the basis for that absence, the fact is that – much later, indeed, than in certain parts of Europe or of the so-called Third World – Pierre Bourdieu is only now, at the onset of the twenty-first century, barely beginning to be noticed, read, utilized, cited, taught and critiqued in the English-speaking sociology of religions (Swartz 1996 is an important exception). This is true even as several other disciplines and fields (anthropology, ethnology, art history, linguistics or literary criticism, as well as the 'sociologies of' culture, education, language, literature, etc.), in many cases within and beyond the US, were taking serious note, in some cases for decades, of Bourdieu's crucial contributions to the study of cultural processes.

Gladly, things now seem to be veering in a different direction, at a faster pace.

This work of Terry Rey is a more than welcome gift to the social-scientific study of religion. It does the much needed groundwork not only

of presenting Bourdieu's life, work, influences and thought to a reader-
ship interested in the social-scientific study of religion, but also of sum-
marizing at length the works of Bourdieu most relevant for such disciplinary focus (too many of which, sadly, are yet to be translated into English),
of developing what a Bourdieuan 'Theory of Religious Practice' would
look like, and of suggesting several ways in which Bourdieu's ideas might
help the specialists conduct their research on religion – all without skirting
the critical task of pointing out the biases, weaknesses and limitations that
(like any and all other theories in every discipline) Bourdieu's work has for
such a task.

   Welcome to a unique study of Pierre Bourdieu's crucial contributions
to the sociological study of religions!

Otto Maduro
Drew University, Madison, NJ

Acknowledgements

dans la géographie des siècles
sur la terre comme au ciel
  la détresse de l'Ancêtre m'est familière
                    Robert Berrouët-Oriol, 'Aux tribus trépassées', 2005

This book is dedicated to John C. Raines, mentor, colleague and friend, who encouraged me to write it and provided invaluable feedback on earlier drafts. John also first introduced me to the work of Pierre Bourdieu about fifteen years ago, when I was preparing my doctoral dissertation on the cult of the Virgin Mary in Haiti. It was a theoretical epiphany for me; Bourdieu made perfect sense for interpreting religion in a former French colony, one characterized by drastic class distinctions, where a Catholic hierarchy, in alliance with the State and the economic elite, has historically waged campaigns to squelch a heresiarch in the form of the Vodou priest or priestess. I am deeply grateful to have had John as a teacher, as I know are many other scholars in my field today, and I'm most gratified to now be his colleague in the Department of Religion at Temple University. Thanks, also, to several other colleagues at Temple, namely Rebecca Alpert, Lucy Bregman, Jon Pahl, Leonard Swidler, David Harrington Watt and Benjamin Zeller, for sharing relevant and important insights and ideas with me on the sixth floor at Anderson Hall. I can think of no other place that I would rather call my intellectual home, where just last year I subjected the students of my graduate seminar in 'Religion, Race, and Ethnicity' to reading an early draft of Chapter 4 of this book; for their having done so critically, and for having responded with excellent comments and suggestions, I'm grateful to Mary Virginia Cale, Kipp Gilmore-Clough, Rachael Kamel, Dave Krueger, Elizabeth Lawson, Markus Lere Dawa, Charles Bryan MacAdam, Suzanne Parlier and Tricia Way.

Many other people helped or supported me during the writing of this book in a variety or ways, big and small, from reading parts or all of the manuscript and providing feedback, to sharing a single reference, citation, image, or idea. I'll spare you the details of how they each helped, though not out of any lack of appreciation whatsoever. Abundant thanks thus to Thomas Alkemeyer, Omer Awass, John Bailly, Jesse Bull, Katie Cannon, John F. Clark, Bishop Dillon, Julian Edward, Bridget Fowler, Istar Gozaydin, Hans Haacke, Valerie Hall, Leon-François Hoffmann, Mathew Hunter, Janet Joyce, Gereon Kopf, Lene Kühle, Sarah Mahler, Sarah

Norman, Lesley Northup, Deborah O'Neil, Marie-Christine Rivière, Claudia Schippert, Franz Schultheis, David J. Silverman, Beril Sözmen, Alex Stepick, Oren Baruch Stier, Jörg Stolz, R. Christopher Stone, Stanley Stowers, Ivan Strenski, James H. Sweet, Alfons Teipen, Loïc Wacquant, Joseph L. Walsh, R. Alan Warde, R. Stephen Warner, and of course to Steven Engler for inviting me to write this book in the first place, for providing critical comments on earlier drafts, and for editing the important series in which *Bourdieu on Religion* takes its place. Extra special thanks to Otto Maduro, one of the pioneers in the Bourdieuian interpretation of religion, for reading earlier drafts of parts of the manuscript, providing excellent feedback, and for writing such a wonderful preface to grace *Bourdieu on Religion*. And last but most, I would like to thank my family for their love and support, and for their patience with my occasional incursions into virtual absenteeism while writing this book. *Entonces, muchas gracias desde el fondo de mi corazón a María de los Ángeles, Nathaniel Joseph, Thoraya Marie, Isabella Linda, y Fabio. Ayibobo!*

Philadelphia, Ash Wednesday 2007

Introduction

I am not Jesus Christ. I am a sociologist, not a prophet. I refuse the chalice that one extends to me, asking me to take upon myself all the misery of the world. And nevertheless, I can hardly keep myself from doing so, revolted but resigned to drink this bitter chalice to the dregs. . . (in Passeron 2003, 26).[1]

'*The prestructured is everywhere*', in Pierre Bourdieu's vision of the social world. 'The sociologist is literally beleaguered by it, as everybody else is' (in Bourdieu and Wacquant 1992, 235). We are indeed born and raised in a world that we did not create, and we go forth into it, negotiate it, and die in it without critically reflecting upon—at least in any sustained fashion—why things are the way that they are. We go through life dutifully abiding by our societies' laws and adopting its conveyances in a generally rather automatist fashion, thus 'socialized and led to feel "like a fish in water"' (ibid.). We speak languages that only become ours because from birth we are bombarded by them and not others, and we go about speaking, hearing, reading and writing them as second nature, largely inconsiderate of just how it is that they came to be our native tongues in the first place. We learn in schools that were built by others before us and follow a prefabricated curriculum therein; we pray in churches, mosques or synagogues where we are told God resides, in ways we are told that God ordains; and we buy things that we believe that that we need, often regardless of whether or not we really do. Our possibilities in life are thus largely determined by the proverbial hands that we are dealt, and most of us simply accept this, more or less, as fate, happenstance, or God's will, and we exert ourselves as best we can so as to avoid pain and suffering for ourselves and those dependent upon us along life's way. And even if we wish to analyze and understand why things are this way, most of us haven't the time, energy or wherewithal to do so. Hence very few people actually manage to even periodically engage in such forms of critical social reflection; fewer still devote a lifetime to such an endeavor, and only a handful gain international renown thereby. Pierre Bourdieu was one such rare person, endowed, as he was, with an ever rarer genius. His massive body of work questions the authorities, traditions and assumptions that determine most things for most people in human society, and it questions them in ways that are as radical as they are sometimes even shocking. Bourdieu (1990a, 127) tells us, for instance, that honor is nothing less than a lie that dupes us into accepting the injustices of our world, just like religion.

Reading Bourdieu—especially of course if he convinces you—can thus be a tremendously disconcerting experience, though one that, paradoxically, inspires at the same time a striking sense of liberation.[2] This experience is beautifully described by Annie Ernaux (2005, 163–64), one of contemporary France's greatest writers:

> Bourdieuian sociology . . . produces a real uprooting of the self; [it's] brutal. All the beliefs that prior oriented one's very functioning, on which one constructs her life, her future, her way of life, briskly collapse. The veil is torn, yes… [I]t completely changed my outlook on the global function of society, on its hierarchies, the use of languages . . . It really had a liberating effect, to the extent that knowing things, understanding how domination functions, simply to understand why one has ever felt socially inferior; [t]his clarified, elucidated the social foundations of the very struggle to be, of the malaise that, until then, was experienced in darkness, and in suffering. From the moment one can explain things socially, in one fell swoop, it's a wholesome breath of freedom!

Bourdieu is certainly not alone in thus shaking up his readers' sense of who they are and of what the world is all about. In this regard, he takes his place in a long line of iconoclastic thinkers in the history of Western philosophy who radically, and often convincingly, question how reality is constructed and perceived. Since the great pre-Socratic Greek philosopher Parmenides, they tell us that things are just not as they appear. Think Plato's cave, Rousseau's free-born man in chains, Berkeley's nonexistent unperceived things, Marx's opium of the people, Nietzsche's transvaluation of values, Heidegger's being-for-another, Sartre's nothingness, and so forth. And, lest one find it curious that I allude here to *philosophers* to introduce one of the contemporary world's most famous *sociologists*, I am justified in doing so for a couple of important reasons: for one thing, Bourdieu was trained as a philosopher and not a social scientist, and certain Western philosophical ideas are as strongly influential on his 'theory of practice' as any that derive from sociology or anthropology proper; and for another, Bourdieu (1990b, 28) conceived of his own professional academic work as something like '*fieldwork in philosophy*', and as a 'sociology of knowledge' designed to 'realize one of the eternal ambitions of philosophy—discovering cognitive structures . . . and at the same time uncovering some of the best-concealed limits of thought' (ibid., 16).

By the end of the twentieth century, Pierre Bourdieu (1930–2002) was widely considered to be one of the greatest social theorists of our time, having effectively cemented his place among such 'masters of the hermeneutic of suspicion', in the descriptive words of Paul Ricouer (1970, 32). His hundreds of essays, dozens of books and numerous interviews cover such a broad range of topics as to defy convenient generalizations or neat schemes of classification,[3] and it is almost unthinkable that anyone could read and understand everything that he wrote (thus, his readers should always employ a hermeneutic of suspicion of their own anytime a commentator or critic says something like, 'Nowhere does Bourdieu account for X...'). For one thing, there is a great deal of it, while for another, it is mostly written in highly complex language that often requires painstaking analysis and careful unpacking in order to be soundly comprehended. Despite this complexity, his influence has been enormous in areas that most occupied him directly, namely the study of education, cultural production, social structures and human practice, while it has also spread into realms about which he wrote little or nothing. Such breadth of interpretive applicability is explicable in terms of the brilliance, flexibility and subtlety of his 'theory of practice', or his model for the analysis of human action ('practice') in 'social space' or 'fields', which has already stood the test of time and been demonstrated to be of powerful use in the analysis of virtually any aspect of social life, from *haute cuisine* in Paris, to gender relations on the floor of the stock exchange; from divination in Nigeria, to elementary education in Japan; from funerary practices in Denmark, to the use of toys among American children, and so on.

If Sartre was France's leading intellectual during the first half of the twentieth century, Bourdieu was during the second. This century was not nearly finished before its epic violence had inspired clichés in disbelief: 'The twentieth century is the most violent in human history'; 'There have been more wars in the twentieth century than in any other century'. Major advances in technology, to be sure, played a central role in creating the premises on which these clichés were founded: electronic communications, atomic energy, air travel, to name a few. As much as these changed the world forever, they certainly also served as handmaidens to the unprecedented global violence that marked and perhaps indeed defined the twentieth century. This is not to suggest, however, that humans are any more violent nowadays than we ever were. We are as much the 'noble savage' today as we were in 1762, when Rousseau opined that we are 'born free' but are 'everywhere in chains'. Put otherwise and more broadly, things are not as they appear. This is one of the oldest and most constant assertions in the history of the Western philosophical tradition to which Rousseau and Sartre belong, and in which Bourdieu was initially trained. By 'in chains' Rousseau meant that we are corrupted,

limited, and arbitrarily misshaped by society in such a way that our peaceful coexistence would require some kind of a 'social contract'.

With the advent of the Industrial Revolution and its creation of new
forms of misery for the urban underclasses of Europe and North America,
it had become apparent to some social philosophers that humanity could
not accept on 'good faith' any 'social contract' that was worded by the
wealthy or otherwise dominant sectors of society. As Marx and Engels
(1976, 67) argued in 1845, 'the ideas of the ruling class are in every
epoch the ruling ideas', and thus society is structured arbitrarily to their
advantage in such a way that members of the underclasses exhibit a kind
of 'false consciousness' that causes their unwitting ascent to processes
and forces that actually harm them. About 100 years later, Sartre (1984,
291) wrote in a similar vein that any facile acceptance of the way that
things are (or of the status quo) was simply an expression of 'bad faith', or
that 'determined attitude which is essential to human reality and which is
such that consciousness instead of directing its negation outward turns
toward itself'. In simpler terms, we act in 'bad faith' when we accept as
true any uninvestigated claim that belies the *existential reality* that we,
and we alone, are absolutely responsible for what we are and what we
become; because there is no essential grounding to our existence, we
are 'condemned to be free' (ibid., 707). Adherence to any form of belief,
religious or other, that grounds or legitimates itself on some putative essence is, for Sartre, 'bad faith' and a manifestation of deplorable human
irresponsibility.

This kind of hermeneutic of suspicion quite naturally engenders dis-
sent and is akin to what Bourdieu (1992) termed 'radical doubt', which
consists of 'scrupulous epistemological attention' (Lee 2005, 352) to the
arbitrary assumptions that inevitably underlie all forms of knowledge. In
other words, all truth is relative, all absolutes are illusory, and to exercise
radical doubt sociologically is to be on the lookout especially for those
assumptions and putative absolutes that establish and perpetuate social
inequalities and injustice because '[a]ppearances are always in favor of
the apparent' (in Bourdieu and Wacquant 1992, 246): 'In the social sciences, as we all know, epistemological breaks are often social breaks,
breaks with fundamental beliefs of a group and, sometimes, with the
core beliefs of the body of professionals, with the body of shared certain-
ties that found the *communis doctorum opinio*. To practice radical doubt,
in sociology, is akin to becoming an outlaw' (ibid., 241). Radical doubt is
a means by which the social theorist sustains consideration of 'what ought
to be the object of knowledge, that is, everything that constitutes the
practical sense of the social world, the presuppositions, the schemata of
perceptions and understanding that give the lived world its structure', or

of '*everything that makes the doxic experience of the world possible*, that is, not only the preconstructed representation of this world but also the cognitive schemata that underlie the construction of this image' (ibid., 247, original italics). By 'doxic experience of the world' is meant, colloquially speaking, the often tacitly accepted 'rules of the game', be it the game of education, art, politics or religion.

Bourdieu thus inherits the spirit of radical doubt from some of the major figures in the history of Western philosophy, and his driving aim as a scholar was to transform this *philosophical spirit* into a *scientific sociology* that could effectively reveal the causes of the reproduction of domination in human society. His is thus a 'strong sociology', as Robert Castel puts it in language echoing the Gospel of John, one that is 'based on the essential recognition that *in the beginning was constraint, and constraint was made society*, and that it is comprised first and foremost of constraints' (2003, 349; italics added). Or, as Loïc Wacquant (in Bourdieu and Wacquant 1992, 14) explains, 'the whole of Bourdieu's work may be interpreted as a materialist anthropology of the specific contribution that various forms of symbolic violence make to the reproduction and transformation of structures of domination'. By 'symbolic violence', Bourdieu means the imposition by the dominant of arbitrary forms and systems of meanings of the social order that are 'misrecognized' by the dominated as somehow un-arbitrary and natural, or that form of violence that 'can be exercised only with that sort of complicity . . . via the effect of misrecognition encouraged by denial, by those on whom that violence is exercised' (Bourdieu 1991d, 210). To claim, for instance, that one person's poverty and another's wealth are the will of God, and that they therefore must be accepted, is a glaring case in point, and to 'impose' this belief upon others, or to 'inculcate' it into their 'vision of the world' is, for Bourdieu, an act of symbolic violence par excellence. Therein lies one of the main reasons why Bourdieu is so useful to the study of religion: to demonstrate the role of religion in the establishment, legitimization and reproduction of social inequality and all of its incumbent injustices.

But whatever *good* that religion has contributed to humanity is seemingly of no interest to Bourdieu. Likewise, his work pays virtually no attention to spirituality as the widespread human phenomenon that it is, to say nothing of mystical experience. 'Bourdieu himself was not religious' (Swartz and Zolberg 2004, 5), he 'manifested no inclination for religious activity' (Dianteill 2004, 84), and, as Derek Robbins's (1991, 96) careful reading demonstrates, he 'argued, in the face of the pre-notions of centuries of belief reinforced by 100 years of analytical sociology of religion, that no attitudes of beliefs are intrinsically religious'. The numinous and the sacred, the transcendent and the holy, as it were, are out of bounds to the scientistic sociology that Bourdieu promoted and practiced. As Deborah Reed-Danahay (2005, 43) observes, furthermore, '[n]either in his work on rural France nor on his work in urban settings, did Bourdieu explicitly take into account the existence of the church, despite the enormous influence that the Catholic Church has had on French society. I am not suggesting that he was not aware of that influence but, rather, that he chose (or his habitus predisposed him) to marginalize that influence in his own work'.[4] And, so, religious people, theologians and scholars of religion concerned with the positive side of religion, which consists of course in significant part in its demonstrable capacity to inspire compassion, charity, and peace of mind, will probably find Bourdieu's positions on religion to be ultimately limited, disappointing and frustrating.[5] God, for Bourdieu, is but a socially constructed illusion, and religion is an ultimately unnecessary system of symbolic meaning that serves chiefly to perpetuate social domination by duping people into accepting their stations in society as somehow being natural or, worse still, divinely sanctioned. Religion thus forges no true anchor for humanity, affords little of substance to improve the human condition, and is in the end but a desperate attempt to create meaning in an otherwise meaningless world.

It is important to note, though, that Bourdieu (2000b, 123) *does* affirm that religion provides people with meaning:

> The Weberian definition is indeed satisfying to me: religion is a systematic answer to the question of life and death; isn't that a fine definition? Of course there are 'existential' questions, but in conjunction with them one should also be sure to consider the 'transcendental', i.e. the collective conditions of the transcendental; questions about life and death, the death of people we love, the 'ultimate' questions, illness, human suffering. Questions to which humans never find answers on their own; religion provides them answers to such ultimate questions, or rather: quasi-systematic answers, not systematic as in logic. It gives coherence to those discontinuous events of our lives, provides concrete coherence for abstract contingencies; in doing so it resembles philosophy, a 'total' explanation of the world.[6]

However, even if they are to 'ultimate questions', the answers that religion provides and religion's 'total explanation of the world' are themselves, for Bourdieu, in the last instance entirely groundless: 'Doomed to death, that end which cannot be taken as an end, man is a being without a reason for being. It is society, and society alone, which dispenses, to different degrees, the justifications and the reasons for existing' (Bourdieu 1990b, 196). And so Bourdieu (ibid., 15) speaks of the '[w]retchedness of man without God or any hope of grace—a wretchedness that the sociologist merely brings to light, and for which he is made responsible, like all prophets of evil tidings. But you can kill the messenger: what he says is still true, and has still been heard'. For this reason does our French sociologist *cum* prophet find 'ridiculous' any intellectual designs 'to save spiritual values from the threat of science' (ibid., 14).

It is thus not surprising that Bourdieu's position vis-à-vis religion and/or key aspects thereof have been variously described as 'hostile' (Urban 2003, 355) and 'pessimistic and static' (ibid., 364); 'Voltairean', 'unidimensional' (Verter 2003, 151) and 'too insular' (ibid., 156); 'essentially Latin' (Robertson 1992, 154); 'mechanistic' (Dillon 2001, 411); 'hypermaterialistic' (Schultheis, forthcoming); 'culturally homogenous' and 'instrumentalized' (Friedland 1999, 307); 'first and foremost, a sociology of Catholicism' (Dianteill 2004, 71); and an 'atheist materialism' (Dubuisson 2003, 164); one that is plagued by 'a sort of historicist assumption' (Tanner 2005, 15) and by a narrow-mindedness that misses entirely 'the possibility of a struggle toward a noncompetitively defined religious field' (ibid., 23); and that sees religion to be just another of the 'artificial discourses' (Robbins 1991, 96) constructed principally by the dominant of human society. Elsewhere in this book I add 'top heavy' and 'generally adversative' to this list. And, yet, none of this is stopping a growing cadre of scholars of religion (even some theologians![7]) from employing Bourdieuian theory with much profit, and for the most part they are doing so in ways that are *not* negatively disposed or antagonistic toward their subject.

Although Bourdieu was clearly no friend to religion, and although he wrote relatively (by his standards) little on the subject, religion is a—if not *the*—most fundamental influence on his understanding of society. That is to say, along with capitalistic economics, religion, or at least the hierarchical Catholic form that dominated much of Western European history, provided Bourdieu with *the* most useful paradigm for identifying and critiquing *all* institutionalized systems of meaning that help create, legitimate and reproduce unequal and unjust social orders, and which give people a 'practical sense' of their positions therein and of what they can expect from life. Religion, furthermore, is one of several such 'symbolic systems'; and whereas it was once dominant among them, its power in contemporary Western society, especially from the modern European perspective from which Bourdieu observed the world and wrote about it, is, he felt, in rather serious decline, being today surpassed by the State as the most powerful agent of consecration (Engler 2003). Hence for Bourdieu (1982, 21), the primary task of critical social theory is to unveil 'the *self deception*, the lie which is collectively maintained and fostered and which, in every society, is at the foundation of the most sacred values', be they 'the most sacred values' of the Catholic Church, the United States Government, or the International Monetary Fund.

Bourdieu's critique of religion is thus aimed, almost exclusively, at religion's function in the creation and consecration of social distinctions and inequalities, or in the reproduction of social domination. In this regard, though, he by no means singles out religion for critique (*nothing* is sacred, so to speak, for Bourdieu, and hence everything is open game), however much religion, along with economics, serves as a paradigmatic model for Bourdieu's decidedly anti-institutional social theory at large. This is evinced by his frequent use of religious metaphors to speak of everything from education and art, to politics and society—all of which are subjected in Bourdieu's work to the sustained and monumental program of critique of this 'master of suspicion' and 'fierce adversary of all forms of deification' (Bège 2004, 273).[8]

'Orthodoxy', 'heresy', 'sacred', 'consecration', 'priest', 'prophet', 'sorcerer', 'heresiarch', 'dogma', 'doctrine', 'transubstantiation', 'sacraments', 'veneration' and 'theodicy' count among the terms that Bourdieu frequently adopts from a religious vocabulary to explain a whole range of 'secular' social institutions and practices. For one colorful example from among the dozens, if not hundreds, that pervade his work: 'The religion of art also has its integrists and modernists, though ones who stand in agreement toward posing the question of cultural salvation in the language of grace' (Bourdieu and Darbel 1969, 13). David Swartz (1997, 47) demonstrates how Durkheim's sociology of religion, furthermore, especially his famous sacred/profane distinction, provides Bourdieu with one of the most important paradigms in his social theory, though this particular instance, it must be said, is clearly more metaphoric than analytical:

> Bourdieu extends Durkheim's sacred/profane opposition to an analysis of contemporary cultural forms. . . More generally, Bourdieu believes that the religious sacred is but a particular case of the more general idea that social distinctions, whether applied to individuals, groups, or institutions, assume a taken-for-granted quality that elicits acceptance and respect. Symbolic power is a power 'to consecrate', to render sacred. He thus associates the concept of the sacred with legitimation, particularly in high culture and art where boundaries are particularly strong. In this sense, he can declare that his sociology of culture is in reality a 'science of the sacred'.

In other words, for Bourdieu (in Monod 2002, 245) '[a]ll that is sacred has its complementary profane, and all distinction produces its vulgarity'. It is in this light, moreover, that we are to understand Bourdieu's (1994b, 132) assertion that 'the sociology of culture is the sociology of religion of our day'.

As will be discussed at length in the chapters that follow, clearly exceeding Durkheim in this regard, the great German sociologist Max Weber is the most powerful influence on not only Bourdieu's sociology of religion but his sociology in general. Bourdieu's (1990b, 46) locating religion's 'practical logic' in economics, for a prime example, derives from Weber in the sense that 'economics is one of the major reference points for sociology. First and foremost because economics is already part of sociology, largely due to the work of Weber, who transferred numerous models of thought borrowed from economics into the area of religion'. Thus over and above providing him with metaphors, as oriented by Weber's sociology of religion, Bourdieu's observations of the social functions and the 'practical logic' of religion had an important role in shaping on a fundamental level his entire theory of practice, and contributed to the development of some of its most essential concepts. 'In Bourdieu's work', as Erwan Dianteill (2004, 66) demonstrates, 'the notions of "belief", "field" or "*habitus*" always result from the social sciences of religion (sociology, anthropology, history). From this point of view, Bourdieu's work is almost a "generalized" sociology of religion (with religion representing in paradigmatic fashion properties common to all spheres of symbolic activity)'.

For Bourdieu, all powerful social institutions, in effect, behave like religions (and especially the medieval Catholic Church) in producing in people the belief that it is by some divine ordinance that most people are powerless while a relative few are powerful, and the belief in the transcendent power of the 'sacraments' that, beginning with religion, all powerful social institutions produce: 'The sacrament is the paradigm of the ritual of institution, act of constitution, of constituent nomination . . .; it transfigures the consecrated thing or person through the effect of a collective sanction, conferred by a sacred character, in a consecrated place . . . to durably transform the reality to which it applies by transforming the collective representation of this very reality' (Bourdieu and de Saint Martin 1982, 43). Bourdieu's creative use of religious metaphors continued throughout his career, moreover, as evident in this gem from an interview with a German journalist in 2001: 'The Catholic church is not anti-capitalist. It would really only like to pour some communion wine into the water of neoliberalism. Its vision of Europe is neoliberalism plus Catholicism, or capitalism plus paternalism' (Bourdieu, with Leick 2001).[9] Not unreasonably, Reed-Danahay (2005, 43) suggests that such religious metaphors, especially in Bourdieu's writings on education, might well amount to 'veiled criticisms of the church'.

Somewhat ironically, a number of Bourdieu's critics also use religious metaphors in speaking of him. One of his own mentors, someone who was in no small part responsible for Bourdieu's rise to prominence in academia, the great French sociologist Raymond Aron (1990, 239) calls him 'the leader of a sect' who counted among his students certain fanatical 'disciples' who blindly accepted 'the gospel according to Bourdieu' (ibid., 316). Similarly toned, in a sarcastic play on the second syllable of Bourdieu's name (which in French of course means 'God') some commentators employ the term *'Bourdivins'* (Bourdieu found the term abhorrent, given that *'divin'* means 'divine' in French) for Bourdieu's 'acolytes' as opposed to *'Bourdieusien'*, the entirely 'secular' term in wide currency in francophone academia and in the French media (each term is also used in French as an adjective).[10] Meanwhile, Bourdieu's (1998b, 73–74) fierce and sustained denunciation of the media as 'a factor of depoliticization' that bespeaks 'demagogy and subordination to commercial values' has provoked the ire of many journalists, including two from France's leading newspaper, *Le Monde*, who called him 'a scientistic pontiff, a Cardinal Ratzinger of science, keeping watch over the scientistic orthodoxy of everything written in newspapers' (Lanzmann and Redeker 1998). Similarly, he has been called the 'Savanarola of the French social sciences' (in Robbins 1991, 175), and his work an ideological 'High Mass' (Verdès-Leroux 2001, 57) conducted by and for 'a demiurge' (ibid., 241). As early as 1979, furthermore, when relatively little of Bourdieu's work had yet been translated into English, Paul DiMaggio (1979, 1472) predicted that eventually 'he will probably attract American disciples, if not a cult'.

Whatever else they do, such criticisms (excluding DiMaggio's neutral prediction) reflect the high probability that institutions with the power to 'inculcate' (this was seemingly one of Bourdieu's favorite words) in human beings the belief, or at least the tendency to believe, that the social world should be accepted the way that it is, would find Bourdieu's entire intellectual project to be threatening—as they well should. Moreover, as Bernard Lahire (2001a, 16) notes, to some interpreters 'Bourdieu's sociological vision appears to be violent and warlike, and thus excessive', but only to those who 'have never been victims of the most brutal forms of domination to which members of the dominated classes of our societies are routinely subjected (first economically and then culturally)'. And historically, for Bourdieu, no institution has wielded such power of inculcation to the degree to which religion has, which is largely why he found such incisive usefulness in religious metaphors to theorize all forms of institutional power. Bourdieu was primarily driven to understand the 'paradoxical submission' of human beings to social systems that actually oppress the vast majority of them. Furthermore, he was firmly convinced that institutions like the church, the school, the media and the state are chiefly to blame for cultivating in people such unreflective submission, and that social science could and should be put to the service of revealing precisely how and why they are to blame. '[T]he whole logic' of Bourdieu's work compels investigation precisely of this *'paradox of doxa'*:

I have always been astonished by what might be called the *paradox of doxa*—the fact that the order of the world as we find it, with its one-way streets and its no-entry signs, whether literally or figuratively, its obligations and its penalties, is broadly respected; that there are not more transgressions and subversions, contraventions and 'follies' (just think of the extraordinary concordance of thousands of dispositions—or wills—implied in five minutes' movement of traffic around the Place de la Bastille or Place de la Concorde . . .); or, still more surprisingly, that the established order, with its relations of domination, its rights and prerogatives, privileges and injustices, ultimately perpetuates itself so easily, apart from a few historical accidents, and that the most intolerable conditions of existence can so often be perceived as acceptable and even natural (Bourdieu 2001, 1).

This astonishment endured over the entirety of Bourdieu's professional career, fueled in part by his provincial origins, reflected in his accent and mannerisms and how they marked him as a culturally inferior outsider in Parisian high society. This was especially acute in the elite schools that he attended in the French capital, where he experienced a kind of 'social racism that cannot but make you perceptive; being constantly reminded of your otherness stimulates a sort of permanent sociological vigilance' (in Bourdieu and Wacquant 1992, 209). In Chapter 1, I trace Bourdieu's remarkable ascendancy from his lower-middle-class roots in rural southwestern France to the pinnacle of French academia, summarize his massive body of literary production, and explain briefly the major intellectual influences on the development of his celebrated 'theory of practice'. By offering explanations of each of its key features, I then introduce the central concepts and basic workings of Bourdieuian social theory at large in Chapter 2.

The subject of religion receives only scant attention in Bourdieu's most important books and is seldom a focal concern in any of his publications. Nevertheless, Bourdieu *did* think a great deal about religion and he wrote a substantial amount on the subject—admittedly not substantial if measured by the immense volume of his overall scholarly output, but a sub-corpus of writings that could themselves comprise at least a couple of books.[11] Chapter 3 provides summary and analysis of these, Bourdieu's direct writings on religion, publications that span most of his career and that cover topics including rural Algerian Islam, Weber's theory of charisma and prophecy, and the French Catholic episcopate. This provides important groundwork for the subsequent two chapters: Chapter 4 is a description of Bourdieu's vision of the 'religious field' and a careful definition of its components, functions and applications, with reference to a substantive example (mine, not Bourdieu's) from the religious field of colonial New England; Chapter 5, meanwhile, explains and assesses several suggestive scholarly uses of Bourdieu's theory of practice to the study of religion, namely Otto Maduro's (1982) sociological interpretation of the Latin American religious field, Catherine Bell's (1992) theorization of ritual practice, Thomas Csordas's (1994, 2001, 2002) 'cultural phenomenology' of Charismatic Christianity, Joan Martin's (2000) analysis of the Christian work ethic of enslaved women of color in the United States, and two of my own (Rey 1998, 2005) considerations of, respectively, charisma and syncretism in Afro-Atlantic Catholicism. Chapter 5 also provides reflection upon several limitations that scholars claim to have identified in Bourdieu's theory of practice respective to the study of religion. A brief summary of the material covered throughout the book and glimpses down potentially prosperous avenues of further Bourdieuian theorization of religion are presented in this book's final essay, which is duly, simply, and predictably entitled 'Conclusion'.

How to Read this Book

This book is designed primarily as an introduction to Pierre Bourdieu's theory of practice as it pertains to the study of religion. It includes:

- a summary of Bourdieu's life and intellectual history, his scholarly production, and his leading scholarly influences, which should be carefully considered as the context out of which Bourdieu's thinking about society emerges. The main items from this chapter are briefly outlined on p. 32;
- a concise explanation of his broader social theory, in Chapter 2, which should serve as the context into which his direct writings on religion should be placed. For a list of the key components of Bourdieu's social theory that are discussed in this chapter, please see p. 56 and refer accordingly to the Concise Glossary of Key Terms that begins on p. 154;
- a discussion of Bourdieu's direct writings on religion, in Chapter 3. These writings are listed on p. 60 and the key points from the two most important of Bourdieu's essays on religion are encapsulated on p. 78;
- an extraction of his theory of religion as contained therein, in Chapter 4. The key points this chapter are listed on p. 106;
- a demonstration with several examples of how Bourdieu's theory is being used in the study of religion today, and an assessment of various criticisms that have been leveled against his theory as pertaining to the study of religion comprises Chapter 5; lists of those discussed in this chapter may be found on p. 131.

Chapter 1

The Life, Work and Influences of a 'Master of Suspicion'

I believe that, whatever slight chance I may have of not being finished off by consecration, I owe to the fact that I have worked to analyze consecration. I even think that I might be able to use the authority that this consecration has given me to give more authority to my analysis of the logic and effects of consecration.
(in Bourdieu and Wacquant 1992, 210)

Life

For someone who eventually became quite a public and politically engaged figure of iconic national stature and international renown, Pierre Bourdieu was rather guarded about his background and personal life. To date, the closest English-language text to a biography of Bourdieu, Michael Grenfell's *Pierre Bourdieu: Agent Provocateur* (2004), consists of merely five pages of 'Personal Biography', followed by a much longer and excellent discussion of the French 'Intellectual Climate' in which Bourdieu was educated and rose to prominence. Bourdieu held biography in general in contempt: 'To try to understand a life as a unique and self-sufficient series of events with no links other than the association with a subject whose constancy is no doubt merely that of a proper name, is nearly as absurd as to try to make sense of a route in the metro without taking into account the structure of the subway network, that is, the matrix of objective relations between the different train stations' (Bourdieu 1986a, 71). As for autobiography in particular, the great French sociologist was loath to engage in something that he viewed as tantamount to 'erecting oneself a mausoleum which is also a cenotaph' (in Bourdieu and Wacquant 1992, 213). Hence the first passage of Bourdieu's most (dare I say?) autobiographical book, *Esquisse pour une auto-analyse* (*Outline for a Self-Analysis*), which sits alone on a single page, reads: 'This is not an autobiography' (Bourdieu 2004, 6). Bourdieu was apprehensive that details of his personal life could readily be (ab)used by his critics to discredit him and/

or to try and explain away some element or another of his work (Bourdieu and Wacquant 1992, 202–204; Carles 2001). He even expresses relief that certain hints about his background embedded in some of his earliest work did not circulate widely, thereby effectively pre-empting any 'ill-intentioned or voyeuristic readers' (Bourdieu 2002, 12). But, because, as Gisèle Sapiro (2004, 77) rightly interprets Bourdieu to mean, any person's 'early experiences are determinant because they condition later experiences (through the integrative effect of the habitus)',[1] it behooves us to take a brief look at Bourdieu's background for insight into the development of his understanding of the social world. As his own theory of human development would suggest, therefore, Bourdieu's personal rejection of religion, for instance, and the generally adversative attitude toward religion in his work are in considerable measure the products of his upbringing in a society that, especially among intellectuals just prior to and since the French Revolution, has long harbored deep collective suspicion of institutional religion.

Béarn

Pierre-Félix Bourdieu was born on the first day of August in 1930 to lower-middle-class parents in Denguin, 'a tiny and remote village in Southwest France, a very "backward" place as city people like to say' (in Bourdieu and Wacquant 1992, 204). Denguin is located in the region of Béarn, not far from the Pyrenees Mountains, in the *Pyrénées-Atlantiques* department of the republic. His native village counted only a couple of hundred residents at the time of Bourdieu's birth, most of them peasants, and did not eclipse the mark of 500 until sometime in the 1960s (Mairie de Denguin, n.d.). It was so remote that Bourdieu's schoolmates in the town of Pau, just 20 kilometers away, had never heard of it—and so they mocked it (Bourdieu 2004, 109). Bearnese, one of four sub-dialects of the Gascon language, is the language of quotidian life in Denguin, though Bourdieu recalls his father, Albert Bourdieu, recounting stories from his past 'in a vague mix of Bearnese, Spanish, and French' (ibid., 111). Some of these stories reflected the kinds of leftist values and commitments that distinguish Bearnese political culture (Bège 2004), such that Bourdieu's own 'left of left' political position derived in large part, as Loïc Wacquant (2005b, 11) explains, from 'his upbringing in a remote region of southwestern France where support for socialist ideals ran strong amidst the ambient conservatism, as did sympathy for the *frente popular* during the Spanish Civil War and the Communist-led Resistance to German occupation during World War II'. Pierre Bourdieu's father, moreover, himself possessed 'an anarchist and rebellious streak, which he also bequeathed to his only son'.

When Noemi Duhau married Albert Bourdieu she did so against the will of her parents. This was because they regarded Albert, the sharecropper who had left school at the age of fourteen, as someone socially below them, who by the standards of the local peasantry were *'une grande famille'* (Bourdieu 2004, 112).[2] Their material difficulties notwithstanding, Pierre Bourdieu seemingly had excellent parents who remained supportive of him throughout his education, his stint in the army, and as he embarked on his professional career as a scholar. He speaks fondly of his father's self-effacing concern for the most destitute of the village and of his delight in helping them: 'He taught me without speaking, and above all with his attitude, to respect "the lesser", among whom he counted himself, and also, even if he never explicitly said it, their struggles' (ibid., 111). In the retrospective words of Jacques Darringrand (in Bège 2004, 274), a onetime schoolmate of Pierre Bourdieu's, we can see that such lessons indelibly marked the future French intellectual giant in ways that would also come to distinguish his professional work:

> There is no one he respects more than the street child, the laboring artisan, the disconcerted student, the unemployed, the homeless, the undocumented, the hopeless. He believes that to awaken to misery, injustice, and inanity is to lash out against them. He thinks that our society must find the where-with-all to fundamentally change and improve.

If his father's respect for local poor and destitute peasants was one of the young Pierre Bourdieu's first lessons in the realities of social inequality, the divergent backgrounds of his parents' respective families, and the resultant tensions over how he should be raised, was another. Being, as she was, from *'une grande famille'*, Noemi Bourdieu was far more intent than her husband on inculcating in their only son the same 'respect for conventions and conveyances' that she herself had been raised to embody. Especially interesting for our purposes, this included of course religion, against which the young Bourdieu rebelled, showing early in his life the kind of revolt against convention that would come to so strongly characterize his scholarly work:

> With a most oppositional and somewhat anarchistic air, she clashed with my father when she wanted to impose upon me, without believing in them, a minimum of external conformity to local customs, especially religious, which I refused (above all because I was distressed by a veritable panic at the very idea of walking through the entire church, on Sunday, to take my place in the boys' pew), or distinctive ways of dressing or appearing in public, a white smock one day, and long pants another (not to mention the impeccable part that she insisted in making in my hair, which I would mess up the moment I got out the door), which revolted me because it all distinguished me from the others and exposed me to their ridicule (Bourdieu 2004, 113–14).

Despite having as rich a Protestant history as any region of France, Catholic customs have always predominated in the Bearnese religious field. Bourdieu's native Denguin is about forty miles from Lourdes, the most important Catholic pilgrimage destination in all of France, and one of the most important in the world. The nearest city to Denguin is Lescar, a commercial center that was on the path of thousands of Catholic pilgrims from throughout medieval Europe who made their way to Santiago de Compostela in Spain. It is interesting to speculate that during his childhood Bourdieu was fully aware of the religious significance of these places, as he may also have been of the story of the *cagot* community that once existed just outside of Denguin (Centre Généalogique des Pyrénées Atlantiques 2006). Consisting chiefly of lepers, but in some cases also of religious heretics, the *cagots* were the social outcasts of medieval France, comparable to the 'untouchables' of India, who suffered persecution and ostracism on par with some of the worst forms of racist oppression in the modern world. They were the 'wretched of the earth' in medieval Béarn, victims of the most extreme instances of what Bourdieu calls 'symbolic violence', which sometimes took Catholic forms, like receiving the Eucharist on the end of a long stick and having a separate receptacle of holy water for their exclusive use.

On the elementary level Bourdieu shined as an exceptional student at the Lycée Louis Barthou in Pau,[3] the largest town near Denguin, from 1941 to 1947. From there he continued his studies in Paris upon his admission into the prestigious Lycée Louis le Grand, an originally Jesuit school that counts Diderot, Voltaire, Molière, Hugo and Sartre among its graduates, not to mention Jacques Chirac and two other presidents of the Fifth Republic. After three years at Louis le Grand, 1948–1951, Bourdieu scored highly enough on the standardized national examination to be counted among *la crème de la crème* of France's young adults that are admitted each year into the famous Ecole Normale Supérieure, also in Paris, the country's most prestigious preparatory school (which might more accurately in American terms be called a 'teachers' college') and alma mater to most of the celebrated French intellectuals of the twentieth century: Durkheim, Bergson, Sartre, Lévi-Strauss, Merleau-Ponty, Foucault and Derrida, the latter a classmate of Bourdieu's there.

It is noteworthy that Bourdieu's scholarly achievements were probably only made possible by the fiercely anti-clerical French Revolution, which wrenched education from the hands of the Catholic Church and guaranteed free access to it for all *citoyens*. Consideration of this momentous historical event and its sociocultural inertia in France provides some useful background for viewing Bourdieu's own iconoclasm. In a similar vein, a brief look at Béarn's history can also help illustrate features of French religious culture that shaped, as much as anything, Bourdieu's conceptualization of the 'religious field'. Denguin was named after Guy de Lons, the Bishop of Lescar who, in addition to participating in the Crusades against the Moors, commissioned the construction of the Cathedral of Our Lady of the Assumption for Béarn's most important historical city in 1120. The Cathedral's own history, moreover, can serve as a microcosm of French religious history and the rise of the Catholic monopolization of the European religious field that is the dominant image one takes from reading Bourdieu on religion, just as it is a dominant paradigm in his social theory at large: 'Bourdieu's sociology of religion is, first and foremost, a sociology of Catholicism', as Erwan Dianteill (2004, 71) explains:

> The accent thus falls on the process of monopolization of power by a single institution: The Catholic Church. From this point of view, the highest concentration of hierocratic power is reached in Western Europe before the Reformation. It is the genesis of this monopolization that most interests Bourdieu.

The Protestant Reformation radically altered the French religious field, as much in Béarn as anywhere. By the middle of the seventeenth century there were 30,000 Protestants (locally called 'Huguenots') in the region, for example, while the town of Pau itself, where Bourdieu would attend primary school three hundred years later, was already one-third Protestant. In Lescar, meanwhile, Protestants pillaged the cathedral during the reign of Jeanne III, the Queen of the Kingdom of Navarre from 1555–1572 who had imposed Calvinism on her subjects after her own conversion in 1556. Parts of southern France, including Béarn, belonged to Navarre up until 1620 and were ravaged during the French Wars of Religion from 1562 until the signing of the Edict of Nantes 1598, which granted to Protestants the same rights that Catholics enjoyed as the kingdom's subjects. Lescar's Cathedral of Our Lady of the Assumption, meanwhile, was duly emptied of its idols in 1563 and remained a Protestant church until 1620, when it became Catholic once again.

The cessation of religious violence wrought by the Edict of Nantes was short-lived, however, as King Louis XIV (reigned 1643–1714), along with his powerful prime minister, the Catholic Cardinal Mazarin, overruled the Edict of Nantes with the signing of the Edict of Fontainebleau in 1685, which made Protestantism illegal in *their* kingdom. A wave of religious persecution followed, as the Catholic Church, in conjunction with the crown and its army, took extreme measures to reestablish its monopoly over the French religious field. Central to this initiative was the crown's infamous *dragonades* campaign, in which the royal soldiers (dragoons, hence the term *dragonades*) were quartered in the homes of Protestants in part to forcibly convert them to Catholicism. Consequently they drove as many as half a million Huguenots out of France. The relatively heavily Protestant region of Béarn was especially beleaguered by the *dragonades*. In and around Bourdieu's native village of Denguin, for instance, the local crown governor (*intenerand*), Nicolas-Joseph Foucault, combined Catholic zeal and military violence to personally succeed in making 20,000 converts, destroying their Protestant churches all along the way. In Lescar, meanwhile, restorations were underway on the city cathedral, which was by then back under Catholic control.

But the icons of the Cathedral of Our Lady of the Assumption would be destroyed once again, albeit for secular reasons this time, about 100 years later during the French Revolution, and its doors were closed to the Catholic faithful in the name of Reason, to whose goddess the famous Cathedral of Notre Dame in Paris was dedicated in 1793. Also during the Revolution, the guillotine came to Béarn, where in Pau six Catholic priests were beheaded in 1794 (Goity n.d.). Some semblance of 'normalcy' was finally restored for the Catholic Church with the signing of the Concordat of 1802 between Napoleon and the Vatican, though much of its property, privilege and power in France were lost forever, along with any and all hope of ever reestablishing its monopolistic dominance of the French religious field. It is one example—and for Bourdieu the example that hits literally closest to home—of the decline in institutional religion's symbolic power that Bourdieu seemed to think inevitable for the modern world, a world in which the State replaces the Church as the chief instrument of consecration (Engler 2003). This goes far in explaining the relatively little attention that Bourdieu pays to religion in his massive body of work (Dianteill 2004; Verter 2003).

The history and nature of the French religious field is of course far more complex than my cursory sketch intimates. This glimpse is intended, nonetheless, to provide some cultural and historical illustration of the world in which Bourdieu's own habitus was formed, including, most importantly for our purposes, his attitude toward religion. The generally anti-clerical tone of his writings on religion, for instance, is not his alone but part of a characteristic sentiment of French intellectuals since the Enlightenment, a sentiment behind the French Revolution that remains inert in contemporary French society, especially among the French intelligentsia. According to Dianteill (2004, 81), furthermore, this also had an important influence on Bourdieu's development as a scholar and especially on his thinking about religion:

> The end of the nineteenth century was thus a violent period of anti-clericalism, one that led to the 1905 law separating church and state. The Catholic Church lost its status of official religion at this time. It is in this anti-clerical context that

French sociology is born. It constituted itself largely in opposition to the intellectual hold of religion, and singularly against Catholic influence in the university at the turn of the twentieth century. In one sense, being a sociologist necessarily meant not being *'one of them'*. . . Bourdieu was not exempt from this form of anti-clericalism.[4]

Education

It is somewhat surprising to learn that Bourdieu never underwent formal training in sociology, a craft in which he was essentially self-taught, and that he never earned a doctoral degree in any subject. His concentration of studies on the university level, at Ecole Normale Supérieure, instead was in philosophy, a discipline that Bourdieu would eventually find relatively impotent to make critical sense of contemporary society, hence his eventual adoption of sociology. His turn from the philosophy that he learned there notwithstanding, Bourdieu's experience at the illustrious academy of higher learning (ENS) was fundamental to the formation of both his radical spirit of critical inquiry and his consciousness of the outsider-hood that his rural background amounted to in Parisian society. As David Swartz (1997, 18) explains:

> ENS is known for cultivating an abundance of *esprit critique*, and in this Bourdieu excelled. Little escaped his critical flair: peers, professors, the school itself. The reputation that would characterize his later sociological work—that of being a sharp and relentless critic of the French educational establishment—is already in evidence at ENS. What is striking is Bourdieu's self-perception of being an outsider within the academic establishment and his sharply critical attitude toward the very institution that made his phenomenal rise to intellectual renown possible. Bourdieu experienced ENS not only as a miraculous survivor or strenuous academic selection, but also as a cultural and social outsider.

His self-awareness as an outsider in the rarefied Parisian intellectual, cultural and social air helped fuel Bourdieu's incessant, even passionate, quest to uncover the mechanisms that produce distinctions between individuals and groups in society, just as it eventually bolstered his commitment to the marginalized in a rapidly globalizing world. In this respect, the 'social racism' that victimized Bourdieu in Paris because of his provincial origins served to radicalize his thought in ways that mirror the experience of not only his fellow non-Parisian *normaliens* Jacques Derrida and Michel Foucault (Swartz 1997, 18), but also the great Italian Marxist philosopher Antonio Gramsci, a kindred spirit whom Bourdieu virtually never cites because it wasn't until relatively late in his career that he became familiar with Gramsci's important work (Bourdieu 1990b, 27).[5]

The intensive study of languages was crucial to Bourdieu's overall education, and he demonstrated an impressive aptitude especially for Latin, German and English, languages that he eventually mastered to the extent that he could translate them on a most advanced level.[6] With his concentration in philosophy, for instance, Bourdieu produced his thesis at the Ecole Normale Supérieure in 1953, an annotated translation of Leibniz's *Animadversiones* from the original Latin into French, with interpretative commentary.[7] Thereafter he passed the demanding *agrégation* examination, in 1955, which qualifies one in France for teaching on the secondary or university level, though he never proceeded to complete the state doctoral exam or write a doctoral dissertation,[8] in part out of defiance, meaning that once established as a university professor he was disqualified from directing students' doctoral thesis projects. Nonetheless, his *agrégation* marked Bourdieu's entry into the ranks of the French intelligentsia as a *normalien*, itself a mark of the kind of prestige and distinction that are the targets of consistent attack in his work, though one that Bourdieu also benefited from in numerous ways on his remarkable path of upward social mobility.

As is the pattern for many *normaliens*, upon graduation Bourdieu landed a teaching job, in his case as a philosophy professor at a secondary school outside of Paris, the Lycée Théodore de Banville in Moulins. While there, Bourdieu distinguished himself as an enthusiastic and committed teacher. For example, he once brought from Paris replicas of paintings by several masters, like Gauguin, Picasso and Van Gogh, to adorn the otherwise drab philosophy lecture hall (Lallot 2005, 26); he contributed essays to the student literary journal (Ville 2005, 33); and his students in Moulins affectionately nicknamed him 'Pablo', which he took in good humor. Bourdieu also developed a reputation as something of a radical in Moulins, not least of which for ordering twenty copies of *The Communist Manifesto* for the local public library, a move that won him the reproach of the school headmaster (Lallot 2005, 28). As fate would have it, though, he held his position at the Lycée de Moulins only for a year due to circumstances beyond his control, namely the Algerian War of Independence (1954–1962).

Algeria

Bourdieu was forced to vacate his post as professor of philosophy in Moulins in 1956 when he was drafted into the French army and sent to Algeria, where he served for a compulsory two years. This experience had an immeasurable impact on his personal and professional life, as explained by Michael Grenfell (2004, 34):

> Bourdieu refers to 'the shock of Algeria' . . . It has been said that Bourdieu's stay there coincided with some of the most troubled and violent times in Algerian history. The political events which surrounded him at this period stretched beyond Algerian borders and implicated North Africa, the Middle East as a whole, and indeed the constitution of the French Republic. But it was the immediate and first hand experience which was most striking for Bourdieu.

The more that Bourdieu tried to make sense of Algerian society in crisis and transition, the more philosophy's 'social distance' made it seem incapable of helping him to do so, and thus he turned to sociology and ethnography with intensity and vigor. Bourdieu (2004, 93–94) viewed this shift in disciplinary focus as a kind of personal rite of passage: 'the abandoning of the heights of philosophy for the misery of the slums was also a kind of sacrificial expiation of my adolescent unrealisms'. He was still a soldier when he began research for his first book, *Sociologie d'Algerie*, which he wrote 'with the intention of high-lighting the plight of the Algerian people and also that of the French settlers whose situation was no less dramatic, whatever else had to be said about their racism, etc. I was appalled by the gap between the view of French intellectuals about this war and how it should be brought to an end, and my own experience' (in Mahar 1990, 38).

Although sociology was rather undeveloped in France while Bourdieu was a student, and it then held very little attraction for him (had he not studied philosophy he would likely have studied either biology or medicine instead), he found it to be quite incisive for the analysis of the cultural havoc that French colonialism wreaked in Algeria. Thus, upon his discharge from the army he decided to stay in Algeria for several more years in order to conduct serious ethnographic and sociological research both in the capital city of Algiers and among several ethnic groups among the rural Algerian peasantry, namely the Kabyle, the Shawia and the Mozabite. To support himself he assumed a teaching position in the Faculty of Letters at the University of Algiers, where he recruited some of his students into his fieldwork, including Abdelmayek Sayad, with whom he co-authored his third book on Algeria (Bourdieu and Sayad 1964). With the Algerian War of Independence raging, it was, to say the least, a dangerous time and place to be conducting fieldwork: 'It is not easy to put into words, as I experienced them, the situations and events—adventures, maybe—that so profoundly distressed me, to the point where they still return in my dreams' (Bourdieu 2004, 66).

Bourdieu thus witnessed first-hand the horrors of a colonial occupation that was but one episode in a global story that fascinated him as much as it disturbed him: the confrontation of traditional cultures with modernity and the concomitant establishment of new forms of social distinction and inequality. As Tassadit Yasine (2003, 338) notes, Bourdieu's 'position as an ethnographer allowed him to deconstruct the mechanisms of domination of colonialization and their destructive effects on Algerian society and culture'. To put it in the theoretical language that Bourdieu would later develop, French colonizers constructed the social mechanisms that were intended to 'inculcate' in the 'habitus' of colonized Algerians the 'misrecognition' of the emergent and radically unequal colonial social order as natural or just. In Algeria, Bourdieu was already laying the groundwork for such notions as these and the dialectical relationship between habitus and social structures, recognizing, as he did, that this misrecognition among the colonized would likely endure well beyond eventual Algerian independence: 'The peasant cannot be liberated from the colonists without being liberated from the contradictions that colonialism has developed in him' (Bourdieu and Sayad 1964, 170).

Bourdieu's aforementioned turn from philosophy during this period was not tantamount to the abandonment of philosophy.[9] On the contrary, his philosophical training allowed him to interpret sociological theory in innovative ways toward the analysis of Algerian society and culture—ways that prefigure his later social theory. 'This early research experience inaugurates specific motifs and points of method that become recurring themes in Bourdieu's later work', notes Swartz (1997, 49): 'Four fundamental conceptual issues in particular emerge: the problem of relations between individual dispositions and external structures, the problem of agency in structural analysis, the problem of relating cognitive structures to social systems, and more generally the problem of relations between material and symbolic aspects of social life'.

Grappling precisely with these issues while in Algeria, Bourdieu was moving toward the formulation of his trademark concepts of habitus and capital, which are as deeply influenced by western philosophical thought as they are by classical sociological thought, seeing as western philosophy has always been centrally concerned with human perception. As 'a system of lasting, transposable dispositions which, integrating past experiences, functions at every moment as a *matrix of perceptions, appreciations, and actions*' (Bourdieu 1977, 82–83, original italics), habitus was the key to negotiating the first three of these four conceptual issues, while capital, as manifest in *either* material or symbolic form, was the key to negotiating the fourth (in ways, moreover, that would have significant import for Bourdieu's understanding of religion):

> The fourth problem stems from his observation in Kabylia that ritual and ceremony, feasts, and key symbolic observances were no less important to the

maintenance and reproduction of group life than were its economic foundations. Indeed, Bourdieu concluded that in this traditional society it is impossible
to distinguish the material and the economic from the symbolic as a form of
power, a kind of capital, that can be used to generate social advantages as well as
exercise social control (Swartz 1997, 51).

Thus emerging out of Bourdieu's theorization of peasant culture and
society and the nascent urban proletariat in Algerian in the late 1950s,
habitus and capital are the cornerstones of Bourdieu's theory of 'practice', or of what people do and why they do it, meaning that three of his
four signature 'thinking tools' first emerged during his early fieldwork in
Algeria. Concerning the fourth, meanwhile, although the notion of 'field'
initially came to Bourdieu shortly after he had left Algeria, in 1962, and it
first appears in his published work in the mid 1960s, as Alan Warde (2004,
3) points out, it is entirely absent from his most advanced theoretical
analysis of Algerian culture and society, *Outline of a Theory of Practice*
(first published in French in 1972), and it only features briefly in *The Logic
of Practice* (first published in French in 1980); nevertheless, the concept
of field clearly re-emerges later to become 'the primary analytical tool for
his major empirical studies in the 1980s'.

Professional Career

Bourdieu's sociological writings on Algeria greatly impressed Raymond
Aron, France's leading sociologist of the day, who had himself written an
earlier book on the crisis in Algeria (Aron 1957). Aron thus invited Bourdieu
to join him at La Sorbonne to serve as a teaching assistant and to begin
undertaking research at the *Centre Européen de Sociologie Historique*,
which was founded in 1959 with Aron as its director. At the time, sociology was held in relatively low esteem in the French academy, where
even its towering French founding figure, Emile Durkheim, was dismissed
and almost reviled among the French intelligentsia:

> There was a kind of horror of Durkheim. No one wanted to hear him spoken
> about. He was despised . . . I recall when I came back from Algeria, I had a post
> as assistant at the Sorbonne. Aron said to me: 'You are a *normalien*, you are
> capable of teaching Durkheim'. Nothing could be worse. I had read Durkheim as
> a pupil, the *Rules of Method*, etc. Then I had to read them in order to teach them,
> and it is then that I became interested in them since they helped me a lot in my
> empirical work in Algeria (in Grenfell 2004, 16).

Over the course of the next twenty years—a course that Swartz (1997,
16) rightly calls 'an extraordinary trajectory of upward mobility'—Bourdieu

held a variety of positions in the French academy, mostly in Paris but also in Lille. This trajectory, per Grenfell (2004, 82) 'amounted to successful engagement in class struggle and education as a liberating force', which eventually took Bourdieu to the summit of the French intellectual world. In a nutshell, it happened like this:

Bourdieu spent a year at the Faculty of Letters at the University of Paris, La Sorbonne, assisting Aron. That year he also sat in on a seminar at the *Collège de France* by France's most distinguished anthropologist, Claude Lévi-Strauss, who, next to Sartre, was then the nation's leading intellectual figure. From there, Bourdieu moved to the University of Lille for three years. It is significant for our purposes that while teaching a course in the sociology of religion at the University of Lille, Bourdieu experienced something of a theoretical epiphany one day while he was explaining to his student Weber's theory of the economy of salvation, or of the religious market:

> It was the following year [thus, in 1962–1963] that I taught my courses in Lille on the religious field. It was there, moreover, that I came across the idea of the field, while teaching this very course. It was the next year. I was teaching a course in the sociology of religion in which I commented page by page, line by line, on the chapter of *Wirtschaft und Gesellschaft* that I had translated, and that's when I found it . . . I was experimenting, drawing up a diagram on the blackboard, and all of the sudden it occurred to me: obviously it is necessary to place the different figures in relation to one another (priest, prophet, sorcerer) and, because at the same time, during the same period, I worked also on the literary field, I had the idea of the field (in Fritsch 2005, 97; brackets and parentheses in original).[10]

In 1962, Bourdieu married Marie-Claire Brizzard, soon starting with her a family that would eventually count three sons. He returned to Paris in 1964 upon being appointed as one of the directors of *l'Ecole Pratique des Hautes Etudes* (later called *l'Ecole des Etudes en Sciences Sociales*), 'the Parisian power base upon which his subsequent career was initially founded. From this point on we witness an ever-gathering momentum of research activity and publication' (Jenkins 1992, 15).

May 1968 saw clamorous student protests rage in Paris, which eventually escalated into a nation-wide strike. It was an unprecedented crisis in modern France, paralyzing parts of the country and ultimately leading to the collapse of the de Gaulle government. Scenes of riot police surrounding La Sorbonne, firing tear gas and carting off students in handcuffs only fueled national sympathy for the protesting students. At its peak, the movement drew some two-thirds of the nation's work force into its strikes, and over 1 million people marched in Paris on May 13. One protest slogan summed up quite well the motivation for the strikes and protests:

'Pas de replâtrage, la structure est pourrie!' ('No Re-plastering, the Structure is Rotten'). In light of Bourdieu's decidedly anti-institutional bent, and given the fact that one of his own studies on inequality in French education, *Les héritiers, les etudiants, et la culture* (1964, co-authored with Jean-Claude Passeron), was for some university students a veritable manifesto to protest, 'Bourdieu's silence during the May 1968 student uprising was conspicuous, because virtually all other leading French sociologists at the time took public positions regarding the student movement' (Swartz 2004). One of them was Aron, who was appalled by Bourdieu's disruptive influence among the students, his conspicuous silence during the revolts notwithstanding: 'His disciples had spread throughout the Sorbonne, distributing tracts based on the gospel according to Bourdieu and Passeron, calling for the institution of "Estates General of teaching"; the students, for their part, used and abused the ideas of the book *Les Héritiers*' (Aron 1990, 316). Aron and Bourdieu would never work together again. Once split from Aron, Bourdieu founded his own research center, *Centre de Sociologie Européenne*, in 1968.

Bourdieu eventually came to wield a great deal of power and influence in the French 'intellectual field', amassing an inordinate amount of what he would call 'intellectual capital' and investing it in ways that yielded a most handsome return, eventually raising him to the pinnacle of French academia. In addition to his own publications, lectures, commentaries, and the foundation of his research center in 1968, he edited a section of books called 'Common Sense' for *Les Editions de Minuit* from 1964 to 1992, and founded in 1975 an innovative sociological journal, *Actes de la Recherche en Sciences Sociales*, in 1989 a literary review, *Liber*,[11] and in 1996 a radical academic press, *Raison d'Agir*. In one sense, all of these initiatives were parts of Bourdieu's master plan to 'transform sociology into a rigorous research enterprise' (Swartz 2004, 20) and to place sociology at the service of the exposure and critique of domination. One of Bourdieu's closest collaborators at the *Centre de Sociologie Européenne*, Monique de Saint Martin (2003, 325), provides a useful sketch of this overarching research agenda:

> Over the course of thirty years of work and research with Bourdieu, we often analyzed the imposition and the maintenance of domination as well as different forms of domination. . . The dominant class, or more rarely the dominated class, the fields of the dominant class, the struggles between different factions in both the dominant class and the dominated class, dominant culture, the school as foundational to domination and the division of labor of domination were some of the concepts or schemes of analysis applied in research on taste in different social classes, on university students, on preparatory classes in the leading schools, on winners of the national high school academic competition ['*les lauréats du*

concours général'], on management or on the episcopate, to mention but a few subjects of this research.

Ironically, some of his collaborators found 'without question' that 'Bourdieu directed his center in an authoritarian fashion' (Vidal-Naquet 2003, 94), one so 'excessive' in its *'domination* and control' that de Saint Martin could no longer bear to work with him (de Saint Martin 2003, 324, italics added). She was not the only scholar to experience such a 'concrete difficulty' (Castel 2003, 353) in working with this evidently mercurial man who could be, even to close collaborators, 'inaccessible and arrogant, protected by secretaries and answering machines that record no message' (Schusterman 2005, 479). Aron (1990, 239) likewise assailed Bourdieu for being so 'sure of himself and overbearing, an expert in faculty politics, merciless toward those who might challenge him. Humanly, I hoped for something else from him'. Bernard Lahire (2001a, 16), meanwhile, found Bourdieu to be possessed of 'a certain tendency to absolutize his own point of view while denying any significance in others'.[12]

Whatever toes that he may have stepped on along the way, Pierre Bourdieu's extraordinary ascendancy to intellectual acclaim reached its zenith in 1980 when he was elected as Chair of Sociology at *Collège de France*, his country's most prestigious institution of higher learning. As a European social scientist, he could go no higher. Conceivably, such an achievement was the result of a combination of personal brilliance and theoretical creativity (first and foremost), calculating and relentless ambition, self-avowed workaholism, and some measure of each arrogance and audacity. Thus by the 1990s Bourdieu had become France's, if not all of Europe's, leading intellectual, as reflected in his reception of the Gold Medal Award from the *Centre Nationale de Recherche Scientifique* (the National Center for Scientific Research) in 1993, one of the rare few social scientists to be so honored.[13]

The prestige of his position at the *Collège de France*, coupled with the various research and publishing initiatives that he led, brought Bourdieu increasing public notoriety, and his political engagements became more frequent and vocal by the late 1980s. This was a notable change, because in earlier years Bourdieu had largely shunned political engagement outside of the academy and the research field. And whereas this shift might thus seem somehow incongruous (or perhaps contradictory, in light of Bourdieu's [1996, 209] criticism of Sartre as *'the total intellectual'*[14]), in actuality, as Anna Boschetti (2005, 137) explains, Bourdieu's 'direct political action carried out beginning in the late 1980s, far from constituting a break in regards to the earlier period, in its inspiration and its manifestations is the coherent realization of a possibility that is inscribed in his entire oeuvre'. These manifestations, such as the founding of *Raisons d'Agir*, were parts of an effort 'to put the competencies of social science at the service of . . . the *"sans"* (those "without": the job*less*, the home-*less*, and paper*less* migrants) and the emerging transnational currents fighting the spread of neoliberal globalization' (Wacquant 2005b, 13). Bourdieu (in Mauger 2005, 375) expressed the hope that the press would 'little by little, become something of an international popular encyclopedia', one 'animated by a militant will to diffuse indispensable knowledge for politi-cal reflection and action in a democracy'.

The causes to which Bourdieu's own 'militant will' drove him ranged from the opposition to Reagan's and Thatcher's welfare reform programs in the United States and England respectively, to the grievances of striking railway workers in France; from opposition to the 1991 war in Iraq and protests against the repression of intellectuals in Algeria, to the struggle against racism and xenophobia in France and support for the AIDS aware-ness and activist group ACT-UP; and from denunciations of the corruption of the Mitterand government to, perhaps most amply, the struggle against the neo-liberal economics of contemporary globalization. The last of these is perhaps best illustrated by Bourdieu's backing of José Bové, a farmer who gained international acclaim for his destruction of a McDonald's res-taurant in southern France in 1999. 'For him, life itself was a commit-ment', said Bové of Bourdieu (in Riding 2002).

Pierre Bourdieu's life of commitment ended after a brief struggle with lung cancer on January 23, 2002, in Paris. He was seventy-one years old. Richard Schusterman (2005, 478) explains that Bourdieu's death was 'without question an event of international proportions. The President of the Republic Jacques Chirac and the Prime Minister Lionel Jospin were quick to salute the career of this *star* of the theory of *practice*'. It was also 'a huge loss not only for the political causes and the oppressed whose causes he championed, but equally for the numerous disciplines that he helped move forward: philosophy, sociology, anthropology, history, politi-cal science, political economics, the theory of education, feminism, liter-ary theory, art criticism, and communications theory'. Given the recent proliferation of publications using Bourdieu to study religion, furthermore, we can well add 'religious studies' to this ever-growing list.

Work

Bourdieu authored scores of articles and over forty books, some of which have been translated into as many as two dozen languages. The first were published in 1958, and posthumous texts are currently in production. In the 1990s Bourdieu increasingly employed interviews as a means of conveying his ideas in much more accessible language than that in which most of his published work is written. It is as if he came to realize that placing his craft at the service of the world's socially marginalized would require such a shift, one that also saw Bourdieu publish a few slender volumes, late in his career, that are markedly less difficult to read than most of his books and articles. He was, furthermore, an avid photographer, and some of his photos from Algeria have been compiled for publication (Bourdieu 2003b) and for gallery exhibitions. Adding to all of this newspaper editorials, conference papers, and reviews, Bourdieu's profession production is comprised of hundreds of items, obviously far more than can be summarized here. Instead, I follow Grenfell's (2004, 8) helpful cataloguing of Bourdieu's 'major publications into four overlapping phases': (1) his early ethnographic and sociological work on Algeria; (2) publications based on his early research at the *Centre de Sociologie Européenne*; (3) his major studies on French society and culture from 1979–1989; and (4) the polemical works of protest and the 'methodological and philosophical works' (ibid., 9) that appeared during the last decade of his life.

As explained above, Bourdieu spent most of the second half of the 1950s in Algeria, first as a soldier and later as a professor of sociology who engaged in fieldwork both in Algiers and in rural communities in the mountainous Kabylia area east of the capital. He also returned to Algeria for further fieldwork during the first half of the 1960s. During this period, Bourdieu taught himself classical sociology and put what he learned from Marx, Durkheim and Weber to the test in his research for the three books that he published on Algeria, *Sociologie de l'Algérie* (1958), *Travaille et travailleurs en Algérie* (1963) and *Le déracinement: la crise de l'agriculture traditionelle en Algérie* (1964). As Derek Robbins explains (1991, 16), the first of these books, based mostly on Bourdieu's interpretation of ethnographic literature (he had not yet had the opportunity to do serious fieldwork because of his military service), 'offers, first, accounts of the social organization of four different tribal groups—the Kabyles, the Shawia, the Mozabites and the Arab-speaking peoples—and then secondly, offers reflections on the consequences of the collapse of these traditional systems'. Respectively, Bourdieu's other two books on Algeria discuss the impact of colonization on urban labor and agriculture, which were written 'as deliberate contributions to Algerian self-development and social reconstruction. Both arose out of Bourdieu's recognition that the anomie of the Algerian masses which was the consequence of their only partial adaptation to modern values and behaviours meant that they were now particularly vulnerable'.[15]

Bourdieu's next major study, 'Célibat et condition paysanne' (1962), marks an important transition from his work on Algeria to his work on France.[16] The idea for this interesting book on changing marital traditions in his native Béarn came to Bourdieu while at a Christmas Eve dance at a tavern there, where he was struck by the scene of a group of men who stood idly aside, never dancing. He later discovered that social change in the region had essentially doomed these men to lives of bachelorhood, a reality that Bourdieu chose to study sociologically in part as something of an exercise in self-discovery:

> I saw this initial scene as a sort of challenge: at the time I had in the back of my mind the idea of taking as an object of analysis a universe of which I had a familiar knowledge. Having worked in Kabylia, a foreign universe, I thought it would be interesting to do a kind of *Tristes tropiques* . . . but in reverse (this book was one of the great intellectual models that we all had in mind at the time): to observe the effects that objectification of my native world would have on me. Thus I had a small theoretical purpose, and the ballroom raised questions (in Bourdieu and Wacquant 1992, 163).

Thus did Bourdieu plunge into the second phase of his professional output, first while on the faculty at the University of Lille from 1961–1964, and then from his research base at the *Ecole des Hautes Etudes en Sciences Sociales* in Paris.

Turning his attention from the bachelors of his native Béarn, Bourdieu next critically explored the relationship between education and cultural and social inequality in France in two books co-authored with Jean-Claude Passeron, *Les Héritiers* (1964) and *La Reproduction* (1970).[17] These books embodied what might be called the driving motive of Bourdieu's entire academic agenda: the examination of the means by which inequalities and distinctions between people are reproduced in society. A key Bourdieuian concept in this agenda that gains prominence at this juncture is that of 'symbolic violence', defined at the beginning of *La Reproduction* as 'power that manages to impose meanings and to impose them as legitimate by concealing the power relations which are the basis of its force' (Bourdieu and Passeron 1977, 4).

Research at the *Centre de Sociologie Européenne* during this period also produced critical sociological studies of photography and art museums, followed by one of Bourdieu's most important books, *Outline of a Theory of Practice*, which appeared in French in 1972 and in a much revised English translation five years later. In *Outline*, Bourdieu draws on his fieldwork in Algeria to systematically construct 'a theory of practice and of practical knowledge' and 'a theory of the theoretical and social conditions of the possibility of objective apprehension' (Bourdieu 1977, 4). In his typically complex language and sophisticated argumentation, Bourdieu here defines and demonstrates the analytical power of his 'thinking tools': habitus, capital, *doxa*, symbolic violence, practical logic, etc. The book also contains what may well be the most widely cited sentence from the entirety of his voluminous body of work: 'Every established order tends to produce (to very different degrees and with very different means) the naturalization of its own arbitrariness' (Bourdieu 1977, 164). Like most of his studies, *Outline*, as its translator into English, Richard Nice (1977, vii), points out, is a 'text which seeks to break out of a scheme of thought as deeply embedded as the opposition between subjectivism and objectivism', a key issue to which we will return below and again in Chapter 2.

Listing nine of the books that comprise it, Grenfell (2004, 9) explains that the 'third phase' of Bourdieu's scholarly productivity featured 'the appearance of his main anthropological studies of France . . . as well as further methodological and philosophical statements' and a 'major work on language'. The first book from this period, *Distinction*, is also Bourdieu's most famous and is ranked by the International Sociological Association as the sixth most influential social-scientific book of the twentieth century. *Distinction* is a dense and sophisticated sociological and ethnographic study that sold widely when it first appeared in France, and this 'major assault on the notion of pure or innate cultural taste' (Jenkins 1992, 137) sparked wide public debate there. Bourdieu (1979, 35) argues here that culture is no less a site of class struggle than economics, and that cultural tastes are little more than '[r]eproduction strategies' employed consciously or unconsciously by individuals and families 'to maintain or improve their position in the class structure'. Or, per Grenfell (2004, 99), '*Distinction* sets out to establish that cultural consumption (in both senses of the word) is less a means of personal development or enlightenment than many of the cultural missionaries in post-war France had believed. Rather, Bourdieu argued in an iconoclastic way that it was better understood as a medium of social differentiation and, much as education, reproduction'.

The fourth and final phase of Bourdieu's work spans the last ten to fifteen years of his life and is characterized in part by a shift in publication style. To be sure, there appeared during this phase some books of theoretical sophistication, such as *Pascalian Meditations* (2000a), my personal favorite, and extensive sociological analysis and methodological rigor, like *La Misère du monde* (Bourdieu et al. 1993), a dense text (over 1,400 pages!) that is rich in material drawn from interviews with the socially marginalized of France, where it was a bestseller. Meanwhile, the 'shift in the style of his published work' at this juncture is marked by the appear-

ance of published 'collections of interviews, lectures, and conferences
. . . More and more, he adopted the interview format rather than the
highly formalized writing characterizing most of his previous work' (Swartz
1997, 27). In a similar vein, there also appear during this period a few
short books in, by Bourdieu's standard, remarkably accessible language
that tackled subjects that he considered to be of paramount concern to
humanity at the turn of the millennium: globalization, neo-liberal economics, xenophobia, sexism, and class struggle, and the misery and suffering that they cause throughout the world: *Practical Reason* (1998a),
Acts of Resistance (1998b), *Masculine Domination* (2001), and *Firing Back*
(2003a). Perhaps Bourdieu sensed that his time was running out and thus
he needed to reach the suffering masses of the world more directly, and
thus new and even risky measures would be required: 'The older that I
get the more I feel myself driven to crime. I cross lines that I had prohibited myself from crossing in order to bring to the public world values that
are in currency in the intellectual world' (in Mauger 2005, 383).

Influences

> I have never thought of myself in such terms as being 'a marxist' or a follower of
> Weber. I usually object to such questions. Primarily because, when one asks
> these questions . . . it is nearly always with the intention of polemic, to place me
> in a class, to catalogue me, *kategorisieren*, to accuse me publicly: 'Deep down,
> Bourdieu is a Durkheimian'. This is pejorative from the point of view of the one
> who says it: that means: he is not a marxist, and that is bad. Or even: 'Bourdieu
> is a Marxist'. And that is not right either. In any case, the answer to the question
> of knowing whether an author is a Marxist, a follower of Durkheim or of Weber
> produces hardly any information about that author (in Mahar 1990, 31).

The wide array of people cited in Bourdieu's oeuvre is almost dizzying,
ranging from Leibniz to Virginia Wolff, Homer to Sartre, Flaubert to Freud,
and Aristotle to Charles Schulz, the cartoonist of 'Peanuts' fame. And just
as the broad range of his research ventures makes for a defiance of any
neat classification of his work, so, too, does this wide array of citations
make placing Bourdieu in a single intellectual lineage virtually impossible,
something that he seemingly desired. That said, there are about a dozen
figures that predominate among his influences, listed here more or less in
descending order of importance: Weber, Marx, Durkheim, Merleau-Ponty,
Mauss, Bachelard, Pascal, Heidegger, Leibniz, Canguilhem, Lévi-Strauss,
and Sartre. Helpfully Swartz groups most of these figures into two categories, 'Philosophical Thought' and 'Classical Sociological Theory'. In the

Pierre Bourdieu's Life and Work

1930	Born in Denguin, France, on August 1 to Albert Bourdieu and Noemie Bourdieu (née Duhau)
1941–1947	Primary studies at Lycée Louis Barthou in Pau
1948–1951	Secondary studies at Lycée Louis le Grand in Paris
1951–1954	Tertiary studies at Ecole Normale Supérieure with a degreed major in philosophy
1954–1955	Professor of Philosophy, Lycée Théodore de Banville, Moulins
1955–1957	Draftee in the French Army for service in the Algerian War of Independence
1958	Publication of *Sociologie d'Algérie*, Bourdieu's first book
1958–1960	Assistant Professor, Faculty of Letters, University of Algiers
1960–1961	Assistant Professor, Faculty of Letters, University of Paris, La Sorbonne
1961–1964	Assistant Professor, Faculty of Letters, University of Lille
1964	*The Inheritors* first published in French; co-authored with Jean-Claude Passeron
1964–1984	Instructor, Ecole Normale Supérieure, Paris
1964–2002	Founding Director of Ecole des Hautes Etudes en Sciences Sociales, Paris
1971	Publication of Bourdieu's most important two essays on religion
1972	*Outline of a Theory of Practice* first published in French
1972–1973	Visiting Member, Institute for Advanced Studies, Princeton
1975–2002	Founding Editor, *Actes de la Recherche en Sciences Sociales*
1979	*Distinction* first published in French
1980	*The Logic of Practice* first published in French
1982	Publication of 'La sainte famille: L'épiscopat français dans le champs du pouvoir'; co-authored with Monique de Saint Martin
1982–2002	Professor and Chair of Sociology, Collège de France, Paris
1985–1998	Founding Director, Centre de Sociologie Européenne
1993	Recipient of the Gold Medal from the Centre National de Recherche Scientifique
1993	*The Weight of the World* first published in French
1996	Recipient of the Erving Goffman Prize, University of California, Berkeley
1997	*Pascalian Meditations* first published in French
2000	Recipient of the Huxley Memorial Prize, Royal Anthropological Institute, London
2001–2002	Corresponding Fellow of the British Academy
2002	Died of lung cancer, January 23, Paris

first category, Swartz (1997, 34) maps out the various influences on Bourdieu of the philosophers of science Gaston Bachelard and Georges Canguilhem, two of Bourdieu's professors at Ecole Normale Supérieure, most significantly in their calling 'attention to the "constructed" nature of scientific knowledge', and their calling for 'reflexive monitoring of the assumptions that enter into the scientific construction process. Bourdieu adopts this reflexive method as the trademark of his sociology'.

Also included in Swartz's category of philosophical influences on Bourdieu are, among others, Maurice Merleau-Ponty, another professor at Ecole Normale Supérieure during Bourdieu's time there, and the two leading intellectuals in France during Bourdieu's formative years in the academy, Sartre and Lévi-Strauss. Writing before the publication of Bourdieu's *Pascalian Meditations*, in which, seemingly from out of the blue, Bourdieu declares himself to be, if anything, 'a Pascalian', Swartz does not include Pascal here, though we certainly should. In the category of 'Classical Sociological Theory', meanwhile, he lists Karl Marx, Emile Durkheim and Max Weber. We should add a fourth here, Marcel Mauss, if only because he is a primary taproot of Bourdieu's pivotal notion of habitus, as discussed in the following chapter.

Lévi-Strauss's structuralism and Sartre's existentialism respectively ex-emplify the two oppositional poles in social theory that Bourdieu's entire project is designed to overcome. As Rogers Brubaker (2004, 30) explains, in Bourdieu's work at large these figures are:

> set against one another, in a relation of fruitful tension, two radically different approaches to the study of social life: Sartre's voluntarism and Lévi-Strauss's structuralism. Sartre's emphasis on the creativity, freedom, and unstructured power of choice of the individual subject, and Lévi-Strauss's emphasis on the causal power of structures operating independently of the consciousness of agents came to be seen by Bourdieu as antithetical poles of a basic opposition between subjectivism and objectivism.

In fact, Bourdieu (1990a, 1) opens *The Logic of Practice*, his flagship theoretical book, by drawing attention to this quite problematic episte-mological dichotomy in social inquiry:

> Of all the oppositions that artificially divide social science, the most fundamen-tal, and the most ruinous, is the one that is set up between subjectivism and objectivism. The very fact that this division constantly reappears in virtually the same form would suffice to indicate that the modes of knowledge which it distinguishes are equally indispensable to a science of the social world that cannot be reduced either to a social phenomenology or a social physics.

Thus one of Bourdieu's overarching objectives is '[t]o move beyond the antagonism between these two modes of knowledge, while preserv-ing the gains from each of them' (ibid.).[18]

The phenomenology of Martin Heidegger, and especially Merleau-Ponty, rank among Bourdieu's chief philosophical influences. In Heidegger, Bourdieu found 'a way to analyse the relation between individual prac-tice and the world, that was neither intellectualistic nor mechanistic' (in

Mahar 1990, 34). More important still, Merleau-Ponty engendered in Bourdieu's thinking about human agency an awareness of the fundamental importance of the somatic dimensions of human perception and personal dispositions. The magnitude of this for the development of Bourdieu's notion of habitus cannot be overstated, especially as pertaining to the utility of this concept for the study or religious belief, experience and practice, a key issue to be explored in Chapter 5:

> The agent engaged in practice knows the world but with a knowledge which, as Merleau-Ponty showed, is not set up in relation of externality of a knowing consciousness. He knows it, in a sense, too well, without objectifying distance, takes it for granted, precisely because he is caught up in it, bound up with it; he inhabits it like a garment [*un habit*] or a familiar habitat. He feels at home in the world because the world is also in him, in the form of a habitus, a virtue made of necessity which implies a form of love of necessity, *amor fati* (Bourdieu 2000a, 142–43).

Merleau-Ponty also played in Bourdieu's development as a scholar 'a key role by taking seriously into account the social sciences in his philosophical work' (Swartz 1997, 30). As a matter of fact, Merleau-Ponty devotes a chapter of his 1955 book *Les aventures de la dialectique* to Weber. It was while reading this very book, which he calls a revelatory 'little bolt of lightning' (in Fritsch 2005, 92), that Bourdieu (2000b, 112) first heard of Weber, who is clearly the strongest influence on Bourdieu's theoretical understanding of religion.

Among his many philosophical influences, in the end Bourdieu esteems Blaise Pascal to be paramount among them: 'For a long time I had adopted the habit, when asked the (generally ill-intentioned) question of my relations with Marx, or replying that, all in all, if I really had to affiliate myself, I would say I was more of a Pascalian' (Bourdieu 2000a, 1–2). In light of Bourdieu's atheism and Pascal's intense Catholic faith, this declaration should certainly sound surprising. Yet, Bourdieu does with Pascal precisely what Marx does with Hegel, and that is to remove the idealism altogether from the mentor's system of thought toward rehabilitating it for contemporary social theory.[19] Thus stripped of its religious assumptions (one can only wonder what Pascal would have thought!), Pascal's key insight, for Bourdieu, is that 'worldly consolations or consecrations' are nothing more than 'a fallacious refuge against abandonment and solitude and . . . a ruse of bad faith to avoid a resolute confrontation with the human condition' (ibid., 239, n. 36).[20] Bourdieu interprets this to be what Pascal means in speaking of the 'wretchedness of man without God'. In such a reading, the sociological significance of Pascal thus lies in the power that he inspires for the critique of the State, which for Bourdieu has replaced religion as 'the primary site of consecration' (Engler 2003, 450):

> what Pascal describes as the 'wretchedness of man without God', that is, without a reason for being, is sociologically attested in the form of the truly metaphysical wretchedness of men and women who have no social *raison d'être*, abandoned to its absurdity. And one also understands, *a contrario*, the quasi-divine power of rescuing people form contingency and gratuitousness that is possessed, whether one likes it of not, by the social world, that which is exercised in particular through the institution of the State (Bourdieu 2000a, 239–40).

Otherwise, Bourdieu (1990a, 49) praises Pascal for his 'extraordinary analysis of the foundations of belief',[21] and he was 'grateful to Pascal . . . for his concern, devoid of populist naivety, for "ordinary people" and the "sound opinions of the people": and for his determination, inseparable from that concern, always to seek the "reason of effects", the *raison d'être* of the seemingly most illogical or derisory human behaviors' (Bourdieu 2000a, 2). In this sense, Bourdieu modeled himself as a thinker after Pascal.

The three towering figures in classical sociology are also the most powerful influences on Bourdieu's own social theory: Marx, Weber and Durkheim. Many commentators classify Bourdieu as a Marxist, neo-Marxist, or post-Marxist (e.g., Maduro 1977; Garnham and Williams 1980; Guillroy 1993), and there are abundant passages in Bourdieu's writings where he indeed sounds quite 'orthodoxly' Marxist. His central concern with class and capital, as well as his underlying assumption that the social is profoundly economic, clearly derive from Marx; his pivotal notion of misrecognition is an adaptation of Marx's notion of false consciousness; and his commitment to placing critical social theory at the service of radical social and political change is quintessentially Marxist. Pointing out a less obvious, though no less important, influence of Marx on Bourdieu, meanwhile, Richard Jenkins (1992, 19) explains that '[f]rom Marx, particularly the early Marx of the *Theses on Feuerbach*, he derives his interest in practice'. While these influences are clearly far-reaching for Bourdieu, as Brubaker (2004, 46–47, original italics) shows, Bourdieu moves beyond Marx on the central issue of class in that '[t]he conceptual space within which Bourdieu defines class is not that of relations of production, but that of social relations in general. . . Class thus defined is treated by Bourdieu as a *universal explanatory principle*'. In Bourdieu's own words (1985b, 723), to soundly theorize society 'there has to be a break with the economism [of Marxist theory] which leads one to reduce the social field, a multidimensional space, solely to the economic field, to the relations of economic production, which are thus constituted as coordinates of a social position'.

Throughout his work, Bourdieu quite creatively, and with much interpretive profit, synthesizes the ideas of various thinkers, rightly convinced
that this is an invaluable means to advancing social theory. In this way
does he conceptualize correctives for the shortcomings that he found in
classical Marxist theory and in the sociology of Emile Durkheim. For Paul
DiMaggio (1979, 1460), this particular synthesis of ideas underlies
Bourdieu's entire theory of practice, 'an elegantly systematic, if not entirely satisfactory, revisionist approach to the Durkheimian problem of
order—an effort, in some respects brilliant, to mate Durkheim and Marx'.
Durkheim was primarily concerned with the question of how societies
could remain coherent in a modern world that features their ever-increas-
ing internal diversification—on how social order is maintained. One of
the keys to answering this question, for Durkheim, was to analyze the
means by which societies reproduce themselves by influencing the ways
in which people think, feel and behave, or what Bourdieu (1971a, 300)
calls 'the Durkheimian hypothesis of social genesis of schemes of thought,
perception, appreciation and action'. However, just as Bourdieu diverges
from Marx on fundamental counts, so does he diverge from Durkheim,
and here is where his synthesis of Marx and Durkheim is most apparent:

> Like Durkheim, Bourdieu sees symbolic systems as classification systems that
> provide both *logical and social integration*. He emphasizes the social as well as
> cognitive functions of 'collective representations' and 'primitive classifications'.
> But if for Durkheim this integrative force operates to produce a desired consen-
> sual unity for the social order, for Bourdieu it produces domination . . . The
> pressing question for Bourdieu is not, as it was primarily for Durkheim, how
> solidarity is reinforced, but rather how solidarity is constructed and maintained
> in a social order characterized by hierarchy, conflict and struggle (Swartz 1997,
> 48, original emphasis).

If his personal background and his reading of Marx engendered in
Bourdieu a critical awareness of the importance of 'hierarchy, conflict,
and struggle' in society, it is his engagement of Weber's sociology of
religion, and especially Weber's crucial discussion of the competition
between priests and prophets over the control and distribution of 'salvation goods', that allows Bourdieu to transform this awareness into his
own monumental theory of practice. Here Weber employs the economic
language and economic logic to the interpretation of religion that are so
essential to Bourdieuian theory at large. Briefly stated, Bourdieu (1991a,
4) is most impressed by Weber's sociology of religion because it provides
'a way of linking the contents of mythical discourse (and even its syntax)
to the religious interests of those who produce it'. Insofar as they are
arbitrary, for Bourdieu, *all* discourses (e.g., literary, political, artistic, economic, cultural, religious) are 'mythical', and a pressing obligation for

sociology is to uncover the links between its 'content' and the 'interests of those who produce it'.

There are of course other influences on Bourdieu's social thought besides those outlined here,[22] and, despite charges of his overestimating the originality of his work (e.g., Verdès-Leroux 2001), Bourdieu would be, I think, the first to acknowledge them, as he does in fact throughout his writings. Following Swartz's bipartite division of these influences, we may summarize that from philosophy, especially the philosophy of science as reflected in the work of Bachelard and Canguilhem, and phenomenology, as reflected in the work of Merleau-Ponty, Bourdieu derives the bricks and mortar of his own sophisticated epistemology, or his understanding of how people know and perceive. Tested against his fieldwork in Algeria and France, meanwhile, from classical sociology, and especially from Durkheim, Bourdieu derives his conviction that knowledge is always socially constructed, and from Marx the conviction that all social constructions are arbitrary, unequal and unjust, while from Weber he gains sharpness of focus on symbolic goods and the underlying economic logic of society. Brubaker (2004, 33) elucidates the confluence of these last three influences nicely: 'At the risk of crude oversimplification, it may be suggested in summary that Bourdieu attempts to systematize Weber's thought in a quasi-Marxian mode and to "subjectivize" Marxian thought by incorporating the Durkheimian concern with symbolic forms and the Weberian concern with symbolic power and symbolic goods in its systematic view of the social world as a structure of class-based power and privilege'. The greatest challenge facing sociology, for Bourdieu, is to understand how such a 'structure of class-based power and privilege' is reproduced in human society. And in the end, the key to this challenge lies in identifying the social and epistemological processes of mediation implicating the individual perceiver and the social structures and mechanisms that produce everything in and about society that he or she perceives, and that strongly determine the ways in which he or she perceives them. The thinkers discussed here, among others, provide excellent thinking tools from which Bourdieu fashions his own to construct his theory of practice in order to take up this challenge in a powerful and compelling way. The overall result is almost without peer in being 'so systematic, so comprehensive, so creative, or so fertile' and in reaching 'so keenly to the heart of so many analytical issues' (DiMaggio 1979, 1466). In the next chapter we'll take a closer look.

Summary of Key Elements to Chapter 1

- Bourdieu's upbringing in rural southern France (pp. 14–19);
- history of the 'religious field' of rural southern France (pp. 16–18);
- Bourdieu's formal education (pp. 19–20);
- military experience and early fieldwork in Algeria (pp. 20–23);
- professional career, from University of Lille to the Collège de France (pp. 23–27);
- chronological overview of Bourdieu's scholarly work (pp. 27–31);
- philosophical and sociological influences on Bourdieu (pp. 31–37).

Chapter 2

Theory of Practice: Field, Habitus, Capital

I would say that the interview can be considered a sort of spiritual exercise that, through forgetfulness of self, aims at a true conversion of the way we look at other people in the ordinary circumstances of life. The welcoming disposition, which leads one to make the respondent's problem his own, the capacity to take that person and understand them just as they are in their distinctive necessity, is a sort of intellectual love: a gaze that consents to necessity in the manner of the 'intellectual love of God' (in Bourdieu et al. 1999, 614, original emphasis).

Overview

All of its subtlety and sophistication notwithstanding, Pierre Bourdieu's theory of practice may, for introductory purposes, be boiled down to a handful of its most fundamental concepts.[1] The first is *practice*, or what people do in society.[2] Invariably, *practice* takes place in any number of the interrelated and sometimes overlapping *fields* that together constitute society. So much of what people do, furthermore, amounts to self-interested pursuits of forms of *capital*, whether material or symbolic, relative to the respective *fields* in which their *practice* unfolds. And the ways in which people perceive of and pursue *capital* are chiefly generated by their *habitus*, which is that part of their personhood that filters their perceptions, molds their tastes, and casts their inclinations and dispositions. To these four most fundamental Bourdieuian concepts we may add a fifth, *symbolic violence*, which, because of its awesome influence on how people perceive of the social world, is the main mechanism, for Bourdieu, by which distinctions between individuals and groups and forms of domination predicated thereupon are reproduced in society. So central is the concept of symbolic violence to Bourdieu's entire social theory that Loïc Wacquant (in Bourdieu and Wacquant 1992, 14), one of Bourdieu's leading interpreters, is prepared to assert that 'the whole of Bourdieu's work may be interpreted as a materialist anthropology of the specific contribution that various forms of symbolic violence make to the reproduction and transformation of structures of domination'.

This chapter takes a closer look at Bourdieu's signature notions of *field*, *habitus*, *capital* and *symbolic violence* toward introducing his theory of *practice* at large. In this theory, as Deborah Reed-Danahay (2005, 11) succinctly puts it, 'social fields (*champs*) are sites of struggle over "symbolic capital" that are organized around interests such as education, art, politics, and literature. Social agents (Bourdieu's term for individuals) interact within social fields through their habitus (inculcated dispositions and cultural capital—including values, beliefs, tastes, etc.)'. The analysis of these concepts and the ways in which they operatively interrelate is what Bourdieu calls the *'general science of the economy of practice'*, a system of theoretical premises that 'informs all of Bourdieu's more specific theoretical analyses and empirical investigations' (Brubaker 2004, 39), which may thus be said to be the heart of Bourdieuian theory.

Pierre Bourdieu's 'Generative Structuralism'

Taken as a whole, Bourdieu's theoretical project is a critical scientific analysis and explanation of the social influences on what people do and why they do what they do, and of how what they do contributes to the reproduction of these very social influences. Bourdieu (1990b, 14) characterizes this project as a form of 'generative structuralism', or 'genetic structuralism':

> If one wants to give a name to what I am doing, you could call it genetic structuralism. One can use the term in two senses. First, I am trying to describe and analyse the genesis of one's person. That is, habitus or the notion of habitus. The interest is in understanding how what we call the 'individual' is moulded by social structures. That is the problem of the internalisation of social structures and the production of habitus as a generative structure. The concept of habitus is generative structure (in Mahar 1990, 33–34).

Meaning essentially the same thing, Bourdieu (1990b, 123) also refers to his work as *'constructivist structuralism'* and/or *'structuralist constructivism'*: 'By structuralism or structuralist, I mean that there exist, in the social world itself . . . objective structures that are independent of the consciousness and desires of agents . . . By constructivism, I mean that there is a social genesis on the one hand of the patterns of perception, thought and action which are constitutive of what I call the habitus, and on the other hand of social structures, and in particular of what I call fields and groups, especially of what are usually called social fields'.

Relentlessly driven by 'an element of zealous iconoclasm' that 'exposes mercilessly the covert functions of all institutions and their reinforcing ideologies' (Robbins 1991, 175), and ever attuned to his chief objective to formulate a serviceable sociological model for the critique of all forms of social domination, Bourdieu developed his genetic structuralist theory of practice by craftily interweaving ethnographic fieldwork with sophisticated sociological interpretation based on his own critical reading of classical sociological theory and method and the entire history of western philosophy. Monique de Saint Martin (2003, 326), one of his closest collaborators and the co-author of Bourdieu's single most extensive empirical study of religion, sees this concern with social domination as a unifying theoretical thread woven throughout Bourdieu's work—that Bourdieu developed his social theory 'from the outset to unveil domination and the least visible forms of domination, so often hidden by common sense'. In Bourdieu's (in Bourdieu and Wacquant 1992, 198–99) own words, sociology is thus at its best when it serves as:

> an instrument that people can apply themselves for quasi-clinical purposes. The true freedom that sociology offers is to give us a small chance of knowing what game we play and of minimizing the ways in which we are manipulated by the forces in the field in which we evolve, as well as by the embodied social forces that operate within us. I am not saying that sociology solves all the problems of the world, far from it, but it allows us to discern the sites where we do enjoy a degree of freedom and those where we do not.

Put otherwise, the chief purpose of sociology, for Bourdieu, lies in '[p]roducing awareness of these mechanisms that make life painful, even unlivable'. When social science serves this purpose, 'one has to acknowledge the effect it can have in allowing those who suffer to find out that their suffering can be imputed to social causes and thus feel exonerated; and in making generally known the social origin, collectively hidden, of unhappiness in all its forms, including the most intimate, the most secret' (in Bourdieu et al. 1999, 629).

In Bourdieu's (in Calhoun 1993, 69) view, 'the social world can be explained as a multidimensional space that can be constructed empirically by discovering the main factors of differentiation which account for the differences observed in a given social universe, or, in other words, by discovering the powers or *forms of capital* [original italics] which are or can become efficient . . . in the struggle', which centrally characterizes any social field. Society consists of a collectivity of interrelated and 'homologous' spaces, or 'fields'. A field is a competitive arena of social relations wherein variously positioned agents and institutions struggle over the production, acquisition and control of forms of capital particular to the

field in question. For example, academic degrees are an obvious form of
intellectual capital at stake in the academic field; money, in the economic
field; prestige, in the cultural field; 'connections' in the social field; and
so on.

Reflective of the paramount influence of Weber's sociology of religion
on his theory of practice at large, discussed in Chapter 1, Bourdieu sometimes uses the term 'market' interchangeably with the term field. Other
fundamental terms in Bourdieu's theory of practice, such as 'profit', 'interest', 'capital' and 'investment', are also usually associated with economics and thus likewise reflect the strong Weberian (and Marxist) bent
of Bourdieu's work, just as they reflect what John B. Thompson (1991,
16) calls 'the core assumption in Bourdieu's theory': that 'practices never
cease to comply with an economic logic' (Bourdieu 1990a, 122). Understandably, some interpreters have read into Bourdieu's social theory a
rigid economic reductionism or determinism. Yet rather than imputing
any ultimately reductionist form of 'economism', he is in effect asserting
with this language that all fields conform to a certain economic logic, and
thus Bourdieu (1977, 183, original italics) sees 'the science of economic
practices as a particular case of a *general science of the economy of practices*, capable of treating all practices, including those purporting to be
disinterested or gratuitous, and hence non-economic, as economic practices directed towards maximizing of material or symbolic profit'. In non-
economic fields, moreover, forms of capital at stake are generally examples of what Bourdieu calls 'symbolic capital', such as prestige, honor,
professional titles, and the like, which work in consort with material capital by providing an aura of legitimacy to the hording of various forms of
capital by society's dominant individuals and groups or classes. Material
and symbolic profit are thus often mutually reinforcing.

Wacquant (2005a, 2) further describes Bourdieu's theory of practice
as 'an exceptionally sophisticated attempt to develop a coherent theoretical framework for the analysis of the social world', which is 'the product of the resolute application of a small number of analytical principles
and methodological postures'. In Wacquant's helpful estimation (ibid.,
2–3, original italics), there are essentially four such principles of Bourdieuian
analysis: (1) the '*radical historicization*' of the particular field under analysis, and especially of 'its vocabulary, its official discourse and ordinary
representations, its distinctive devises and associations, and, last but not
least, the discipline that claims to study it'; (2) 'the systematic excavation
of the social conditions of possibility' of practice in a given field; (3) the
critical examination of '*those two states of the social* that are objective
systems of *positions* and subjective bundles of *dispositions* deposited in
agents in the guise of the cognitive and conative schemata that inform

their thoughts, feelings, and conduct'; and (4) the devotion of 'special attention to the *specific efficacy of symbolic power* and to the social tricks it plays on us all'.

With these principles in mind as a kind of job description, one good way of gaining a sound understanding of Bourdieu's theory of practice is to take an inventory of his box of 'thinking tools', taking each tool out of the box one-by-one and learning how it works—or rather, learning how each one is to be put to work. Only then can they be used in concert to build the kind of theoretical apparatus that scholars the world over, in an ever-widening range of academic disciplines, are finding to be such a solid structure on which to hang their own analyses. But a cautionary note is warranted here to disabuse the reader of any notions of rigidity implied by the term that I have just used, 'structure'. Bourdieu's theory of practice was a work in progress that was abruptly halted by his untimely death in 2002, and, furthermore, all of the concepts that are essential to his theory are intended to be flexible and adaptable. Although this can cause confusion and leads some critics to allude to putative contradictions in Bourdieu's work, it is also one of the innovative strengths of his theory of practice, as explains Rogers Brubaker (1993, 217):

> In the first place, the core concepts are not—and are not supposed to be— precise and unambiguous. When I first encountered Bourdieu's work, I collected a dozen or so definitions—or what I took to be definitions—of 'habitus' in an attempt to pin down its precise meaning. Only later did I realize that the attempt was not only vain but misdirected, that Bourdieu was not in fact defining but rather characterizing the concept of habitus in a variety of ways in order to communicate a certain theoretical stance or posture, to designate—and inculcate—a certain sociological disposition, a certain way of looking at the world. The same could be said of the other fundamental concepts: interest, capital, strategy, field, and so forth.

Bourdieu's theory of practice thus amounts to 'a *temporary construct which takes shape for and by empirical work*' (in Wacquant 1989, 50, original italics).

That said, in what follows I offer definitions of the three most essential concepts in Bourdieuian theory and brief explanations of what Bourdieu, generally speaking, intends for each one: field, habitus, and capital. By way of conclusion, Bourdieu's pivotal notion of symbolic violence is also introduced in this chapter. Along with these, other important concepts from Bourdieu's theory of practice, like *collusio*, *doxa*, misrecognition, and *illusio*, are better illustrated through application to substantive examples, and thus they will be explained in Chapter 4.

Field

In English the word 'field' generally evokes images of either farmland with amber waves of grain, professional domains like accountancy or education, or sporting confines like baseball diamonds and soccer pitches. If we take away the first of these images from the equation, add 'force field' and 'battlefield' into the mix, and stir them all together, we wind up with something like what Bourdieu means by the term. With the exception of the playing field (which in French is *'un terrain'*),[3] these images are also evoked by the French word *'champ'*. As Stephen Foster (1986, 103) helpfully reminds us, reflected in the connotations of 'force field' and 'battlefield' are the key characteristics of any given social field, per Bourdieu's conception thereof: a field is a 'space of action' and a 'place of struggle'. The struggle is over forms of capital in the field, and the action is comprised of the production of capital, the consumption of capital, and the jockeying for positions among agents (who are *generally* consumers of capital) and institutions (which are *generally* producers of capital) within the field. In Bourdieu's (in Bourdieu and Wacquant 1992, 243) own uncharacteristically succinct words, a field is 'a structured place of social forces and struggle'.

To soundly understand the Bourdieuian notion of field, and to thereby enable oneself to apply the concept toward the investigation of religion or any arena of the social world, it is important to pay close attention to the nature and function of 'positions' in the field and their 'relations' to one another. A field, Bourdieu (in Bourdieu and Wacquant 1992, 97) insists, should be conceived of as:

> a network, or a configuration, of objective relations between positions. These positions are objectively defined, in their existence and in the determinations they impose upon their occupants, agents or institutions, by their present and potential situation (*situs*) in the structure of the distribution of a species of power (or capital) whose possession commands access to the specific profits that are at stake in the field, as well as by their objective relations to other positions (domination, homology, etc.).

Put otherwise, any individual occupies a certain *position* in society's various fields, which is chiefly determined by how much capital, or power, that he or she possesses. Social fields are therefore networks of relations between individuals and institutions competitively engaged in the dynamics of capital production, pursuit, consumption, and/or accumulation. This engagement is invariably in one's *interest*, and thus each of us—by second nature because we have internalized this entire system—develops *strategies* to either maintain or improve our positions in this relational network of power that is the social world. Any given person's *strategy*, moreover, is not so much 'the product of a conscious, rational calcula- tion', for Bourdieu (1990b, 62), as it is 'the product of the practical sense as the feel for the game, for a particular, historically determined game— a feel that is acquired in childhood, by taking part in social activities, especially . . . in children's games'.

Despite their variations in capitals, interests, strategies and positions, all fields are 'homologous', meaning that they are all characterized by same (*homo*) principle (*logous*), or by a uniform logic, according to which they all operate. This is what Bourdieu (1996, 182) means in saying that 'structural and functional homologies exist between all fields'. Further- more, because such 'structural homologies' are shared across social fields, individual fields (e.g., the cultural field, the political field, the religious field) are only 'relatively autonomous' and thus interrelated. This is also due to, just as it allows for, the transferability of capital from one field to another (a process that Bourdieu [1986b, 242] refers to as 'transubstan- tiation'!), and to the fact that all fields are situated in the larger meta-field of power. To illustrate with a specific example, an agent who succeeds in obtaining an MBA from a prestigious university, clearly a highly coveted piece of academic capital (a form of symbolic capital), will be in a position of greater potential to succeed in the economic field and augment his or her sum of economic capital (a form of material capital), namely money; and money, in turn, can be invested profitably in the political field in ways that reify its investor's dominant position in the meta-field of power (e.g., by contributing handsomely to a successful electoral campaign and thereby ingratiating oneself to a politician and perhaps consequently securing po- litical favors).[4] The MBA, furthermore, is a piece of symbolic capital that contributes to the naturalization of the notion that people who hold such a degree are 'smart', 'hard-working', 'entrepreneurial' and have high in- comes, and that's just the way it is; meanwhile, issues of access to quality higher education, like inheritance and racial inequality, are thereby effec- tively masked.

To digress momentarily and to foreshadow our discussion of religion in the following chapters, it is largely because of the transubstantiative ca- pacity of symbolic capital that Bourdieu's theory of practice is so well suited to interpreting the relationship between religion, class and power, especially in societies that are characterized by stark class divisions. Bourdieu calls for a field analysis that focuses on the struggle over forms of religious capital, like those that Weber calls 'the psychological reassurance of le- gitimacy', the 'feeling of worthiness', and '*legitimierende Macht*' (legiti- mating authority). Once transferred into other fields and transformed into other forms of capital, religious capital of this kind enables elite agents or institutions to enhance or augment their holdings of economic and political capital and thereby solidify or improve their positions in the economic and political fields, and thus to dominate in the meta-field of power. Power requires consecration, after all, and, for Bourdieu, religion is the prototypical possessor of the authority to consecrate, having historically done so in ways that inform his entire understanding of the very nature of society.

It is significant for the broader purposes of this book that, as explained in Chapter 1, Bourdieu arrived at the notion of field early in his career while teaching Weber's economy of salvation, in which the priest, prophet and sorcerer struggle over the control of 'salvation goods' to maintain or improve their positions in this economy by satisfying the religious needs of members of the laity so that they either remain or become their followers (through, Bourdieu would add, 'imposing' on them 'a worldview'). In Bourdieu's notion of field, be it the religious field or any other field, issues of relationality, struggle, force and power are therefore crucial: 'That is what I mean when I describe the global social space as a *field*, that is, both as a field of forces, whose necessity is imposed on agents who are engaged in it, and as a field of struggles within which agents confront each other, with differentiated means and ends according to their position in the structure of the field of forces, thus contributing to conserving or transforming its structure' (Bourdieu 1998a, 32).

Habitus

Bourdieu refers to the relationship between habitus (the seat of one's dispositions and the filter of all that one perceives) and field as a 'double and obscure relation' and an 'ontological correspondence'. By 'double relation' Bourdieu (in Bourdieu and Wacquant 1992, 127) means that 'the field structures the habitus' while the '[h]abitus contributes to constituting the field- as a meaningful world'. The structures of the field also imbue the 'social agent' with a particular ensemble of tendencies of perception, appreciation and practice—a habitus. Hence the 'ontological correspondence' between habitus and field: the fields shape the habitus throughout the course of its individual and social development, and the habitus in turn renders the field 'meaningful' through its developmental influence on agents' appreciation and consumption of capital. For this reason, consumers' tastes, needs, and interests have direct and significant influence on the structure of any marketplace (field) and on the kinds and qualities of goods (capital) available therein, while advertising

too oppositional ?
too masculine a reading of
social space 47 ?

strategies and consumers' prior experience with products each play a fundamental role in determining consumer interest. For Bourdieu, one key to understanding the social world and human practice lies, therefore, in an analysis of this 'obscure and double relation', which operates chiefly in accordance with an economic logic of supply and demand. It is in this sense that Bourdieu (1990b, 14) speaks of his theory of practice as '*genetic structuralism*':

> the analysis of objective structures—those of different fields—is inseparable from the analysis of the genesis, within biological individuals, of the mental structures which are to some extent the product of the incorporation of social structures themselves: the social space, and the groups that occupy it, are the product of historical struggles (in which agents participate in accordance with their position in the social space and with the mental structures through which they apprehend this space).

Thus the 'ontological correspondence' between habitus and field helps answer what Luc Boltanski (2003, 157) calls 'the thorny question . . . posed by the tension between, on the one hand, an approach that takes as its objective the discovery of underlying structures . . . and, on the other hand, an approach that intends to root itself in the experience of the subject acting in the world'. Through a socialization process in which an individual internalizes 'objective structures' in his or her habitus—a process in which one's tastes and inclinations are developed and anchored into his or her personality—a '*practical sense*' of the social world is obtained: 'The habitus is this kind of practical sense for what is to be done in a given situation—what is called in sport a "feel" for the game, that is, the art of *anticipating* the future of the game, which is inscribed in the present state of play' (Bourdieu 1998a, 25, original italics). As Bernard Lahire (2005, 301) argues, in developing the notion of habitus in this way, Bourdieu largely succeeds in helping sociology 'to overcome this theoretically sterile opposition between "society" and "the individual", as if one were dealing with two different *things*, like a "a table and a chair" or "a pot and a pan"'. There is no player without the game, of course, and no game without the player, to extend Bourdieu's analogy. The notion of habitus thus allows the sociologist 'to grasp the social in its incorporated form, to apprehend that the social world imbues each one of us, in the form of propensities to act and react in a certain way, with preferences and dislikes, ways to perceive, to think and to feel'.

In the sense that Bourdieu conceived of the habitus as 'the matrix of perception' it is somewhat reminiscent of Kant's *a priori* categories, though more flexible and infinitely more variegated than Kant's triadic perceptive/cognitive filter of space, time and causality. Where Bourdieu's (1977,

78) notion of habitus departs from anything like Kantian categories is that in addition to being 'the basis of perception and appreciation of all subsequent experiences', the habitus' is equally characterized as any individual's 'set of dispositions' that *inclines*[5] the agent to act in a certain fashion, thus to a great extent shaping (or generating) her or his 'practice': 'The structures constitutive of a particular environment (e.g. the material conditions of existence particular of a class condition) produce habitus systems of durable, transposable dispositions, structured structures predisposed to function as structuring structures' (Bourdieu 1977, 72). Habitus is thus both an individual's epistemological ground and her behavioral motor.

Because, as Wacquant (1993, 245) notes, 'many key traits of Bourdieu's sociology remain elusive so long as one lacks a precise picture of the streams of thought that influenced him', to gain a clearer understanding of the crucial notion of habitus it is helpful to briefly outline Bourdieu's creative synthesis of its previous incarnations in the work of earlier social thinkers. By referring to Kant above, I do not mean to imply that Bourdieu was influenced by the great German philosopher in developing his notion of habitus. As far as I know, Kant never prominently employed the term, though a number of other leading figures in the history of western philosophy, in different ways and at times with different renditions (e.g., 'hexis', 'habits', 'mental habits', etc.), have done so, beginning with Aristotle and including Aquinas, Hegel, Husserl, Dewey and Habermas. Furthermore, in sociological theory proper, earlier uses of the term, variously understood, are also made by Durkheim, Weber and, most importantly for Bourdieu, Mauss (Sapiro 2004).[6] Weber's use of the term habitus, however, is less influential on Bourdieu than Weber's (1978, 1186) notion of 'ethos': 'matter-of-fact considerations that . . . determine individual behavior and interpose impersonal forces between the persons involved'. For Weber, ethos is largely a cognitive process that shapes or inspires human practice. From Mauss, meanwhile and more importantly, Bourdieu gains the pivotal insight that a more holistic understanding of habitus requires attention to the somatic dimensions of perception and action. As Gisèle Sapiro (2004, 68) aptly demonstrates, '[h]abitus thus comes to designate this system of cognitive schemes that Weber denotes by the term *ethos* and to which Bourdieu adds, following Mauss, bodily habits'.

Just as vital as Bourdieu's wedding of Weber and Mauss in forging his own conception of habitus was his critical engagement of Erwin Panofsky's *Gothic Architecture and Scholasticism*, which Bourdieu translated into French in 1967, adding his own 'Postface' in the process, in which he praises Panofsky's short but compelling book as being 'without the slightest doubt one of the most beautiful challenges that has ever been mounted against positivism' (Bourdieu 1967, 135).[7] Bourdieu takes considerable licence in his translation of Panofsky, casting numbered subsections in the original as 'chapters' in the French version and giving them titles that do not appear in the original. For example, Bourdieu entitles Chapter 2 '*La force formatrice d'habitudes*' ('The Formative Force of Habits'), and where Panofsky (e.g., 1957, 20) uses the term 'mental habits' in the original, Bourdieu translates it faithfully as '*habitudes mentales*' in the text but chooses to render the term as 'habitus' in his index (Panofsky 1967, 206).[8] Panofsky, furthermore, only uses the term a couple of times in his book, though enough obviously to have a huge impact on Bourdieu, who uses the term about four times as often in his Postface than Panofsky did in the book itself. Be that as it may, Panofsky's demonstration of the mutually influential relationship between architectural structure (as a 'habit-forming force') and 'mental habits' is quite persuasive and is, as such, a decisive influence on Bourdieu's particular development of the notion of habitus. 'The attraction of Panofsky's work was that he had not been content merely to observe patterns of similarity in Gothic architecture', writes Derek Robbins, 'but had gone further to suggest that these patterns were the direct result of the common internalization of modes of scholastic thinking in the period between 1130 and 1270' (Robbins 1991, 61).[9] It is also significant for our purposes that Bourdieu (once again!) found such important insight from a text that is essentially about religious ideas— significant perhaps in part because habitus, as a theoretical concept, is thus inculcated with religious notions in ways that predispose it to be so suitable for the study of religion, as will be shown in Chapters 4 and 5.

Jean-Paul Bronckart and Marie-Noëlle Schurmans (2001, 163) do well to explain that Bourdieu effectively synthesizes these influences in such a way that several characteristics distinguish his own conceptualization of habitus: '*corporeal dispositions* (postural and gestural), qualified as *hexis*; moral dimensions (or the system of values), qualified as *ethos*; cognitive dimensions (or the system of representations), qualified as *eidos*; and . . . linguistic competence as well as the *aesthesis* (aesthetic dispositions or taste)'. I should add here that just as there are thus corporeal, cognitive, linguistic and aesthetic dimensions to the *dispositional* function of habitus, so too are there corporeal, cognitive, linguistic and aesthetic dimensions to its *perceptive* function.

Bourdieu (1977, 80) stresses the 'objective homogenizing of group or class habitus which results from the homogeneity of the conditions of existence', meaning that individual members of the same socio-economic class have relatively homogenous habitus because they have in common many formative experiences, such as family structure, household income, type of neighborhood, quality and degree of education, form of religion, etc., which inculcate in their habitus a particular 'set of dispositions'. Hence, because the habitus is 'embodied history, internalized as second nature' (Bourdieu 1990a, 56), what an agent from, say, the urban American working class expects from life, and how he or she perceives of and reacts to any life experience or social condition, will be similar to the expectations, perceptions and reactions of other urban working-class Americans because their respective habitus have been similarly formed. In other words: 'A social class (in-itself)—a class of identical or similar conditions of existence and conditionings—is at the same time a class of biological individuals having the same *habitus*, understood as a system of dispositions common to all products of the same conditionings' (ibid., 59). Thus, once developed, an individual agent's habitus is always and inevitably a specifically class-ed habitus, which predisposes her or him to perceive, appreciate and act in ways reflective of the material conditions of the class existence that contribute to her or his habitus' formation. Therefore, class identity is the key formative influence on the habitus.[10] This association of habitus and class is one of the most fundamental premises in Bourdieu's theory of practice at large, as Brubaker (2004, 47–48) explains: 'For Bourdieu . . . class and habitus, the twin lynchpins of his metatheory, together explain anything and everything. Dispositions (the habitus) directly govern conduct, and because classes are defined as individuals sharing the same dispositions as well as the same external conditions of existence, class becomes the principle of intelligibility of all conduct, and sociology can take as its aim to "determine how class condition is able to structure the whole experience of social subjects"'. Class difference, meanwhile, is, for Bourdieu, structured by the disproportionate distribution of various forms of capital across society's various fields.

Capital

In *Distinction*, Bourdieu (1984, 101) offers the following formula as an encapsulation of his theory of practice: '[(habitus) (capital)] + field = practice'. Practice is thus the sum product of a person's active engagement of capital in any given field. A person's engagement of capital, furthermore, may take one or more of several forms, depending both upon her respective *position* in the field and upon the inclinations inscribed within her habitus: the production of capital; the consumption of capital; the pursuit of capital; the possession of capital; the employment

[handwritten margin note: does B. reinforce rational choice theory in deciphering religious practices?]

of capital; and/or the accumulation of capital. How individuals engage capital, what forms of capital they esteem, is one of the most important functions of their habitus, or of their internalization of the social world, and how much capital they wind up possessing in various fields ultimately determines their position in the broader field of power. Despite finding Bourdieu's quasi-mathematical formula to be 'problematic', Nick Crossley (2001, 96) ascertains its 'basic gist' to be 'that practice is the result of various habitual schemes and dispositions (habitus), combined with resources (capital), being activated by certain structured social conditions (field) which they, in turn, belong to and variously reproduce and modify'. As such, we may understand Bourdieu to mean here that capitals are 'resources distributed throughout the social body which have an exchange value in one or more of the various "markets" or "fields" which . . . he believes comprise the social world' (ibid.).

The influence of Marx on Bourdieu's notion of capital is obvious,[11] though Bourdieu's expansion of the concept beyond the material into the symbolic is an important and compelling innovation that, as much as anything else, marks Bourdieu's departure from Marx:[12]

> Economism recognizes no other form of interest than that which capitalism has produced, through a kind of real operation of abstraction, by setting up a universe of relations between man and man based, as Marx says, on 'callous cash payment' and more generally by favouring the creation of relatively autonomous fields, capable of establishing their own axiomatics (through the fundamental tautology 'business is business', on which 'the economy' is based). It can therefore find no place in its analysis, still less in its calculations, for any form of 'non-economic' interest (Bourdieu 1990a, 115).

Weber is a less obvious, though no less powerful, influence than Marx on Bourdieu's notion of capital. In this regard, it is especially Weber's economy of salvation that Bourdieu finds so provocative. As explained in the previous chapter and revisited in Chapter 4, Weber's configuration of the religious world as an economic marketplace, in which a Church and its specialists seek to establish and maintain a monopoly in the production and administration of salvation goods, provides Bourdieu with the fundamental paradigmatic model for his entire social theory. Small-scale competitors, in the form of prophets and sorcerers, enter the religious marketplace and seek to gain adherents by marketing to them renegade or subversive forms of salvation goods, which the Church identifies as 'heretical', and the struggle over capital in the religious field thus unfolds accordingly. Weber's concept of salvation goods is thus for Bourdieu the paradigmatic model for his notion of symbolic capital.[13]

Bourdieu (1990b, 112) conceives of symbolic capital as that kind of cultural or social capital that is 'endowed with a symbolic efficacy'. It is this symbolic dimension of Bourdieu's economic paradigm, furthermore, that ultimately exonerates him of the charge of economic reductionism, as Moishe Postone, Edward LiPuma and Craig Calhoun (1993, 5) explain:

> Although the economic is crucially determining, it must be symbolically medi-
> ated. The undistinguished reproduction of economic capital would reveal the
> arbitrary character of the distribution of power and wealth. Symbolic capital
> functions to mask the economic domination of the dominant class and socially
> illegitimate hierarchy by essentializing and naturalizing social position. That is,
> noneconomic fields articulate with, reproduce, and legitimate class relations
> through misrecognition.

nice

As such, symbolic capital, like all forms of capital, is more or less equivalent to power: 'The different forms of capital, the possession of which defines class membership and the distribution of which determines positions in the power relations constituting the field of power . . . are simultaneously instruments of power and stakes in the struggle for power' (Bourdieu 1984, 315–16), whether material or symbolic, which quite often buttress one another in such a way as to perpetuate the status quo. Capital is thus an instrument of both domination and its reproduction in human society.[14]

'Capital, defined implicitly as attributes, possessions, or qualities of a person or a position exchangeable for goods, services, or esteem, exists in many forms', writes Paul DiMaggio (1979, 1463), '—symbolic, cultural, social, linguistic, as well as economic'. There are numerous forms of capital specific to each individual field, such as sacraments and divine sanction in the religious field, academic degrees and endowed chairs in the academic field, electoral offices and legislative authority in the political field, and so on. Their proliferation notwithstanding,[15] all types of capital necessarily take on any one of 'three fundamental guises', for Bourdieu (1986b, 243, original italics), here in effect tripling the theoretical applicability of Marx's notion of capital:

> as *economic capital*, which is immediately and directly convertible into money
> and may be institutionalized in the form of property rights; as *cultural capital*,
> which his convertible, on certain conditions, into economic capital and may be
> institutionalized in the form of educational qualifications; and as *social capital*,
> made up of social obligations ('connections'), which is convertible, in certain
> conditions, into economic capital and may be institutionalized in the form of a
> title of nobility.

Forms of economic capital thus include money and any material possessions that might be considered economic investments, like real estate or stocks and bonds; social capital is one's network of contacts, especially with powerful individuals or groups that may influence one's access to other forms of capital (e.g., Uncle Joe, thanks in no small part to his endowment of a million dollars to the School of Business and his consequent close relationship to key board members, gets his nephew Tim into an elite university despite Tim's low SAT scores and criminal record). Cultural capital,[16] finally, takes a wide range of forms in Bourdieu's oeuvre, from titles of nobility and familiarity with the permanent collection at the Louvre of the Metropolitan Museum of Art, to correct grammar and polished table manners.[17] As a key form of symbolic capital, cultural capital thus reifies and legitimates, and thereby reproduces, social distinctions, and this reproduction is the primary focus of Bourdieu's theory of practice: 'The different forms of capital, the possession of which defines class membership and the distribution of which determines position in the power relations constituting the field of power . . . are simultaneously instruments of power and stakes in the struggle for power; they are unequally powerful in real terms and unequally recognized as legitimate principles of authority or signs of distinction' (Bourdieu 1984, 315–16). Thus symbolic capital, which Crossley (2001, 97) conceives of as something that 'broadly amounts to status or recognition', only gains its 'symbolic efficacy' for Bourdieu (1990b, 112, original italics) 'when it is *misrecognized* in its arbitrary truth as capital and *recognized* as legitimate'. In other words, all forms of capital can be transformed into forms of symbolic capital and thus into weapons of symbolic violence (Terray 2003, 300).

Conclusion: Symbolic Violence in the Field of Power

Not surprisingly, Bourdieu was a great admirer of the iconoclastic English writer Virginia Woolf, and in *Masculine Domination* (2001, 2) he cites the following passage from her 1938 book-length essay *Three Guineas* (1966) as 'an invitation to orient research towards an approach capable of grasping the specifically symbolic dimensions of male domination' and by extension all forms of domination:

> Inevitably we look upon societies as conspiracies that sink the private brother, whom many of us have reason to respect, and inflate in his stead a monstrous

male, loud of voice, hard of fist, childishly intent upon scoring the floor of the earth with chalk marks, within whose mystical boundaries human beings are penned, rigidly, separately, artificially; where, daubed red and gold, decorated like a savage with feathers, he goes through mystic rites and enjoys dubious powers of power and domination while we, 'his' women, are locked in the private house without share in the many societies of which his society is composed.

The relationship between symbolic capital (the red and gold feathers) and symbolic violence (sinking the private brother, the rigid and artificial penning of individuals, locking up the women, *as well as* the mystic rites that give the air of legitimacy this monstrous male's arbitrary and thus 'dubious power of domination') is central to Bourdieu's entire theory of practice, for it is only when armed with symbolic capital that any agent, institutional or individual, can commit acts of symbolic violence and engender in dominated groups and individuals the misrecognition of the social order as something natural. Michael Grenfell (2004, 28, original italics) explains this relationship as follows:

> [C]ompetition operates within *fields* and between them, where there is a struggle to assert particular dominant forms of *capital*, new *capital* definitions, and to devalue others. Bourdieu refers to some *fields* as *markets*—for example, the linguistic market—in order to express that the way they operate is analogous to economic systems. There can also be *symbolic violence*, where there is a struggle between the dominant forms and their representatives; that is, 'a struggle over the power to impose (or even inculcate) the arbitrary instruments of knowledge and expression (taxonomies) of social reality'.

Or, as Cheleen Mahar, Richard Harker and Chris Wilkes (1990, 14) put it, '[t]he work of constructing visions and divisions in the social world supposes a kind of capital (for some) which works effectively in the mechanisms of delegation and dispossession. The outcome of such mechanisms is what Bourdieu calls symbolic violence, because those who do not have "the means of speech", or do not know how to "take the floor", can only see themselves in the words or the discourse of others—that is, those who are legitimate authorities and who can name and represent'. Thus to Emmanuel Terray (2003, 302), all 'beliefs, norms, values, as well as the institutions that support them . . . belong to the universe of symbolic violence', a kind of 'invisible prison, without walls or doors, in which Merlin the wizard is trapped'. What makes symbolic violence violent, furthermore, is 'its imposition of the arbitrary' (ibid.).

To recall, one of the overriding aims of Bourdieu's social theory is to grasp the mechanisms by which distinctions and domination are perpetuated in the social world. Power, as Richard Jenkins (1992, 104) explains, is only rarely exercised as overt physical force, and Bourdieu thus seeks 'to specify in theoretical terms the processes whereby, in all societies, order and social restraint are produced by indirect, cultural mechanisms rather than by direct, coercive social control'. In effect, such mechanisms are, for Bourdieu (1990a, 127), precise forms of symbolic violence: 'that gentle, invisible violence, unrecognized as such, chosen as much as un-dergone, that of trust, obligation, personal loyalty, hospitality, gifts, debts, piety, in a word, all of the virtues honoured by the ethic of honour'. All of these things, furthermore, are symbolically violent because they permit 'relations of domination to be established and maintained through strate-gies which are softened and disguised, and which conceal domination beneath the veil of enhanced relation' (Thompson 1991, 24), and thus 'symbolic violence is the imposition of systems of symbolism and mean-ing (i.e., culture) upon groups or classes in such a way that they are experienced as legitimate' (Jenkins 1992, 104).

nice

In the end, Bourdieu's theory of practice is of course intended to be applied in the analysis of the social world, as already noted, and as Bourdieu insists in numerous places. In Chapter 4, I provide an example of such an application to the interpretation of religion in colonial New England, revis-iting the pivotal notion of symbolic violence there, but for now permit me to draw attention to Bourdieu's (in Bourdieu and Wacquant 1992, 104–105) own explanation that employing his theory of practice at heart is a three-stage process:

> First, one must analyze the position of the field vis-à-vis the field of power . . . Second, one must map out the objective structure of the relations between the positions occupied by the agents or institutions who compete for the legitimate form of specific authority of which the field is the site. And, third, one must analyze the habitus of agents, the different systems of dispositions that they have acquired by internalizing a determinate type of social and economic condition.

Key

In other words, any single field under analysis must be first examined in terms of its relationship to the broader, all-encompassing 'field of power'; a blueprint of its internal structure must be produced; and the nature and functions of its actors' habitus must be taken carefully into account. Along the way, furthermore, one must be diligent to identify any and all forms of symbolic violence manifest in the field, because symbolic violence is the paramount source of distinctions between individuals and groups in society. And only where there is distinction can there be domination.

* a double misrecognition — legitimating both the dominant to the dominant & the dominant to the dominated

Summary of Key Elements to Chapter 2

- Bourdieu defines his social theory as 'generative structuralism', or 'genetic structuralism' (pp. 40–43), meaning that the structures of the social world are internalized by individuals, who in turn contribute to the re-generation of the structures themselves;
- Society is a multidiemensional space, each of whose dimensions is a 'field' (pp. 44–46), in which individual and institutional agents struggle over the production, administration and consumption of forms of 'capital' specific to the field in question (e.g., political capital in the political field, religious capital in the religious field, and so on);
- Social structures are internalized or inculcated in the 'habitus' (pp. 46–50) of individual agents, which is both their 'matrix of perception' and the seat of their dispositions; as such, habitus is essential to personhood and volition, providing one's somatic and cognitive 'practical sense' of the social world;
- One's habitus inclines one to deem various forms of 'capital' (pp. 50–53) as worthy of pursuit; once obtained, material or symbolic capital, as forms of power or resources, determines one's 'position' in any given field and in the metafield of power;
- 'Symbolic violence' transpires whenever distinctions in society are reified through the inculcation in one's habitus of the misrecognition that social distinctions and inequalities are natural instead of arbitrary; any gesture, act, or proclamation in society that promotes such misrecognition constitutes symbolic violence, which ultimately serves to perpetuate domination in human society. For Bourdieu, symbolic violence thus assumes the complicity of its victims (pp. 53–55).

Chapter 3

Bourdieu's Writings on Religion

And acts of nomination, from the most trivial acts of bureaucracy, like the issuing of an identity card, or a sickness or disablement certificate, to the most solemn consecrations of nobility, lead in a kind of infinite regression to the realization of God on earth, the State, which guarantees, in the last resort, the infinite series of acts of authority certifying by delegation the validity of the certificates of legitimate existence. . . And sociology thus leads to a kind of theology of the last instance . . . Durkheim was, it can be seen, not so naïve as it is claimed when he said . . . that 'society is God' (Bourdieu 2000a, 245).

Introduction

Pierre Bourdieu's essays on religion are quite influenced by two seemingly very firm convictions: that religion in the modern world is in decline; and that religion's ultimate social function is to help people make sense of their respective positions in the social order. Consistent with the general raison d'être of his entire sociological project, Bourdieu's commentaries on religion, taken together, thus aim to demonstrate how institutional religions seek to monopolize the religious field by imposing on the laity an 'orthodox' worldview and by denouncing as 'heretical' any alternative worldviews that competitors seek to propagate among the same laity. Another theme that emerges across several of Bourdieu's essays on religion is how the Church (which can be taken as a blanket term for all institutional religious hierarchies) tries to cling to power that is, as a function of modernity, inevitably slipping out of its grasp. Bourdieu's investigations of religion reflect no concern, meanwhile, with some of the central questions that have occupied scholars of religion, especially in the field of religious studies *per se*, such as the origin of religion, comparative religion, theology, spirituality, myth, symbolism, the sacred, and Bourdieu never articulates an extensive definition of religion of his own.[1] And although there is a great deal of discussion of ritual in some of Bourdieu's most important empirical and theoretical work, his emphasis is on ritual as structuring force in society and *not* as a fundamental feature of religion.

The fact that an increasing number of scholars of religion are finding incisive utility in a thinker who actually did not say much directly about religion is, at any rate, impressive testimony to the power and reach of Bourdieu's theory of practice.[2] In this vein, Bourdieu is comparable to Marx and Gramsci, who each wrote even less about religion than Bourdieu but nonetheless have had a tremendous impact on the way that many scholars think about the subject. Like Marx's notion of religion as the 'opium of the masses' and Gramsci's notion that popular religion some- times amounts to an 'active worldview' in opposition to orthodoxy, Bourdieu's notions of religious habitus, field and capital have much po- tential to become staple considerations for studies of religion, especially (though not exclusively) those with sociological and political concerns.

In reading Bourdieu, one should always keep in mind his overarching concern with social distinctions that enable domination. The injustices and inequalities that plague human society are not, he insists, the will of God, monoliths, or historical accidents. They came from somewhere de- monstrably real, and they are perpetuated by something demonstrably real, and all along the way people have been socialized to misrecognize them as being somehow natural and thus acceptable—'well, that's just the way things are, so I guess we're gonna have to live with it'. Bourdieu was driven by the conviction that sociology is a science (or a 'martial art') that has the power to reveal the causes and buttresses of unjust social orders, and the misrecognitions that underlie them—and only once you see that something is in fact arbitrary (and thus not natural and the only way that it can be), can you entertain the notion that it should be changed. Nothing in the social world is unassailable in this regard—not art, not education, not sociology, and certainly not religion. 'It is as if Bourdieu finally witnessed', notes Michael Grenfell (2004, 195), 'the coalescence of the dominating factions of the dominant into one coherent system of rule and subjugation'. In some sense, religion is more assailable than anything else for the unsurpassed role that it has played in human history in forming the *doxa* and providing forms of religious capital that have at times legitimated some of the worst kinds of injustices in human history, like slavery and genocide. Thus the resistance that Bourdieu heralds is necessarily resistance 'against the actual world-view itself' (Grenfell 2004, 195).

Bourdieu's Writings on Religion

By my count, Bourdieu wrote 'only' ten essays that deal centrally (or more or less centrally) with religion, and the subject appears but infrequently elsewhere in his massive body of work.[3] This is not to say that he found the subject to be unimportant, for his early fieldwork in rural Algeria assured him of the central place of religion in social life there, a subject he dealt with then only briefly but most impressively, and his first published scholarly essay treats a controversial religious subject. Furthermore, Bourdieu clearly recognized the awesome influence of religion in the construction of *doxa* and the 'actual worldview itself' that was the target of the resistance that his entire social theory was designed to inspire and equip. The relative infrequency with which he wrote directly about religion, rather, is perhaps best explained by the fact that Bourdieu conceived of himself first and foremost as a sociologist and that a truly scientific sociology of religion was for him difficult to imagine, let alone construct. Can 'the sociology of religion', he asks, 'be a truly scientific sociology? And I respond: difficultly; that is to say, only on the condition that it is accompanied by a scientific sociology of the religious field' (Bourdieu 1987c, 106). In other words, the social-scientific study of religion must always take carefully into account the competitive structure of the religious field, the habitus of practitioners and their interests and strategies, the forms of capital at stake, and related matters. It must also be critically self-reflective—i.e., a reflexive sociology of religion.

Of Bourdieu's ten essays that focus centrally on religion, the earliest, published in 1958, considers the hypocrisy of Tartuffe, the title character of Molière's celebrated (and once-banned) 1664 play; two of them are short lectures published in slightly abbreviated form in his 1987 book *Choses dites* (though omitted in the English translation of this book, *In Other Words*); two other short lectures appear in a similar 1994 volume entitled *Raisons pratiques* (included in slightly varied form in the English translation, *Practical Reason*); one is a short treatment comparing religious piety and artistic devotion; another is a quite trenchant critique of Weber's sociology of religion; one is an extensive co-authored study of the French Catholic episcopate; one is a foray into linguistics that analyzes comments of lament among Catholics about changing liturgical practices; and one is a dense and brilliant presentation of the nature of the religious field. This chapter summarizes these essays and briefly considers discussions of Islam contained in Bourdieu's earliest work on Algeria.

Tartuffe

It is not insignificant for our purposes that Bourdieu's first scholarly publication, 'Tartuffe ou le drame de la foi et de la mauvaise foi' ('Tartuffe, or The Drama of Faith and of Bad Faith' [1958a]), discusses religious hypocrisy as it is so blatantly embodied by the title character of Molière's celebrated comedy *Tartuffe*. Tartuffe is such a compelling figure that his name

---

Bourdieu's Writings on Religion

- (1958a) 'Tartuffe ou le drame de la foi et de la mauvaise foi', *Revue de la Méditerranée* 4/5 (92/93): 453–58.
- (1958b) *Sociologie de l'Algérie*. Paris: Presses Universitaires de France. This book contains two interesting subsections on religion: 'Puritanisme et capitalisme' (pp. 50–54) and 'L'Islam et la société nord-africaine' (pp. 107–15).
- (1987b and 1987c) 'La dissolution du religieux' and 'Sociologues de la croyance et croyances de sociologues'. Lectures republished in *Choses Dites*. Paris: Éditions de Minuit.
- (1982) 'La sainte famille: L'épiscopat français dans le champ du pouvoir', *Actes de la recherche en sciences sociales* 44/45: 2–53. Co-authored with Monique de Saint Martin.
- (1987a) 'Legitimation and Structured Interest in Weber's Sociology of Religion'. Trans. Chris Turner, in Scott Lash and Sam Whimster (eds.), *Max Weber, Rationality, and Modernity*. London: Allen and Unwin, 119–36.
- (1991a) 'Genesis and Structure of the Religious Field'. Trans. Jenny B. Burnside, Craig Calhoun and Leah Florence, *Comparative Social Research* 13: 1–44.
- (1991c) 'Authorized Language: The Social Conditions for the Effectiveness of Ritual Discourse'. In Pierre Bourdieu, *Language and Symbolic Power*. Cambridge, MA: Harvard University Press, 107–16.
- (1994a) 'Pieté religieuse et devotion artistique. Fidèles et amateurs d'art à Santa Maria Novella', *Actes de la recherche en sciences sociales* 105: 71–74.
- (1998a) 'The Laughter of Bishops' and 'On the Economy of the Church'. The former is a subsection (pp. 112–23) and the latter an appendix of Chapter 5 of *Practical Reason* (pp. 124–26).

---

has entered the English language as a word meaning, according to the *American Heritage Dictionary*, 'a hypocrite, especially one who affects religious piety'; the word 'tartuffery', meanwhile, indicates the related condition. Molière masterfully portrays Tartuffe as a deceitful scoundrel who parades as a deeply pious Catholic in order to endear himself to a wealthy man named Orgon. Behind the veil of trustworthiness that Tartuffe creates through his apparent piety, he attempts to seduce Orgon's wife and manages to have Orgon sign over to him all of his property. The drama unfolds around the attempts of Orgon's family and friends to reveal Tartuffe's true nature and designs. It is thus unsurprising that the play, whose second run carried also the title *L'imposteur* (*The Imposter*), outraged the French Catholic hierarchy, who successfully pressured King Louis IV to ban it in 1667. It is equally unsurprising that Bourdieu would be so taken by the play, as the attempts to unmask Tartuffe and demonstrate his use of religion as a means of duping Orgon into ruin presage in interesting ways elements of Bourdieu's theory of (religious) practice that were still over ten years away from being published. The euphemistic nature of religious language, misrecognition, symbolic violence, religion's legitimating power—all of these notions are embedded in the story of Tartuffe.

Bourdieu's 'Tartuffe' is perhaps best described as a kind of existentialist consideration of one of Molière's most celebrated characters. The essay assumes both familiarity with the play and with the central notion to French existentialism, Sartre's 'bad faith'[4]—familiarity he could safely expect among the French intellectuals who were his likeliest readers. It is a relatively short composition, merely six pages, written in a free-flowing prose that nowhere states clearly its purpose. It is nonetheless worth speculating that Bourdieu's exposé of Tartuffe's 'bad faith', which is hardly in itself impressive given the character's obvious and cruel hypocrisy, was intended as a criticism of religion itself, with Tartuffe representing the institutional church and its abundantly euphemistic language, and Orgon representing the laity as the victim of symbolic violence because of his grave misrecognition of Tartuffe as pious and thus good and believable: 'The seducer, when he speaks the language of the devout, only arrives at the depth of his own logic. He employs the words of the cult and of prayer so as not in the least to be discovered a sinner and to endeavor to believe that his creaturely appetites are actually part of the devotions that one must render to the Creator' (1958a, 457). Lest my suggestion that Bourdieu's 'Tartuffe' is a metaphoric criticism of institutional religion sound implausible, I should add that he retrieves the figure from this all-but-forgotten and rarely cited essay nearly twenty-five years later in criticizing the euphemistic and duplistic discourse of the French Catholic episcopate, where Bourdieu (1982, 46) equates the bishops with Tartuffe insofar as they are all 'masters of euphemism': 'And to take Orgon's things by persuading him that doing so was out of heavenly interest is to inscribe oneself in the economy of the offering, a denied economy, and to appropriate for oneself the things of this world by calling them the things of the other world, or, more subtly, in the name of a moral person, the Church'.

Religion in Algeria

It is clear that Bourdieu was deeply impressed by the pervasive and profound influence of Islam in the lives of the Algerians with whom he came into contact both during his military service and his ethnographic fieldwork there. This is especially evident in his first book on Algeria (his first ever book), *Sociologie de l'Algérie*, originally published in 1958: 'The entire Maghreb carries the imprint of Islam . . . [which] exercises so complete and sovereign a dominion', having 'planted such deep roots' that one is led to wonder whether it is 'the only key to Algerian society and *religion in the culture wars generated by globalization*

psychology' (1958b, 107). Bourdieu found Algeria to be so fascinating and rich a terrain for sociological analysis largely because cultural traditions there were so squarely (and brutally) confronted with modernity, due primarily of course to the French colonial enterprise in North Africa—an enterprise in which Bourdieu himself participated as a soldier: 'it is in Algeria, in effect, where the shock of the encounter between autochthonous and European civilizations is felt with all of its force' (ibid., 5). The society of Algeria's Kabyle peasants that Bourdieu analyzed was in tumultuous disarray, its culture's very existence seriously threatened, and yet religion provided perhaps the only true means of cultural self-preservation: 'all disintegrating influences are countered by the extremely lively pressure that the group places on all members through the intermediary of doctrine, with its cohesion determined by the intense effervescence of the religious life, the presence in the life and hearts of all religious law that is at once lived as a rule imposed from beyond and the internalized meaning of conduct' (ibid., 51).

Though written before he developed his theory of practice,[5] Bourdieu's early observations about Islam in Algeria, however briefly stated, are as impressive as anything that he ever wrote about religion. Like any religion, Islam among the Mozabites is a 'cultural fact' (ibid., 108) that requires careful historical and sociological inquiry in order for its nature and influence to be soundly understood. Equally insightful, Bourdieu posits that the historical reception of Islam in Algeria resulted from a dialectical process involving local traditional religion and Islam that operated according to:

> the laws that govern the phenomenon of loaning and borrowing (the existence of resources of a common civilization as a basis of the communication and reinterpretation of borrowed traits in function of the context of the reception). As a result, if the Muslim religion makes any sense to [traditional] Algerian culture, it is because there exists between the two a pre-established harmony in which the dogma and precepts of the one do not contradict in any way the fundamental values of the other and, furthermore, respond to essential needs (1958b, 108).[6]

Bourdieu further considers the pastoral nature of Mzab life and its closeness to the earth to be taproots for those 'reinterpretations that give Algerian Islam its original style' (ibid., 115).

In another perceptive discussion, Bourdieu argues that gender divisions in North African Islam may actually function to enhance feminine power and autonomy: 'The separation of masculine and feminine societies is almost total (a veil that only reveals one eye; reserved place in the mosque, etc.), but does not go without conferring [to women] a certain autonomy'. The space of this autonomy is found 'in the margins of the official religion that is the affair of men'. It is thus fundamentally a reli-

This can be expanded to the unintended results of the success of the civil rights movement → erasure of race in the upper middle class

'religion' were 18st cent. style

gious space, whether in women's ritual washing of the dead or in 'the sort of particular cult' that is entirely comprised of women and distinguished by 'their own kind of sorcery with particular rituals; songs that are uniquely theirs; special tasks or special techniques for communal works; a form of speech that is original in its phonetics, vocabulary, and phraseology' (ibid., 54). In other words, gender divisions in Algerian Islam actually serve to produce feminized spaces of autonomy, or creatively developed 'hidden transcripts', to employ James Scott's (1990) term, in which women's agency is asserted and maintained.

The voice of Weber in Bourdieu's treatment of religion is nowhere more resoundingly echoed than in the title of one of his first published discussions of the subject, 'Puritanism and Capitalism', a subsection of the fourth chapter of *Sociologie d'Algérie*, a kind of homage to the cynosure of Weber's classic argument in *The Protestant Ethic and the Spirit of Capitalism* (1976). Of course, neither Puritanism nor any other form of Christianity has ever exercised significant influence in Algeria, but Bourdieu found that Islam served equally effectively, at least locally, to create a fertile atmosphere for the accumulation of wealth among his subjects in Mzab, a northern region of Algeria. In addition to providing the strongest ground for the resistance to the cultural dissolution provoked by colonization (Bourdieu 1958b, 51), Islam inspired in the Mozabites a kind of detachment from the things of this world, including profits from trade initiatives. Thus discouraged by Islamic asceticism from spending their earnings on luxuries, the Mozabites in Bourdieu's first book had no recourse 'but to reinvest them' (ibid., 53). Surely Weber would delight to know that one of the most important social theorists in his intellectual succession thus demonstrates that economics sometimes *are* directly determined by religious ideas, and not just vice versa, as Marx would have it.

Bourdieu's brief consideration of religion in *Algeria 1960* (1979) also centrally employs a key notion from Weber's sociology of religion, as clearly reflected in the title of the volume's longest essay, 'The Disenchantment of the World'. The growing influence of capitalism and modernization on Algerian culture and society created 'radically new problems' that unseated 'the assurances provided by religion': 'The break with tradition, emigration, the relaxation of collective pressure linked to the anonymity of urban life, contact with a technical civilization entirely devoted to profane ends, the explicit and diffuse teachings of the school, all these influences combine to produce a thorough transmutation of values and to destroy the soil in which traditional religiosity was rooted'. In effect, Algerian society was becoming increasingly 'differentiated' in such a way that the traditional 'religious field' enters a state of 'dissolution' in which formerly religious agents 'can only choose between indifference and superstition' (Bourdieu 1979, 69–70). 'Bourdieu's conviction that religion is a *declining institution* in differentiated societies', as Erwan Dianteill (2004, 82, original italics) explains, thus emerges from both his ethnographic fieldwork in Algeria and his reflections on modern European (and especially French) religious history, which largely explains the relatively infrequent empirical investigations that Bourdieu made of religion during his prolific career. And even the many references in *Outline of a Theory of Practice* and *Logic of Practice*, Bourdieu's most explicit and important theoretical forays, to features of Algerian culture that one might normally consider to be 'religious', are of more interest to Bourdieu as 'rituals, magic, institutions of magic, and illocutionary force, and particular cases of symbolic power' (Dianteill 2004, 68).

The *Chose dites* Essays

In 1987 Bourdieu published a collection of lectures entitled *Choses dites*, which in English means simply 'Things Said'. Two of these lectures were on the sociology of religion: 'Sociologue de la croyance et croyances de sociologues' ('Sociologist of Belief and Beliefs of Sociologists') and 'La dissolution du religieux' ('The Dissolution of the Religious'). The former was originally delivered in 1982 to the Association Française de Sociologie Religieuse (French Association of the Sociology of Religion). The latter, meanwhile, was originally delivered as a lecture in Strasbourg in 1982 and was published in slightly longer form, under a different title, as a chapter in an edited volume on religious leadership in 1985.

The second essay explores the effects that certain facets of modernization (like urbanization, the privatization of life, and women's increasing access to education) have had upon the religious field and the nature of religious leadership. Because, as Bourdieu explains, the law of supply and demand goes far in structuring the religious field (as it does all fields), shifts in human practice in industrial societies have given 'birth to a demand of salvation services of a new type' (1987b, 122), which has in turn caused changes in the religious field that ultimately result in 'the dissolution of the religious'. By 'dissolution' Bourdieu does not mean to imply that religion is disappearing like salt dissolving in water, but rather to illustrate that the religious field is increasingly witnessing the veritable erasure of its borders and a reshaping of its identity as a subfield of the broader 'field of the salvation of souls', which is itself a subfield of the field of 'symbolic manipulation':

> Today we are moving in imperceptible stages from ancient clerics . . . to members of sects, to psychoanalysts, to psychologists, to doctors, to sexologists, to *expression corporelle* teachers, to Eastern martial arts, to life counselors, to

Very nice statement on the diffusion of authority once monopolized by the church

social workers. They all take part in a new field of struggle over the symbolic manipulation of the conduct of private life and the orientation of one's vision of the world, and they all develop in their practice competing and antagonistic definitions of health, of healing, of the treatment of bodies and of souls (1987b, 119).[7]

Thus the incursion of relatively new forms of professionals and specialists into therapeutic and 'theological' or pastoral arenas, which were once largely monopolized by orthodox institutions and their 'religious specialists', has redefined the boundaries of the religious field and diminished significantly the once powerful role of the religious cleric in human society. But lest one think that Bourdieu somehow reveled in this observation, it should be underlined here that to him the new competitors in the field of symbolic manipulation, those responsible for this leveling of the playing field of worldview and well-being, are motivated by an agenda 'to impose truths and values that clearly are no more or no less scientific than those of the religious authorities of the past' (1987b, 123).

It is noteworthy that Bourdieu was obviously uncomfortable with the term 'new clerics', which is the unifying theme of the volume (*Les nouveaux clercs. Prêtres, pasteurs et spécialistes des relations humaines et de la santé* [The New Clerics: Priests, Pastors and Health Human Relations Specialists]) in which his essay first appears. For Bourdieu, the term is 'dangerous' because it tends to imply that the field of 'new clerics' is somehow fundamentally 'new'. To the contrary, although fields can change, certainly, and although their borders can become practically invisible, the logic that structures them is itself unchangeable. This is, for Bourdieu, a fundamental law of social life, hence one can only speak of 'new clerics' or 'new fields' insofar as one can think of 'new forms of struggle', because the struggle remains *essentially* the same in terms of its structuring function (1987b, 118).

'Sociologue de la croyance et croyances de sociologues' focuses primarily on the question as to whether the sociology of religion can be truly scientific when so many of its practitioners belong to the traditions that they study ('indigenous' sociologists of religion), to which Bourdieu (1987c, 159) refers as the problem of 'double belonging' and the 'double game'. For Bourdieu, an affirmative response to this question is very difficult to muster *unless* the sociology of religion is itself subjected to careful sociological analysis; that its *illusio* be subjected to as careful critique as the *illusio* of its subject of analysis, the religious field. Only this can allow for the objectivity that is prerequisite to sound scientific inquiry: 'The scientific sociology of religion presupposes the most complete as possible objectification of the field within which it is produced and of the position in the field of those who produce it' (1987c, 159).

In a very revealing passage toward the end of this short essay, Bourdieu criticizes scholars of religion in general for their 'propensity to treat beliefs as mental representations or as discourses', when in reality 'religious belief . . . is above all a corporal hexis associated with a linguistic habitus' (1987c, 160). This is perhaps Bourdieu's definitive statement on what religious belief ultimately *is* (he of course has much to say about what religious belief *does*), and here we see the depth of influence that phenomenology has on his thought, for Bourdieu is clearly stating that religious belief is *embodied* in the believer, which is reflective of what Bourdieu's mentor Merleau-Ponty (1962, 146) meant by saying that 'the body is our medium for having a world'.

The *Raisons pratiques* Essays

Raisons pratiques: Sur la théorie de l'action (translated into English as *Practical Reason*) is a selection of some of Bourdieu's more accessible writings, originally delivered as lectures, which he gathered here as a representation of 'what I believe to be most essential in my work, that is, its most elementary and fundamental characteristics', and as a means 'to show foreign publics the universal validity of models constructed in relation to the specific case of France' (1998a, vii). As such, this book is one of the best places for readers new to Bourdieu to start in order to gain preliminary insight into his thought in general. That Bourdieu chose to include two brief discussions of religion in this slender volume, 'The Laughter of Bishops' and 'Remarks on the Economy of the Church' (the latter essay being merely a three-page appendix to the former), testifies as something of his acknowledgment of the importance of religion in the contemporary social world, its gradual dissolution notwithstanding. Two terms that Bourdieu italicizes in the preface remind us of some essential analytical contours of all of his work, including its pertinence for the study of religion: that it is '*relational* in that it accords primacy to relations', and that it is '*dispositional* which notes the potentialities inscribed in the body of agents and in the structure of the situations where they act, or, more precisely, in the relations between them' (ibid.).

'The Laughter of Bishops' takes its title from Bourdieu's observation that Catholic bishops in France seem unable to employ 'the language of objectification in relation to the economy of the Church' without laughing. In other words, the logic of the real economics underlying the Church's very existence require euphemisms in order for Church officials to speak of them in seriousness, and not with tongue-in-cheek laughter or winks. 'The religious enterprise is an enterprise with an economic dimension which cannot admit to so being and which functions in a sort of permanent negation of its economic dimension'. For example, 'a pilgrimage enterprise', for Bourdieu, is in reality nothing more than a 'tourism business' whose true economic motivations are concealed by 'a systematic usage of euphemisms: a trip to England will be a "discovery of ecumenicalism"; a trip to Palestine, a "cruise with a religious theme, following the steps of St. Paul"; a trip to Russia, a "reencounter with orthodoxy"' (1998a, 115).[8] Likewise, priests do not receive a 'salary' but 'special treatment from their bishops'; nor are they ever 'promoted' but gain transfers to more prestigious or powerful posts through 'recognition'.

Bourdieu argues that because of this 'double game' that relies so heavily on euphemism and misrecognition, and because '[t]he truth of religious enterprise is that of having two truths: economic truth and religious truth, which denies the former', sociological analysis of religion needs 'to use two words superimposed on each other as if in a musical chord: apostolate/ marketing, faithful/clientele, sacred service/paid labour, and so forth' (1998a, 114). This 'structural double game' is thus structured by religious language's permanent function 'as an instrument of euphemization' (1998a, 118), which permits religious institutions, 'both practically and symbolically, to euphemize social relations' (1998a, 116), which is their own 'permanent function'. As a substantive example of this, Bourdieu analyzes the content of a magazine founded by lay workers in the French Catholic Church as a means to voice their material concerns in an organized, union-like way. Bourdieu finds this example to be so interesting because of its attempt to take an 'anti-economic sub-universe' like the Church 'brutally back to its "economic" truth' (1998a, 113), and thereby 'dissipate the clouds of euphemistic discourse' (1998a, 115).

For another example, and in keeping with *Practical Reason*'s overarching objective to demonstrate the applicability of critiques like this of French society to human society universally, Bourdieu refers to Jacques Gernet's 1956 study of the economic dimensions of Buddhism in China, *Les aspects économiques du bouddhisme dans la société chinoise du cinquième au dixième siècle*, as 'a beautiful analysis of sacred commerce and of the Buddhist temple as a sort of bank—denied as such—which':

accumulates sacred resources, gifts, and offerings based on free consent and volunteerism, and profane benefits, like those sought by usurious or mercenary practices (loans of cereal, collateral loans, taxes on mills, taxes on products of the land, and so forth). These resources, which are not used for the support of members of religious orders or buildings, or for worship services, feasts, official ceremonies, services for the dead, and so on, are accumulated as if in an 'inexhaustible Treasury' and partially redistributed in the form of gifts to the poor or the sick or as free lodging for the faithful. Thus, the temple functions objectively as a sort of bank, but one which cannot be perceived and thought of as such, in fact, provided that it is never understood as such (1998a, 114).

Surely some readers will be taken aback by Bourdieu's comparison of Buddhist monks with mercenaries or usurers,[9] notwithstanding his affirmation of the charitable dimensions of their financial enterprise. Such reactions in readers are, for Bourdieu, inevitable because 'basically the role of the sociologist is probably to say things that no one wishes to hear' (cited in Grenfell 2004, 195).

Authorized Language

Bourdieu's 'Authorized Language', originally published in French in 1975, is more an essay about linguistics than religion, though it uses 'the crisis of institutionalized religion and the crisis in the ritual discourse which it upheld and which upheld it' as a 'quasi-experimental verification' of the article's main argument, which is a refutation of a central point in J.L. Austin's philosophy of language. Bourdieu (1991c, 111, original italics) is critical of Austin (and, by extension, Habermas) for allegedly positing that 'symbolic expressions . . . possess *in themselves*' the power that makes them authoritative and persuasive. For Bourdieu (ibid., 107), this ignores 'the social conditions in which words are employed' and thus misses the fundamental point that '[t]he power of words is nothing other than the delegated power of the spokesperson and his speech'. In other words, 'authority comes to language from outside', and thus 'the language of priests, teachers, and, more generally, all institutions . . . all stem from the position occupied in a competitive field by these persons entrusted with delegated authority' (ibid., 109).

Over and above being a critique of Austin's philosophy of language, 'Authorized Language' is one of a number of Bourdieu's important articles on linguistics that together seek to explain the fundamental importance of language in the homologous struggles that characterize all fields. In his 'Introduction' to the volume in which the English translations of some of these essays appear, John B. Thompson (1991, 8–9, original italics) sums this up quite well:

Hence the efficacy of the performative utterance presupposes a set of social relations, an institution, by virtue of which a particular individual, who is *authorized* to speak and *recognized* as such by others, is able to speak in a way that others will regard as acceptable in the circumstances. It follows that the myriad of symbolic devices—the robes, the wigs, the ritual expressions and respectful references—that accompany occasions of a more 'formal' or 'official' kind are not irrelevant distractions: they are the very mechanisms through which those who speak attest to the authority of the institution which endows them with the power to speak, an institution which is sustained, in part, by the reverence and solemnity which are *de rigueur* on such occasions.

In this sense, Bourdieu (1991c, 115) is commenting as much in this essay on ritual as on language: 'For ritual to function and operate it must first of all present itself and be perceived as legitimate, with stereotyped symbolic serving precisely to show that the agent does not act in his own name and on his own authority, but in his capacity to delegate'.

To illustrate his arguments Bourdieu extracts from a book by a Catholic priest (Lelong 1972) some two dozen quotations from conservative lay Catholics. They are voiced complaints about any of eight kinds of 'errors'[10] that these Catholics perceive in new and alternative forms of liturgical practice that began to gain popularity on the heels of the Second Vatican Council (e.g., women and the laity distributing the host 'like lollipops', Masses in private homes, baguettes used as the Eucharist, etc.). Taken together, the perceived or alleged errors are indicative of a serious crisis in the Church that is marked in significant part by the laity's reclamation of the 'capacity to delegate':

> The indignation of the faithful underlines the fact that the conditions which render ritual effective can be brought together only by an institution which is invested with the power to control its manipulation. What is at stake in the crisis of the liturgy is the whole system of conditions which must be fulfilled in order for the institution to function, i.e. the institution which authorizes and regulates the use of the liturgy and which ensures its uniformity through time and space by ensuring the conformity of those who are delegated to carry it out . . . The outraged faithful are not wrong when they associate the anarchic diversification of ritual with a crisis in the religious institution.

As François-André Isambert (1982, 110) correctly observes, Bourdieu's main point about religion in this essay is that 'the validity that is in question here is a social validity', and the Church's ritual 'effectiveness depends on a global validity of the ceremonial, which is inseparable from the licitness recognized by all'. Or, when the misrecognition on which so much institutional power (religious or other) is predicated begins to unravel among the laity, institutional weakness inevitably results, as with the crisis in a Church that raises questions about its 'social validity' in the modern world.

The Holy Family

'La sainte famille: L'épiscopat français dans le champ du pouvoir' ('The Holy Family: The French Episcopate in the Field of Power') is far and away Bourdieu's most extensive scientific investigation of religion, whereas most

everything else that he wrote on the subject tends to be rather theoretical. David Swartz (1996, 71, n. 1) claims that this is Bourdieu's only
'empirical investigation of religion', though his earliest discussion of Islam
in Algeria, outlined above, could also be counted as an 'empirical investigation', just as 'The Laughter of the Bishops' and 'Authorized Language'
are based in part on empirical analyses, even if they are nowhere as
critical or methodologically sophisticated as 'The Holy Family'. Co-authored
with Monique de Saint Martin, and lending homage to the 1845 Marx and
Engels book by the same title,[11] this essay is very long, a total of forty-
nine double-columned pages in fine print, and very dense, comprising
numerous tables, graphs, statistics, photos, seventy-six notes (some of
them hundreds of words in length), photos, plates of ecclesial documents,
and an appendix. It could easily be a book. In typically complex Bourdieuan
language (the opening sentence is well over 100 words long!), the essay
provides a detailed portrayal of the French Catholic episcopate, providing
careful longitudinal analysis of the backgrounds and intellectual postures
of France's Catholic bishops from the end of World War II to the early
1980s.[12]

'The Holy Family' contains numerous sub-arguments that need not
detain us here.[13] Instead, we may consider two of the article's main
points and, more importantly for the larger objective of this book, glean
from certain passages a fuller understanding of Bourdieu's attitude toward religion, which, overall, one would not be incorrect to label as adversative, thus bespeaking his intellectual debt to Marx. The main points
made in 'The Laughter of Bishops' are also the main points made in 'The
Holy Family', only in this essay they are much further developed and
more strongly supported by extensive statistical analysis. We read in 'The
Holy Family', for instance, a great deal about the abundant euphemisms
employed strategically by the bishops to project an image of unity and
legitimacy toward maintaining an upper hand in the religious field. In
reading Bourdieu and de Saint Martin's very opening salvo, an advertising
slogan from Canon Cameras featuring tennis great Andre Agassi comes to
mind: 'Image is Everything': 'Of all groups of representation, there is
doubtless none that works in such a conscious and systematic manner on
its own image as a body as the episcopate' (1982, 4).

In spite of the bishops' valiant efforts to project an image of unity,
however, Bourdieu and de Saint Martin demonstrate that in reality this
'constituted body' is comprised of two quite different units, or 'poles,
which are the product of the coexistence of two modes of recruitment'
(1982, 5):

> On one side the *'oblates'* who . . . are entirely invested in an institution to whom they owe everything; who are disposed to give everything to the institution that has given them everything, without which and outside of which they would be nothing. On the other side, the bishops who, ordained later in life, possessed, before their entry into the church, besides inherited social capital, considerable educational capital, and who derive from this a more distant, more detached relationship . . . with the institution, its hierarchies, and its ventures.

Thus the community of bishops is itself a 'field of struggle, but *of weak tension*, between agents endowed with an objectively orchestrated habitus' (1982, 31, original italics). The bishops' very existence, moreover, relies on projecting an image of unity, for what would the laity make of dissention and division in the ranks of its most powerful leaders? Bourdieu and de Saint Martin argue that the appearance of unity is central to the bishops' fundamental raison d'être (the raison d'être of all religious specialists, in fact): to impose and inculcate a worldview (1982, 23). As such, the bishops are not only specialists of the religious field but of the broader field of power that shapes society and legitimates and perpetuates the status quo, hence the subtitle of the article: 'The French Episcopate in the Field of Power'.

Religious Piety and Artistic Devotion

In 1982 Bourdieu visited Santa Maria Novella, a thirteenth-century basilica in Florence located just across from the railway station of the same name. Twelve years later he ruminates upon the church's celebrated art in an essay entitled 'Piété religieuse et devotion artistique. Fidèles et amateurs d'art à Santa Maria Novella' ('Religious Piety and Artistic Devotion: The Faithful and the Art Connoisseurs at Santa Maria Novella'), which carries the header 'Croyance Religieuse et Croyance Esthétique' ('Religious Belief and Aesthetic Belief'). This relatively short article is divided into two untitled subsections, the first of which is essentially comprised of some of Bourdieu's field notes from his visit, and a second that reflects upon the relationship and distinction between religious piety and artistic devotion, as the title implies. His field notes contain descriptions of several frescoes and sculptures by the likes of Florentine masters Giovanni Battista Naldini and Jacopo Coppi. Significantly, Bourdieu includes details of religious and other objects near and related to the images, such as how many candles there are, what color they are, and whether or not they are lighted; the presence of roses and kneelers; and his guess at the weight of the basilica's chandelier. Also described are the people present and the things that they are doing. For example: 'in the central nave, [there is] a row of pews aligned perpendicularly to the church's main altar and facing the Madonna. In the pews and on the kneeler are many believers of both sexes and of every age (one young boy with a folder under his arm deposits a coin to light a lamp); they come and go, light a candle, sit and pray' (1994a, 72).

Bourdieu uses his observations at Santa Maria Novella as a backdrop to consider issues that some scholars call 'visual piety,' which David Morgan (2005, 6) defines as 'the constructive operation of seeing that looks for, makes room for, the transcendent in daily life'. In this regard, Bourdieu focuses on the function of the images' 'realism' in effecting such a 'constructive operation of seeing':

> [I]t is as if the effect of religious belief, which causes one to address the figure represented in the *imago pietatis* as a quasi-present person endowed with real powers, can only function as such an *imago* and produce the effect of the real to the extent that there is resonance between its respective immanent stylistic structures and the mental structures that the believer applies to it . . . However, in the case of some paintings of by-gone eras . . . the effect of the real has been neutralized, as certain potential religious viewers are no longer possessed by the practical state of the categories of perception that are indispensable to sight-reading them (1994a, 74).

Over and above such considerations of the differences between religious viewing and aesthetic viewing, perhaps this article's most compelling insight from the standpoint of religious studies lies in its comparison of popular religion and 'popular aesthetics', which are each 'condemned' in similar fashion by the power brokers of, respectively, the religious and cultural fields: 'Because the kind of religiosity that is called "popular" is deemed ritualistic and magical is condemned by the church's clergy, it reflects something of the "popular aesthetic", which is likewise condemned by the educated' (1994a, 74). Such parallel condemnations by the gatekeepers of the respective religious and cultural fields, Bourdieu explains, are based on a virtually homologous kind of 'evolutionary schema' that designates certain objects as 'high art' and others as 'popular art', read 'low art'. In each of 'the two cults of images', furthermore, such divisions between the powerful and the popular are 'the product of the conditions of very unequally distributed economic and social opportunity' (ibid.). Catholic priests and museum curators, in other words, thus serve to perpetuate the very economic and social forces that provide them with distinction and authority through their strategic preservation of their fields' respective *doxas*.

On Weber's Sociology of Religion

Seemingly no book had a greater impact on Bourdieu than Max Weber's *Economy and Society*, especially its chapters on religion. Over and above

[handwritten note: gatekeepers of the respectable — i.e., practices which deserve respect]

its fundamental influence on Bourdieu's interpretation of religion, Weber's classic provides a framework for Bourdieu's theory of practice at large, as Scott Lash (1993, 195) explains:

> In the early 1970s Bourdieu was much influenced by Weber's sociology of religion, recasting the latter's model of religious change in the framework of the cultural markets. Thus Weber's (bureaucratic) priests and (charismatic) prophets are producers of 'symbolic goods' competing for consumers from among the 'laity'. In this formulation we already have the three elements of the economy of culture: (1) the supply side, or the producers of cultural goods; (2) the symbolic goods, or products themselves; and (3) the demand side, the consumers of cultural goods.[14]

In thus extracting Weber's categories and processes from his discussions of religion in *Economy and Society*, as already explained in Chapters 1 and 2, Bourdieu secured the fundamental paradigm for his field theory of society, which goes far in explaining the religious metaphors that often appear in Bourdieu's work. This also in part helps explain how, in spite of Bourdieu's relatively few publications on the subject, scholars of religion are finding increasing value in his theory of practice, *because it is based most centrally upon considerations of religion's essential social function*. The use of Bourdieu by others to interpret religion is thus something of a refraction of Weber's sociology of religion.

Bourdieu's reading of Weber, for all of its power and influence, was not without contention:

> I taught Weber and I found the notion of 'field' which I had confused in my head while teaching him. I did not succeed in teaching the chapter on religious agents. That bored me a lot. It was totally destructive: a series of types with exceptions. I did not see the logic. And then, one day, I began to make a sketch on the board, and I said to myself, it is obvious—it is necessary to study people in relation . . . I had a kind of structural matrix. If I was able to do that, it was because I was doing structuralist-type research on parenthood, and on the Kabyle house. I read pre-structuralist texts with a structuralist mode of thinking (in Grenfell 2004, 15–16).

His criticisms of Weber's once-'destructive' typologies are among Bourdieu's most important contributions to the study of religion, and they receive central attention in his essay on Weber's theory of religion, 'Une interprétation de la théorie de la religion selon Max Weber', which is slightly modified in an English translation, 'Legitimation and Structured Interest in Weber's Sociology of Religion'.

In seeking to understand the legitimation of human authority, Weber adopted the Greek term used in the New Testament, *karism* ('gifts of the

Spirit'),[15] to refer to an inherent quality that makes certain people natural and effective leaders:

> The term 'charisma' will be applied to a certain quality of an individual person-ality by virtue of which he is considered extraordinary and treated as endowed with supernatural, superhuman, or at least specifically exceptional powers or qualities. These are such as not to be accessible to the ordinary person, but are regarded as of divine origin or as exemplary, and on the basis of them the individual concerned is treated as a leader (1978, 241).

Weber articulates three typologies of religious leaders: the prophet (a natural leader), the priest (an appointed leader), and the magician (an entrepreneurial diviner), which obviously often overlap. Clearly the prophet, 'the purely individual bearer of charisma, who by virtue of his mission proclaims a religious doctrine or divine commandment', is the most dy-namic of the three despite possessing less power than the priest (Weber 1963, 46). Concerned primarily with 'religion as a source of the dynamics of social change' (Parsons 1963, xxx), Weber (1963, 9) employs the re-lated notions of charisma and prophet to theorize 'the effect of religious views upon the conduct of life'. It is the prophet, thus naturally endowed with charisma, who most abundantly produces such an effect.

Bourdieu's (1987a, 129) strongest criticism of this model is that 'Max Weber never produces anything other than a psycho-sociological theory of charisma, a theory that regards it as the lived relation of a public to the charismatic personality'. This model is deficient for ignoring the interac-tions between prophet and laity and instead viewing 'charisma as a prop-erty attaching to the nature of a single individual' (1987a, 131). Weber's account is thus flawed because it ignores the structures of the religious field and the relationships between these structures and the religious *habitus* ('the matrix of perception') of the laity, which, for Bourdieu, must be the primary object of analysis for the sociology of religion:

> Any analysis of the *logic* of the interactions that may develop between agents in direct confrontation with one another must be subordinated to the construction of the structure of the objective relations between positions these agents occupy in the *religious field*, a structure that determines both the form their interactions may assume and the representations they may have of these interactions. The interactionist view, strictly speaking, seeks the explanatory principle of practices and representations in the logic of symbolic interactions (1987a, 121, original italics).

Put otherwise, 'Weber consistently fails to establish a distinction be-tween (1) direct interactions and (2) the objective structure of the rela-tions that become established between religious agencies'. For Bourdieu, 'The latter is crucial ... [since] it controls the form that interactions may take. . .' (1987a, 126). While clearly echoing Weber's insistence that the final measure of true prophecy is its capacity to produce effective religious and/or social change, Bourdieu (ibid., 131) goes on to argue that '[p]rophecy can play such a role only because it has as its own generative and unifying principle a habitus objectively attuned to that of its addressees', which allows for the prophet's articulation of readily graspable goals towards whose achievement collective action can be oriented and organized.

Genesis and Structure of the Religious Field

Originally published in French in 1971 and in English twenty years later, 'Genèse et structure du champ religieux' ('Genesis and Structure of the Religious Field') is Bourdieu's most important and most widely cited direct consideration of religion.[16] He opens this essay by lauding as unsurpassed the contributions that Marx, Durkheim and Weber have made to the sociological understanding of religion. Bourdieu then suggests certain drawbacks or limitations of each before quite brilliantly synthesizing them to establish the groundwork for what we might call his 'Theory of Religious Practice'. It would not be inaccurate to say that in this essay Bourdieu synthesizes Marx's central concern with class and Durkheim's rooting of human thought and perception in society to illustrate both the 'genesis', 'structure', 'function' and 'functioning' of the religious field:

> If one takes seriously both the Durkheimian hypothesis of the social origin of schemes of thought, perception, appreciation, and action and the fact of class divisions, one is necessarily driven to the hypothesis that a correspondence exists between social structures (strictly speaking, power structures) and mental structures. This correspondence obtains through the structure of symbolic systems, language, religion, art, and so forth; or, more precisely, religion contributes to the (hidden) imposition of the principles of structuration of the perception and thinking of the world, and of the social world in particular, insofar as it imposes a system of practices and representations whose structure . . . presents itself as the natural-supernatural structure of the cosmos (1991a, 5).

Bourdieu rounds off these influences of Marx and Durkheim with a careful distillation of Weber's economy of salvation to construct his model of the religious field.

Roughly forty pages in length, 'Genesis and Structure of the Religious Field' is a dense and tightly argued essay that seeks first (in a subsection entitled 'The Progress of the Division of Religious Labor and the Process of the Moralization and Systematization of Religious Practices and Beliefs') to demonstrate the historical conditions that permitted the religious field to establish itself as 'autonomous' in human society. Social change

breeds religious change, for Bourdieu. Most importantly, as human societies developed, transitioned from land-based subsistence livelihoods,
and became settled in urban centers, people's religious needs and interests, and religion itself, 'rationalized' and 'moralized'. Bourdieu adopts
these points directly from Weber (1946, 155), as reflected in one of the
latter's most famous quotes: 'The fate of our times is characterized by
rationalization, intellectualization, and the disenchantment of the world'.
This means that certain features of religion lose their sway, like 'magic',
to be replaced by the 'moralization' characteristic of 'salvation' religions,
which seek to explain existence in a more 'rationalized' way.

Of paramount importance from Bourdieu's perspective is that the process of urbanization results in the delineation of borders to the religious
field, whereas in pre-urban societies religion and/or magic were all-perva-
sive and provided, in the relative absence of scientific understanding,
systems of meaning about virtually everything. This sweeping range of
premodern religion's explanatory reach meant that the authority of religious interpretation (notwithstanding the role of the shaman in prehistoric
cultures, which Bourdieu altogether ignores in this essay) was much more
universal and religious capital thus more equally distributed. As important, urbanization and rationalization created the conditions that permitted 'the development of a body of specialists in the administration of
religious goods', which insight Bourdieu (1991a, 6) calls '[t]he greatest
merit of Max Weber'. These specialists, furthermore, gained monopoly
over the production and administration of religious capital to the measure
that they succeeded in dispossessing the laity thereof: 'the constitution of
the religious field goes hand in hand with the objective dispossession of
those who are excluded from it and who thereby find themselves constituted as the *laity* (or the *profane*, in the double meaning of the word)
dispossessed of *religious capital* (as accumulated symbolic labor) and recognizing the legitimacy of that dispossession by the mere fact that they
misrecognize it as such' (ibid., 9, original italics). It is interesting to add
that these very processes, for Bourdieu (ibid., 12), also lie 'at the heart of
the opposition between the *sacred* and the *profane*', which is one of the
central subjects of debate in the study of religion at large.

Besides creating the social conditions that engendered the autonomy
of the religious field, the processes of urbanization and rationalization
also led to a manifest increase in the division of labor in human society,
which resulted in distinctions between individuals and classes and which
markedly increased and intensified competition over all forms of capital
across various and diversifying social fields. Some gained and horded much
more capital than others, and eventually they devised ways in which to
legitimate the resultant inequalities as natural; in other words, a *doxa*

settled over the social world that consisted in large part of the dominant's securing of legitimacy and consecration, and of the dominated's falling victim to untold degrees of symbolic violence, causing them to misrecognize and thus accept this consecration as valid and true. In the second section of this essay, 'Strictly Religious Interest', Bourdieu (1991a, 16) argues that the nature and function of religion changed radically as a result, because a new and pressing religious need emerged in class-divided society: 'If there are social functions of religion and, consequently, if religion is amenable to sociological analysis, it is because laypeople do not—or not only—expect from it justifications for existence capable of freeing them from the existential anguish or contingency and dereliction or even biological misery, sickness, suffering, or death, but also and above all justifications for existing in a determinate social position and existing as they exist, that is, with all the properties that are socially attached to them'. Furthermore, because the religious field, like any field, conforms to the logic of supply and demand, such a powerful new religious need could only lead to a reconfiguration of the religious field.

The second half of 'Genesis and Structure of the Religious Field' consists of two subsections, 'The Specific Function of the Religious Field and its Functioning' and 'Political Power and Religious Power'. Taken together, they constitute Bourdieu's most original argument about the nature and function of religion in human society, being a masterful application of his theory of practice to the religious field. Where the first half of this dense essay concerned itself with, as the title implies, the 'genesis' of the religious field as an autonomous field, the second half seeks to outline its 'structure' and functions. Put briefly, as with any field, for Bourdieu, the religious field is *structured* by a struggle between variously positioned agents and institutions over religious capital, and this struggle is in large part governed by an economic logic of supply and demand (1991a, 22). Being ultimately interested, furthermore, in 'the question of the political function that religion fulfills for various social classes in a given social formation' (ibid., 5), Bourdieu concludes in this essay that religion has two fundamental social functions that have far-reaching political ramifications: (1) to consecrate the social order as legitimate; (2) to provide people with a means to make sense of their positions in the social order.

These structures and functions of the religious field will be further explained in Chapter 4, especially pertaining to Bourdieu's (1991a, 32) argument in the final subsection of this essay ('Political Power and Religious Power') that 'the church contributes to the maintenance of the

---

Key Points in Bourdieu's 1971 Essays on Religion

'Genesis and Structure of the Religious Field'

- Marx's emphasis on class and Durkheim's rooting of religious thought in society are the foundation for the sociological analysis of the religious field;
- Historically speaking, the religious field emerges as autonomous from other social fields due to an increase in the division of labor in society;
- The resultant division of the religious field between religious specialists and the laity is the central structure of the religious field;
- The Church (orthodoxy) 'inculcates' in the religious habitus of the laity the need to consume the religious capital that the Church produces;
- Through acts of 'symbolic violence' the Church seeks to portray competing religious specialists like prophets as heretics in order to maintain a 'de facto monopoly' of the religious field;
- The religious field is thus, like all fields, characterized by a struggle that is shaped by the dialectic between habitus, capital, practice, and the structures of the field;
- The chief social functions of religion are to legitimate the social order and to provide people with a justification of their place in the social order.

'Legimation and Structured Interests in Weber's Sociology of Religion'

- Weber's theory of charisma and prophecy is important but fundamentally flawed because it ignores the relationship between the various social positions occupied by priests, prophets, and members of the laity in the religious field;
- Instead, understanding charisma and prophecy requires consideration of various 'religious interests' that generate both priestly and lay religious 'practice';
- Religious interests are centrally determined by the need to justify one's position in the social order;
- The notion of religious needs in Weber is 'weakly elaborated' and can be improved by understanding religious needs as 'dispositions' and as extensively shaped by the supply and demand logic of the religious field;
- Charisma is only successful if and when there develops a 'quasi-miraculous harmony' between the content of the prophetic message and the religious interests of its lay audience;
- The religious field is centrally structured by the competition between Church and heresiarch over 'the power to modify . . . the worldview of lay people, by imposing on and inculcating in them a particular religious habitus'.

---

political order, that is, to the symbolic reinforcement of the divisions of this order, in and by fulfilling its proper function, which is to contribute to the maintenance of the symbolic order. It does this by imposing and inculcating schemes of perception, thought, and action objectively agreeing with political structures and grants these structures the supreme legitimation of "naturalization"'.

A Brief Conclusion

The hermeneutic of suspicion underlying Bourdieu's writings on religion mirrors that which pervades his larger body of work. Religions 'impose' worldviews upon people, by 'inculcating' into their habitus modes of perception and thought. Religions are thus prolific producers of people's 'misrecognitions' that the social word is only unequal because of karma, God's will, or some other 'euphemistic' linguistic construct that 'legitimizes' (by 'naturalizing') the order of things, the status quo. Religion is therefore not trustworthy, for Bourdieu, because it can and does provide Tartuffe the means to dupe Orgon into signing over to him his property, just as it can and does provide real humans with the powers of consecration that have proven capable of legitimizing the worst horrors of which we have so far as a species proven ourselves capable, such as the crusades, the transatlantic slave trade, the holocaust, and the Rwandan genocide, to mention but the most glaring examples that spring to mind. Or, in Bourdieu's (1991a, 4) own words, 'religion conserves the social order by contributing . . . to the "legitimation" of the power of "the dominant" and to the "domestication of the dominated"'. He adds that Weber is in perfect accord with Marx in this regard, which is perhaps the central lesson that Bourdieu learns from each.

It would be a mistake, however, to characterize Bourdieu's assessment of religion as being overly reliant on Weber and Marx and perhaps truncated by Bourdieu's selective reading on the subject. Far from limiting his reading on religion to the thinkers who most influenced his social theory at large, Bourdieu was seemingly widely read in theology and in scholarly literature that can be considered sympathetic to or even supportive of religion. He cites in clear admiration, and without criticizing, for example, William James, Martin Buber, Teilhard de Chardin, Reinhold Niebuhr and Gershom Scholem, among others, while referring to Ernst Troeltsch's *The Social Teachings of the Christian Churches* as 'monumental' (1991a, 18), and, as explained in Chapter 1, Bourdieu was quite fond of Blaise Pascal, a deeply religious thinker, to say the least. Bourdieu's early writings on Islam in Algeria, meanwhile, bespeak a keen appreciation of some of the inarguably positive effects of the religion on the lives of the people whom Bourdieu began his career studying. Whatever positive affirmations that Bourdieu made concerning religious thought or religious practice, though, his overarching mission ultimately drove him to focus instead on religion's function in the establishment and reproduction of social distinctions and domination. Empirical investigation of anything that religion posits as an objectively real holy, sacred, or transcendent being or order is *per force* outside of the pale of scientific investigation. 'The sacred only exists for those who have a sense of the sacred, who none the less, when faced with the sacred itself, still experience it as fully transcendent' (Bourdieu 1990b, 195). What religion does to and in society, and the social interactions and misrecognitions that allow it to do what it does to and in society, is, for Bourdieu, the principal concern of the sociology of religion. As for God: 'God is never anything other than society. What is expected of God is only ever obtained from society, which alone has the power to justify you, to liberate you from facticity, contingency, and absurdity' (ibid., 196).

Chapter 4

Outline of a Theory of Religious Practice: Eternalizing the Arbitrary in Colonial New England

This island of the sacred, ostentatiously opposed to the profane, everyday world of production, a sanctuary for gratuitous, disinterested activity, offers, like theology in other periods, an imaginary anthropology obtained by denial of all negations really performed by the 'economy' (Bourdieu 1990b, 134).

Overview

Pierre Bourdieu conceives of the religious field as one of numerous distinct yet interrelated fields that together constitute human society. Fields are characterized and structured principally by the struggle or competition that takes place within them, as explained in Chapter 2. For Bourdieu (1987a, 126), the religious field is characterized by a '[c]ompetition for religious power [that] owes its specificity . . . to the fact that what is at stake is the monopoly of the legitimate exercise of the power to modify, in a deep and lasting fashion, the practice and worldview of lay people, by imposing on and inculcating in them a particular religious habitus'. Struggle in the religious field, furthermore, unfolds principally between the Church (*Eglise*) and its priests versus the prophet (or 'heresiarch')[1] and his believers, or orthodoxy versus heterodoxy, over the production, administration and consumption of religious capital and the adherence of the laity to whom it is marketed. Bourdieu (1971a, 305) stresses that the Church's primary interest (an interest concealed by the Church's trademark use of euphemisms) is 'the monopoly over the legitimate production of religious capital' and the 'institutionalization of their dominance in the religious field'. As I will illustrate with examples from colonial religious history in New England, the Church and its specialists institutionalize domination by employing various 'weapons of symbolic violence'

in a concerted effort to 'eternalize the arbitrary'. This secures the misrecognition, and hence the recognition, of the legitimacy of both their
dominant position in the religious field and the inequalities of the broader
social order, which obviously benefits elites at the expense of the subjugated. It is thus pertinent for orthodoxy's religious specialists to inculcate
in the laity a religious habitus that permits orthodoxy's (and the allied
economic and political elite's) 'misrecognized domination' (Krais 1993,
177), and doing so requires a systematic crafting of the religious field's
doxa (the field's informal and tacitly accepted rules) and *illusio* (people's
'feel' for the field and their inclination to invest in it).

   This chapter discusses Bourdieu's sociological theory of religion, or his
theory of practice as it pertains to the religious field.[2] It is in keeping with
the overarching aim of Bourdieu's lifework, which is the exposure of the
sources of social inequality and its reproduction, that his model of the
religious field is especially apt for studies of the relationship between
religion, class and power; religion, race and ethnicity; and religion and
colonial conquest. This is not to suggest, however, that other aspects of
Bourdieu's theory of practice hold little or no potential for fruitful applications to the study of religion. On the contrary, some of the most impressive Bourdieuian interpretations of religion thus far, like Thomas Csordas's
(1994, 2001, 2002) cultural phenomenology of Charismatic Christianity
and Catherine Bell's (1992) theory of ritual practice, do not, technically
speaking, use his model of the religious field at all, as will be demonstrated in Chapter 5.[3] My intention here, meanwhile, is to provide an
outline of Bourdieu's conceptualization of the religious field and explanations of each of its key components, such as religious habitus, religious
capital, the goods of salvation, misrecognition and symbolic violence. In
addition, I suggest ways in which other Bourdieuian concepts, like *collusio*,
illusio and *doxa*, can be integrated into Bourdieu's model toward expand-
ing its usefulness. In the spirit of Bourdieu's (in Bourdieu and Wacquant
1992, 96, original italics) 'permanent reminder that concepts have no
definition other than systematic ones, and are designed to be *put to work
empirically in a systematic fashion*', and to illustrate with a concrete example of how Bourdieu's theory may be applied to a specific case, I
consider in this chapter the religious field of colonial Martha's Vineyard,
New England, as portrayed by David Silverman in his excellent 2005 book
*Faith and Boundaries: Colonists, Christianity, and Community among the
Wampanoag Indians of Martha's Vineyard, 1600–1871.*

Religion and Colonialism

It is wholly unsurprising that Bourdieu's model of the religious field is so useful for theorizing the role of religion in colonial conquest. For Bourdieu, historically the religious field only emerges as autonomous from other social fields when there develop in a given society the kinds of struggle and social distinction that, in extreme forms, characterize colonialism. The explanation for this emergence, as Otto Maduro (1977, 364) aptly observes, 'lies for Bourdieu in the historic genesis of a corps of functionaries specialized in religious labor, that is, in the task of responding by a certain type of practices and discourses to a particular category of needs characterizing certain social groups'.[4] In colonial societies (and in class-segmented societies in general), furthermore, dominant social groups require of religion its legitimating authority, while dominated groups require of religion compensation for their suffering and a way to make sense of their place in the social order. For Bourdieu (1991a, 22), these are religions' most important social functions, and the religious field is shaped by, and operates according to, the economic logic of supply and demand: the laity's religious needs for religious capital constitutes the demand side of the equation, while the Church and its specialists and/or the prophet produce and supply religious capital.

How does religion perform these social functions? 'Religion contributes to the (hidden) imposition of the principles of structuration of the perception and thinking of the world', writes Bourdieu (1991a, 5), 'and of the social world in particular, insofar as it imposes a system of practices and representations whose structure, objectively founded on the principle of political division, presents itself as a natural-supernatural structure of the cosmos'. One could allude to abundant examples from the history of European colonial endeavor around the world to illustrate Bourdieu's meaning in this regard. This phenomenon is quite effectively symbolized, for instance, by Columbus' arrival in the Americas on a ship named for the Virgin Mary and the ensuing campaigns of Iberian and French Catholic friars throughout the Americas to convince the subsequently vanquished Native Americans that this woman was not only the Mother of God but also *their* mother, and that she wanted them to accept the new social order as legitimate: 'The conquest was regarded as the work of the Virgin', note Ivone Gebara and María Clara Bingemer (1989, 129), 'the powerful and yet tender lady, who was concerned about protecting the Spanish and Portuguese believers and converting the Indians to faith in her divine son'.

Although Protestant theology of course did not grant its missionaries and colonizers in the Americas such access to the Blessed Virgin Mary and the saints to aid in their conquest of Native Americans, the Bible itself provided ample legitimating authority to the cause, especially once they convinced 'Indians that God's written word was indeed meant for them and was no less sacred when printed in their language than in English' (Silverman 2005, 51). The colonial religious field of Martha's Vineyard is a patent example of the function of Christianity in the establishment and reproduction of distinctions between groups in the social order. It thus provides an excellent opportunity to illustrate the chief structures and mechanisms in Bourdieu's model of the religious field.

Sailing from Amsterdam, where they had taken refuge for about a year from King James's religious intolerance back home in England, to a place in the New World that they would name New England, English Puritans (known also as Congregationalists) first arrived in 1620 on the *Mayflower*. A year later the celebrated 'Pilgrims' signed at Plymouth a treaty with local leaders of the Wampanoag tribe, and by 1630 a governor of the Massachusetts Bay Colony, John Winthrop, was seated in Boston as the political leader of some 900 English settlers. Called *Noepe* by the Wampanoag, Martha's Vineyard is the largest of the islands dotting the southeastern coast of Massachusetts. In 1641, Thomas Mayhew, Sr., an English merchant, missionary, and an extraordinary historical figure, acquired a settlement deed for the island and purchased some of its land from a local Wampanoag chief. Soon his and other families joined him, and by the end of that decade a discernable and permanent community of English Puritans had made the island their home. Mayhew appointed his son, Thomas Mayhew, Jr. as his 'proxy and the community's interim preacher' (Silverman 2005, 17).

Ensuing details about the settlement's development are of course beyond our scope here; please refer instead to Silverman's account and to various sources in his extensive bibliography, and suffice it to say here that by the middle of the seventeenth century, America's 'manifest destiny' was thus well underway, its blueprint crafted by the Mayhews and others of their ilk, who had no doubt whatsoever that their colonial endeavor was the will of God.

Consecration, *Collusio*, and Conflict

Usually manifest as competition over forms of capital specific to a given field, struggle is unsurpassed in its determination of the nature and contours of social fields, as explained in Chapter 2. In the religious field, the struggle is essentially over the power to consecrate, which, for Bourdieu

(1991a, 14), is the ultimate and paradigmatic form of symbolic power in human society because of its capacity to make people see the world in a certain way: 'The effect of consecration . . . also causes the system of dispositions toward the natural world . . . in particular transmuting the ethos as a system of implicit schemes of action and appreciation into ethics as a systematized and rationalized ensemble of explicit norms. Thus, religion is predisposed to assume an ideological function, a practical and political function of absolutization of the relative and legitimation of the arbitrary'.

As the following analytical survey of the colonial New English religious history will demonstrate, this is very much the case in the religious field when concrete distinctions based on race, class, language or denomination feature prominently in a given society.[5] In such cases is Bourdieu's theoretical formulation of the religious field most apt for interpretive application. For less stratified societies, however, his model is much less serviceable, as Bourdieu himself would clearly agree, because it is devised for interpreting religion in differentiated societies and not in premodern, 'primitive' or undifferentiated societies, which have no autonomous religious fields at all: 'The technological, economic, and social transformations that are correlated with the birth and developments of towns, and in particular advances the division of labor and the appearance of the separation of intellectual and physical labor, constitute the common condition of two processes that can only unfold in a relationship of interdependence and reciprocal reinforcement, namely the constitution of a relatively autonomous religious field and the development of a need for the "moralization" and "systematizaion" of religious beliefs and practices' (Bourdieu 1991a, 5).

A singular conflict between Puritan Christianity and the traditional religion of the indigenous Wampanoag people centrally structured the religious field of colonial Martha's Vineyard. Whereas the Vineyard's English pastors made every attempt to distinguish their religion as superior to Wampanoag tradition and to impose it as the unique path to salvation, in reality the dominated class generally believed that their traditional religion and Christianity formed two intertwined trunks to a single religious tree, or that they amounted to two simultaneous scenes in a single religious epic. This is not to imply that interreligious relations in the colony were harmonious or that English Puritans were at all tolerant of the 'superstitions' of the darker skinned peoples they sought to dominate. On the contrary, there in fact waged in the colonial New English religious field a sometimes violent (both symbolically and less often overtly) struggle between competing religious institutions and their specialists over the production and administration of important forms of religious capital, such as sacraments, community membership, moral sanction, and the assurance of salvation, enlightenment or holiness; i.e., of 'the goods of salvation'.[6] For the English Puritans, meanwhile, the inculcation in the Wampanoags' religious habitus of the recognition of the legitimacy of Congregationalist forms of religious capital, and of the illegitimacy of traditional Wampanoag religious capital, was of paramount importance.

Several of Bourdieu's signature concepts, like habitus, capital and field, can help us understand the nature of the colonial New English religious field. Their application in this regard consists first in conjoining each with the adjective 'religious'. For example, the religious field, like any field, is a 'market' or arena of competition and struggle, in which religious agents and institutions vie for control of the production, accumulation and distribution of legitimate forms of capital particular to the religious field; i.e., over forms of religious capital. In the context of colonial Martha's Vineyard, the struggle took the form of Puritan Christianity against the shaman (*powwow*) and his or her followers (who may collectively be called the 'heresiarchy'), institutions that are in competition over the control and administration of religious capital and the lay audience (consumers) to whom it is marketed. The religious specialists of each the Church and the heresiarchy struggle against one another to make the laity believe that their products, their religious capital, are legitimate, while the adversary's are illegitimate. It thus follows logically, for Bourdieu, that only once the recognition of the legitimacy of a certain form of religious capital is inculcated in the habitus of the laity, the laity will become consumers thereof. The economic metaphors that Bourdieu uses here should be interpreted carefully: Only religious specialists, like priests and prophets, produce and *possess* religious capital; the laity, meanwhile, only *consume* it. But insofar as they are therefore *consumers* of religious capital, they are not identified as such in Bourdieu's model because they *buy religious capital* but because they *buy into* it.

In addition to using the logic of economics to describe the structure and function of social fields, Bourdieu also often uses the logic of sporting competition.[7] The religious field can thus be thought of as 'a game' between Church and heresiarchy. However, from the opening whistle the game is not fair, because the Church, or in the present example the English Puritans, slant the playing field by effectively crafting the *doxa* (the combined doable and thinkable) of virtually every intercultural field on the island. The thereby disadvantaged heresiarchy, or practitioners of traditional Wampanoag religion, are left to make sense of their shifting identities and stations in a radically changing socio-cultural order:

> Every established order tends to produce . . . the naturalization of its own arbitrariness. Of all the mechanisms tending to produce this effect, the most important and the best concealed is undoubtedly the dialectic of the objective chances and the agents' aspirations, out of which arises a *sense of limits*, commonly called the *sense of reality*, i.e., the correspondence between the objective classes and the internalized classes, social structures and mental structures, which is the basis of the most ineradicable adherence to the established order. Systems of classification which reproduce . . . the objective classes, i.e., the divisions by sex, age, or positions in the relations of power production . . . by securing the misrecognition, and hence the recognition, on which they are based. . . This experience we shall call the *doxa*. . . (Bourdieu 1977, 164).

Elsewhere, Bourdieu (2001, vii) refers to this kind of 'naturalization' of 'arbitrariness' as a process of '[e]ternalizing the arbitrary', a process that is powerfully generative of *doxa* and *illusio*—hence the subtitle of this chapter.

Based on religious, cultural, and especially (and increasingly) racial difference, the English settlers in Martha's Vineyard managed to establish quite a rigid system of social distinctions in colonial New England. It was a system of functional inequality that was fundamentally justified by Christianity. Not only were people thereafter classified as either English or Indian (or later as either white or black), but as English Christians, Indian Christians ('praying Indians', who were widely regarded by the English as inauthentic Christians) and heathen Indians. Furthermore, material and symbolic power were increasingly concentrated largely toward the top of this emergent socio-religious hierarchy, resulting from a degree of racism among the English that proved too strong for their Christian ideals to overcome:

> Englishmen had to account for . . . their . . . insistence on treating praying Indians—fellow Christians, after all—as third-class members of colonial society or resident aliens. For if Christian Indians remained a people apart after all their reforms, clearly what made them distinct was something else besides the outward manifestations of culture such as religion, government, or dress, as earlier theorists had proposed. Increasingly, settlers explained this conundrum away and their role in perpetrating it by appealing to race (Silverman 2005, 119).

In general, colonialism's introduction of new forms of social distinctions, such as white versus black and Christian versus pagan, is accompanied by a directly related diversification of respective *collusio* among members of particular status groups. *Collusio* is one item that most scholars have left in the Bourdieuian thinking toolbox, in part surely because Bourdieu himself only rarely picked it up. Nonetheless, the concept holds great potential for thinking about race, ethnicity, class and religion, even if it nowhere features in Bourdieu's writings on religion. Bourdieu (2000a,

145) defines *collusio* as 'an immediate agreement in ways of judging and acting which does not presuppose either the communication of consciousness, still less a contractual decision, [which] is the basis of practical mutual understanding, the paradigm of which might be the one established between members of the same team, or, despite the antagonism, all the players engaged in a game'. It would not be unfair to think of *collusio* as a kind of collective habitus, or at least as the predictable and relative uniformity in the habitus of all members of a given delineated collectivity or social status group, be it a family, class, race or ethnicity. Or, *collusio* can be seen as any social group's collective grounding in the *doxa*. Because 'everything is social' and socially constructed, characteristics of the members of any given collectivity can generally be explained in terms of the socially (and culturally, politically, religiously and economically) environmental factors that shape them. Members and participants in any given collectivity thereby coherently belong and participate by virtue of *collusio*, or the shared 'feel for the game' that their common socializations have inculcated in their habitus:

> Just as habitus is not an instantaneous being . . . but . . . a force endowed with a law, and therefore characterized by constants and constancies . . . equally it is not the isolated, calculating subject of the utilitarian tradition and the economists (and coming after them, the 'methodological individualists'). It is the site of durable solidarities, loyalties that cannot be coerced because they are grounded in incorporated laws and bonds (of which family loyalty is a particular form), the visceral attachment of a socialized body to the social body that has made it and with which it is bound up. As such, habitus is the basis of an *implicit collusion* among all the agents who are products of similar conditions and conditionings, and also of a practical experience of the transcendence of the group, of its ways of being and doing, each agent finding in the conduct of all his peers the ratification and legitimation ('the done thing') of his own conduct, which, in return, ratifies and, if need be, rectifies the conduct of others (2000a, 145, original italics).

Catholics can go anywhere in the world and, even without understanding the language of Catholics whom they encounter in the foreign places that they might go, they can understand one another on a fundamental level because they partake of the same religious *collusio*, having had their religious habitus formed by the same 'catholic' religious institution that features a very centralized and unifying liturgical spine. The same can be said for social class, race and ethnicity in such a way that minimizes physical appearance as a putative or assumed condition for group membership, or at least in such a way that allows us to consider internalized race as opposed to objectified race (race-in-itself as opposed to race-for-another, to adapt Sartre's famous ontological paradigm, if you will).

One day on the subway in North Philadelphia, for example, I overheard two young black men, evidently working class, speaking about a white coworker whom they perceived of as white only in appearance because he shares their own *collusio*: 'He's a white boy, but he from da' hood and shit—he's a brother'. Their white brother's habitus, having been formed in the same streets, schools, parks, churches and workplaces as theirs, has incorporated the 'durable solidarities' that enable him, though white by appearance, to be exempted from everything implied by the statement (constructed by blacks and intended for whites) 'It's a black thing you wouldn't understand', membership and participation in the *collusio* being requisite, as they are, to understanding (and confirming and adhering to) 'the done thing'—or the 'black thing'.

Cultural (and racial, ethnic and religious) assimilation thus implies the erosion, whether partial, gradual or complete, of one's participation in an original or objectively expected *collusio* and one's adaptation of or entry into another. The annals of European expansionist conquest comprise a bevy of examples of the colonizer's effectively destroying, or at least reducing the range and reach of, the *collusio* of the colonized through the (super)imposition of a new and Eurocentric *collusio*. Thus in colonial Martha's Vineyard, animal husbandry, over and above animal hunting, became for the Wampanoags 'the done thing', as did land ownership, financial debt, and the worship of Jesus Christ. However, if the Wampanoags' motivation for investing in such a *collusio* shift was, at least in part, 'ideological in character', as Silverman (2005, 38) argues (i.e., driven by their 'anticipation of worldly goods', which was 'ultimately grounded in their conviction that a spirit of unrivaled power favored Christians for their adherence to him'), it was an investment that in the end yielded quite limited, at best, returns, at least as concerns the things of this world, like material and symbolic power:

> even the Wampanoags' long and troubled history with the English could not have prepared them for the vast tumult about to enter their lives – epidemic diseases, a new religion, land loss, and political upheaval, followed by dept peonage, exogamous marriage, racial castigation, and much more. Mayhew's colonists were quite unlike the roughneck crews that the Wampanoags had [previously] confronted, but they came with an agenda far more threatening, if also more subtle: had no plans to force the Indians into slavery, but they did want them as servants; they would not ship Indians to distant lands, but they did encroach upon the Natives' very lands. And what was more, the colonists intended to stay, not to strike quick and sail off. . . . English good fortune was bought at the Wampanoags expense, leading to the gradual disintegration of [Wampanoag culture] (Silverman 2005, 7).

[handwritten marginalia: "making suffering sufferable — but what of resistance? rebellion"]

Misrecognizing the *Illusio*

Like Marx and Weber before him, Bourdieu emphasizes religion's function as a key source of the legitimation of wealth and power, and hence
of social distinctions and of domination. Religion also provides the
underclasses with the means to make sense of and endure their lot,
which thereby contributes to their 'misrecognition' of the social order as
legitimate and to their partaking in the field's *illusio*. For Bourdieu (1971b,
10, original italics), these are the 'two major types' of 'religious demands'
that determine the supply side of the religious economy, thereby strongly
influencing the forms taken by the systems of relations and interactions
between people and institutions that structure the religious field: 'Religious demands tend to be organized around two major types that corre-
spond to the two major types of social situations, that is, the *demands for
legitimation* of the established order for the privileged classes, and the
demands for compensation for the underclasses (religions of salvation)'.
In further elaborating on the former of these religious demands, Bourdieu
(1987b, 125) uses two terms from Weber to identify what turn out, in the
final analysis, to be for the dominant social groups two 'irreplaceable'
forms of religious capital: '*das unvergleichliche Mittel der Domestikation
des Beherrschten*' ('the incomparable means for domesticating the subjects') and '*legitimierende Macht*' ('power of legitimation').[8] Each of these
were clearly at stake and fully operational in the colonial New English
religion field, as they were in the entirety of Europe's conquest of the
New World.

Bourdieu does advance a number of criticisms of Weber's sociology of
religion, though with the exception of the one concerning charisma, discussed below and in Chapter 5, they are mostly inconsequential. Where
Bourdieu's analysis is more sophisticated, however, is in its demonstration of the operative function of religious capital in reinforcing the status
quo, or in describing how '[r]eligious capital is a power resource', to use
David Swartz's (1997, 43) expression. Available to the dominant in the
religious field is that extremely powerful form of religious capital that
Weber (1963, 107) calls 'the psychological reassurance of legitimacy',
which, for Weber, is the only thing that elites truly need of religion.
Whereas Weber points to these, Bourdieu explains how they function.
As James C. Scott (1990, 67) similarly asks, does not religion operate 'as
a kind of self-hypnosis in ruling groups to buck up their courage, improve
their cohesion, display their power, and convince themselves anew of
their high moral purpose?' Such 'self-hypnosis', Bourdieu would argue,
moreover, is a product of the interactive relation between habitus and
capital—just like virtually everything else in human society.

Marx and Engels (1964, 41) influentially argue that elites also use religion to veil their interests and the arbitrariness of the unjust social order, thereby duping the masses into submission: 'man makes religion, religion does not make man'; 'the ruling ideas of each age have ever been the ideas of the ruling elite' (Marx and Engels 2002, 241). Elite religiosity thus promotes 'false consciousness' (or, to use Bourdieu's comparable term, 'misrecognition' [*méconnaissaince*]) in the masses by creating the illusion (*illusio*) that elites are religious and therefore moral and deserving of their power and privilege, and that participation in the fields (religious or other) that they almost invariably dominate is unquestionably worthwhile:

> This *illusio* implies, on the one hand, an investment in the game as such, the inclination to play the game (instead of leaving it, or of losing interest in it). On the other hand, it implies a 'feel' for the game, a sense of the game mastered in the practical form of an embodied principle of relevance that guides investments (in time, labor, and also in affects) by allowing one to differentiate between *interesting, important* things (problems, debates, objects, lectures, masters, etc.), and insignificant things, devoid of interest. (The two dimensions of the *illusio*, inclination and ability, are inseparable: the ability to differentiate—'taste'—distinguishes those who, being capable of differentiating, are not indifferent, and for whom certain things matter more than others, from those to whom, as the saying goes, 'it's all the same') (Bourdieu 1991b, 7).

It thus follows that, for both Marx and Bourdieu, religion is the 'opium of the people' in two senses: it anesthetizes the people to ease their pain, and it inebriates them to such a degree that they see the entire game as fair and worth playing, when in reality it is unfair and it fuels their opium addiction.

In a real sense, *illusio* is what allows any 'established order . . . to produce (to very different degrees and with very different means) the naturalization of its own arbitrariness . . . by securing the misrecognition, and hence the recognition, of the arbitrariness on which' it is in reality based (Bourdieu 1977, 164). The reproduction of the social order, after all, requires the complicity of the dominated groups, which is assured by the *illusio*. It is, furthermore, a product of the relationship between habitus and field: 'The habitus and the field maintain a relationship of mutual attraction, and the illusion [*illusio*] is determined from the inside, from impulses that push toward a self-investment in the object; but it is also determined from the outside, starting with a particular universe of objects offered socially for investment' (in Bourdieu et al. 1993, 512).

With the notions of illusio and misrecognition, Bourdieu (1991a, 19, original italics) supersedes Marx and Weber by showing precisely how the ideas of the ruling class, as they pertain to religion, become the ruling ideas of the age:

> In a society divided into classes, *the structure of the systems of religious representations and practices* belonging to the various groups or classes contributes to the perpetuation and reproduction of the social order . . . by contributing to its consecration, that is, to sanctioning and sanctifying it. As soon as it presents itself as officially one and indivisible, it organizes itself in relation to two polar positions: 1) the systems of practices and of representations (dominant religiosity) that tend to justify the existence of the dominant classes as dominant and 2) the system of practices and representations (dominated religiosity) that tend to impose on the dominated a recognition of the legitimacy of the domination founded on the misrecognition of the arbitrariness of the domination and of the symbolic modes of expression of this domination (that is, the lifestyle and religiosity of the dominant classes).

Misrecognition thus produces and reproduces the *illusio* and plays an irreplaceable and effective role in the legitimation of elites' power and dominant social status, thereby perpetuating the inequalities of the social order. In the religious field, orthodoxy's tendency 'to justify the existence of the dominant classes as dominant' breeds in the habitus of the dominated classes a decisive form of misrecognition, thereby contributing to the structuring and reproduction of the *illusio*.

Religious Habitus

As explained in Chapter 2, the habitus is the 'set of dispositions', 'the basis of perception and appreciation of all subsequent experiences', that predisposes the agent to perceive and behave in a certain fashion. It is both the 'matrix of perception' and the seat of one's dispositions, and as such is very essential to what it means to be a human being. It is also, in my view, the single most important concept in Bourdieuian theory for the study of religion chiefly because of its trenchant power for explaining the nature of human belief and practice, which are obviously so fundamental to religion at large—more on this in Chapter 5.

The religious habitus is the specifically religious dimension of an individual agent's habitus that manifests itself most apparently, though not exclusively, in the religious field. It is the principal determining subjective (though objectively defined) influence on what particular religious interests, tastes, dispositions and needs that anyone has, on how she or he perceives of, responds to, and uses religious symbols and/or engages in rituals, on her or his reactions to religious leaders, on what forms of religious capital she or he deems worthy of pursuit, and generally on how she or he fares in the religious field. Bourdieu offers two explicate definitions of religious habitus: (1) 'a lasting, generalized and transposable disposition to act and think in conformity with the principles of a (quasi) systematic view of the world and human existence' (Bourdieu 1987a, 126); and (2) 'the principal generator of all thoughts, perceptions and actions consistent with the norms of a religious representation of the natural and supernatural worlds' (Bourdieu 1971a, 319). Nested in these definitions is one of the most central and important points that Bourdieu makes about religion: *that the perception and appreciation of the meaning and function of religious symbols and doctrines (not to mention belief itself) are attributable mainly to the agent's religious habitus and the power relations, both institutional and personal, that unfold in and structure the religious field; i.e., the conflicts of interests and the struggle over religious capital.*

Thus equipped with the notion of 'religious habitus' as our thinking tool, we can more incisively understand the function of religion in the establishment of and perpetuation of the inequalities and injustices that characterized colonial New English society. Yes, religion provided the *legitimierende Macht* for the English conquest of the region's natural and human resources—clearly. But the issue is more complex than this. In a real sense, the scales were tipped from the outset in favor of the English by the respective nature of their and the Wampanoags' religious habitus, because the English Puritans' theological absolutism strongly predisposed them to dismiss Wampanoag indigenous religion as diabolical superstition, witchcraft and magic that was totally devoid of any theological merit or divine truth, and thus Mayhew preached of 'the wekenesse and wickednesse of the Pawwaws power' (Silverman 2005, 24). The Wampanoag religious habitus, meanwhile, centrally featured a belief in divine power (*manit*) that imbued all of creation, which fostered in the Native Americans the openness to the possibility that it also imbued the Bible, leading them in turn not only to esteem the Bible's store of religious capital as worth their while, but to also esteem literacy as an important form of cultural capital. Indeed, Mayhew's brilliant translation of Christianity into Wampanoag terms succeeded in large part for its focus on this belief:

> [R]eligious translation was more than a temporary expedient in the hope of future purification, for Christian and Native beliefs were indeed analogous at several critical points. For instance, to encourage the Natives' acceptance of monotheism, Mayhew . . . proposed that they had 'an obscure Notion of a greater god than all, which they call *Manit*, but they knew not what he was and therefore had no way to worship him'. Now they did, since Mayhew argued that God was the wellspring of all the *manit* in the world (Silverman 2005, 34).

English colonization and evangelization of course caused a tumultuous disruption of the traditional Wampanoag religious habitus. 'Much was at stake', writes Silverman (ibid., 24). 'At risk was the continuity of beliefs and rituals that had evolved with the Wampanoags throughout the ages to help them make sense of their world'. Once the Wampanoag were 'dispossessed' by the English of the powers to consecrate and to make sense of the world, which are, for Bourdieu, the ultimate forms of religious capital, the Puritans were able to establish a 'de facto monopoly' in the Vineyard's religious field.[9] Maintaining this monopoly, meanwhile, required the Puritans' sustained inculcation of their righteousness into the Wampanoags' radically altered religious habitus; or, in Bourdieu's (1991a, 25) terms, it required the Puritans 'to make them misrecognize the arbitrariness of the monopolization of a power and a competence [i.e., religious authority] in principle accessible to anyone'. And, for Bourdieu (ibid., 22, original italics), religious authority is the 'power durably to modify the representations and practices of laypersons by inculcating in them a *religious habitus*'.

Further elaboration on the nature and function of the religious habitus, especially regarding its somatic dimension, and on the critical importance of the relationship between religious habitus, religious capital, and religious field may be found in Chapter 5, with reference to substantive examples from a later period in United States history, the historical emergence of Afro-Catholic religions in the Atlantic world, and others. For now, it suffices to re-emphasize that one's religious habitus inclines one to find certain forms of religious capital as appealing or even absolutely necessary in life and others as actually satanic and eternally perilous. At any rate, such subjective religious inclinations both shape and are shaped by the objective structures of the religious field, in Bourdieu's generative structuralist view of the social world.

Religious Capital

What precisely, it needs to be asked, are the forms of religious capital that interest agents, and over which religious institutions and specialists struggle, and which the laity consume? There are of course many types (and 'sub-types') of capital at stake in the religious field, such as the legitimation of the social order, the sanction of wealth and power, and the sense of meaning that religion brings to people's lives, and each of these is highly coveted. As Bradford Verter (2003, 157) helpfully explains:

> The product of accumulated labor, religious capital has two forms: religious symbolic systems (myths and ideologies), on the one hand, and religious competencies (mastery of specific practices and bodies of knowledge), on the other.

> The church manages its fund of religious capital by maintaining a steady demand for the goods of salvation among the laity, and by ensuring a steady and monopolistic supply of these goods through its reproduction of a pool of authorized producers and distributors of the sacred and its exclusion of rivals, whom the church identifies as blasphemers, heretics, and magicians—that is to say, as illegitimate.

Among the 'different types and subtypes' (Bourdieu 1986b, 242) of religious capital, Bourdieu most often refers the 'the goods of salvation', meaning especially sacraments and any officially recognized membership in an ecclesial community that is regarded as requisite to salvation. Bourdieu esteems the goods of salvation to rank among the preeminent forms of religious capital because of their contribution to the misrecognition that religions, in the words of Lora Stone (2001, 23), 'are not following material interest, but rather are pursuing salvation, opposing evil, or realizing the sacred'. Such 'misrecognition denotes "denial" of the economic and political interests present in a set of practices', as David Swartz (1997, 43) notes. This in effect causes the underprivileged masses to seek meaning, consolation and salvation in religion, rather than looking elsewhere for the power to change the misrecognized and unequal social order: 'The laity expect of it [religion] not only justifications of their existence that can offer them deliverance from the existential anguish of contingency or abandonment, or even form physical woes, suffering, sickness or death. Religion also has social functions in so far as the laity expect justification of their existence as occupants of a particular position of the social order' (Bourdieu 1987a, 124).

As noted in Chapter 1, Bourdieu (1990b, 36) is most impressed by Weber's sociology of religion for its elucidation of the economic logic of the religious field, and for its emphasis on the relations between producers and consumers of salvation goods and the interests of each that shape the religious market, in which the priest and the prophet play central roles:

> Weber built up a veritable political economy of religion; more precisely, he brought out the full potential of the materialist analysis of religion without destroying the properly symbolic character of the phenomenon. When he states, for example, that the Church is defined by the monopoly of the legitimate manipulation of the machinery of salvation, far from proceeding from one of those purely metaphoric transfers of economic language . . . he produces an extraordinary leap forward in understanding.

This 'extraordinary leap forward' notwithstanding, Bourdieu is critical of Weber's view of the prophet as being naturally endowed with charisma and thus possessing the powers of *creatio ex nihilo* of religious capital; Bourdieu insists instead upon the economic logic underlying religious practice and the relations between Church and laity, one that ironically is inherent in Weber's own model. Forms of religious capital and their market value are to a considerable degree determined more by the needs of the consumer than by the powers of the prophet, hence the prophet, for Bourdieu, is not *vox Dei*, as Weber has it, but rather *vox populi*.[10] In other words, Bourdieu (1987a, 129) takes issue with Weber for positing charisma, a central concept in Weber's sociology of religion, 'as a mysterious quality inherent in a person or as a gift of nature', whereas Bourdieu (1987a, 130) argues that charisma is more socially grounded: 'The prophet embodies in exemplary conduct, or gives discursive expression to, representations, feelings, and aspirations that existed before his arrival . . . In this sense he brings about, in both his discourse and his person, the meeting of the signifier of the pre-existing signified . . . It is, therefore, only by conceiving the prophet in his relationship with the laity . . . that one may resolve the problem of the initial accumulation of religious capital'.[11]

As an independent producer and peddler of religious capital, the prophet thus emerges as an upstart 'player' in the religious game, or as something of a subversive entrepreneur in the religious marketplace, whose primary objective is in one sense the same as that of the representative of the Church, or the priest: the prophet, like all other religious 'agencies, individual or institutional', takes part 'in the competition for the monopoly of the management of the goods of salvation' (Bourdieu 1971a, 318–19), which, in the end, is a struggle to get people to believe certain things about the world to be true, or inculcate in them a religious habitus that is amenable to the respective interests of either the Church or the heresiarch. The prophet is obviously in a disadvantaged position in this struggle, unless of course he or she succeeds in inspiring a revolutionary shift of power in the religious field. Understanding sociologically how the prophet or any other religious specialist or agency fares in the competition, moreover, demands careful analysis of 'the actual state of the structure of objective relations between the religious demand (i.e., the religious interests of the different groups or classes of the laity) and the religious supply (i.e., religious services, whether orthodox or heretical)' (ibid.).

Here we can see reflected several essential structural elements of the religious field as Bourdieu understands it: the operation of an economic logic, particularly that of supply and demand; the social grounding of religious interests; the positions of, and relations between, various agents and institutions and their specialists; and the central competition between orthodoxy (the Church) and heterodoxy (the heresiarchy) over religious capital as a 'resource of power'. It would be somewhat misleading, however, to overemphasize issues of power in this regard (as I believe that Bourdieu does) and thereby overlook other less political forms (or the less transubstantiative forms) of religious capital that were also, to return to our substantive example, of decisive interest to the Wampanoag, or to dismiss the kinds of religious capital that their indigenous religion continued to provide, at least *in spirit*, even as they adopted Christianity. In addition to investing in Christianity to gain leverage 'to broker an alliance with' the English (Silverman 2005, 13), to maintain some of their land in the face of English greed, and to obtain guns, credit, and other material goods, the Wampanoag adopted the new religion for its rich stores of what Verter (2003) calls 'spiritual capital',[12] such as its faith healing (Silverman 2005, 22), its protection from witchcraft or shamanistic sorcery (ibid., 21, 36), its communal dimensions (ibid., 26), and above all its God, whom they seemed to accept quite sincerely and with no ulterior motive as the supreme guardian spirit and the completion of their own indigenous theology (ibid., 16, 26). They thus made Christianity their own by finding in it the same kinds of 'spiritual capital' (which is something like religious capital only de-institutionalized, freer, more freely accessible, and sometimes the production of members of the laity themselves) that previously was produced by the shaman.

Religious capital, meanwhile, derives so much of its importance in society because it is transferable into forms of political capital, which is only possible because fields, for Bourdieu, are only 'relatively autonomous' and thus interrelated, as explained in Chapter 2. Furthermore, the transferability of capital from one field to another, as John B. Thompson notes (1991, 6), determines that 'those who occupy dominant positions in the political field will be identical with, or in some way closely linked to, those who occupy dominant positions in the field of economic production'. The possession of large sums of capital in one field usually translates for an individual into advantageous positions in other fields.[13] Because of this nuance, Bourdieu's theory of practice is especially useful for analysis of the relationship between religion, class and power, especially in places like colonial Martha's Vineyard where a rigid hierarchical system of social class, based, in this case, fundamentally on racial difference, emerged with the English conquest of the region. A Bourdieuian interpretation of our substantive example (and all substantive examples, for that matter) would thus call for a field analysis that focuses on the struggle over forms of religious capital, like *legitimierende Macht*. Once transferred into other fields and transformed into other forms of capital, religious capital thus enables elite agents or institutions to perform better in the economic, political and cultural fields.

From Silverman's (2005, 159–72) account, the remarkable life of a Native American man named Zachariah Housseit (d. 1772) can serve as an excellent case study of such inter-field transferability (and mutability) of religious capital. Though born into an abjectly poor family with an alcoholic father deeply indebted to 'a shameless liquor peddler' (Silverman 2005, 159), Housseit's mother's formidable Christian piety eventually transformed his father into an upright and sober citizen, and instilled in their son a healthy dose of the Protestant work ethic. With this ethic's sense of frugality and 'inner-worldly asceticism', to use Weber's famous term,[14] decidedly inculcated into his habitus, Zachariah Housseit managed to embark on a path of upward social mobility that was unsurpassed among the Wampanoag of his day. He did so chiefly by garnering an unprecedented amount of political capital among the colonized Wampanoag, a feat that he could never have accomplished had he not, in 1740, left the emergent Baptist heresiarchy to become one of orthodoxy's (i.e., Congregationalism's) leading religious specialists. Illustrating the transferability of religious into political and economic capital, Silverman (ibid., 165) suggests that in converting from Baptist to Puritan Christianity, Housseit's 'motivation might have been a larger flock with a bigger salary and stronger ties to colonial elites, all to better serve his political ambitions'. In effect, he became a very influential Congregationalist preacher and about as 'true' a Christian as a Wampanoag could be in the eyes of the English. Being also a teacher, a magistrate and a trader, he was of course much more than a preacher, but the religious capital (his reputation as being honest and trustworthy and therefore deserving of large credit lines at local depots, for one thing) that he amassed he quite effectively reinvested in other fields (e.g., political, social economic) to become arguably the most prominent Wampanoag leader in the colonial history of Martha's Vineyard.

The competition over religious capital (a 'game' that Houssueit had mastered as much as its *doxa* would allow any Wampanoag to master) on the island unfolded on many levels and among and between a series of polar oppositions: between opposing socioeconomic classes; between different 'religious specialists' in a given 'subfield'; between religious specialists and the laity; and, most importantly, between Church and heresiarch. Each pole in these juxtapositions had specific interests 'at stake' in the competition. Such confrontational relationships both structured the island's religious field and, in cyclical fashion, were reproduced by the very structures that they created, which reflects well what Bourdieu (in Bourdieu and Wacquant 1992, 132) means in describing fields in general as 'structured spaces of social forces and struggles'. In the 'structured space' of the colonial Martha's Vineyard religious field, the struggle over the control of religious capital became even more complicated with the emergence of Baptist Christianity, especially in the wake of the First Great Awakening in the 1730s and 1740s. With the Congregationalists' domination of the field at stake, Puritan religious specialists employed a strategy of symbolic violence against the Baptists, at first by labeling them 'petulant Congregationalists who had been "brought under the Church-dealings for their vile immoralities",' as Thomas Mayhew put it (Silverman 2005, 162), and later by investing their political capital to convince 'Christiantown's guardians . . . to pull down the Indians' meeting house to keep it from being used by "secteries and itinerants"' (ibid., 240). Indeed so much more was at stake than the Congregationalists' monopoly of the colonial New English religious field: to Wampanoags and African-Americans alike, two of the most appealing messages preached from Baptists pulpits were racial equality and a 'theodicy of compensation', to use another of Weber's terms, which assured a turning of the tables and a meting out of justice, if not in this world then in the next.[15]

Symbolic Violence in the Religious Field

'Symbolic violence is the coercion which is set up only through the consent that the dominated cannot fail to give to the dominator (and therefore to the domination) when their understanding of the situation and the relation can only use instruments of knowledge that they have in common with the dominator, which, being merely the incorporated form of the structure of the relation of domination, make this relation appear as natural' (Bourdieu 2000a, 170). The specific forms of symbolic violence that manifested in colonial Martha's Vineyard, it may be argued, laid the foundation for an entire history of what Robert Bellah (1967, 346), in a groundbreaking and much-debated essay, calls American 'civil religion': 'a genuine apprehension of universal and transcendent religious reality as seen in or, one could almost say, as revealed through the experience of the American people'. From the very beginning on the *Mayflower*, English Puritans perceived of and portrayed their entire colonial endeavor as God's plan, just as today the President of the United States justifies invading a sovereign foreign nation in the name of God:

> Mayhew, like most Puritans, thought of New England's colonization as a religious undertaking. They believed that God would reward them with blessings on this earth—if not necessarily the next one—if they created a society that upheld proper worship, biblical law, and Christian neighborliness. The Indians' conversion to Christianity was supposed to be part of this vision, as exemplified by the

Massachusetts Bay colony seal that pictured an Indian pleading 'come over and help us' (Silverman 2005, 19).

Nearly 400 years later, we see the very same elements of civil religion at play in President George W. Bush's rationalization of the American invasion of Iraq:

George Bush has claimed he was on a mission from God when he launched the invasions of Afghanistan and Iraq, according to a senior Palestinian politician in an interview to be broadcast by the BBC later this month. Mr. Bush revealed the extent of his religious fervour when he met a Palestinian delegation during the Israeli-Palestinian summit at the Egyptian resort of Sharm el-Sheikh, four months after the US-led invasion of Iraq in 2003. One of the delegates, Nabil Shaath, who was Palestinian foreign minister at the time, said: 'President Bush said to all of us: "I am driven with a mission from God". God would tell me, "George, go and fight these terrorists in Afghanistan". And I did. And then God would tell me "George, go and end the tyranny in Iraq". And I did' (in MacAskill 2005).

A compelling point may thus be made here by using Bourdieu against Bourdieu, so to speak. As indicated earlier, Bourdieu sees religion as being of diminishing importance in the contemporary world, and yet consideration of his own concept of symbolic violence as operative in American civil religion demonstrates how wrong he is in this regard. As an examination of their symbolically (and too often overtly and physically) violent effects reveals, religious ideas (e.g., American civil religious ideas) have tremendous influence in the contemporary world, with literally millions of human lives in the balance.

In a subsection poignantly entitled 'Symbolic Productions as Instruments of Domination', Bourdieu (1991d, 166) explains the overall social effect of symbolic violence: 'The dominant culture contributes to the real integration of the dominant class (by facilitating the communication between its members and by distinguishing them from other classes); it also contributes to the fictitious integration of society as a whole, and thus to the apathy (false consciousness) of the dominated classes; and finally, it contributes to the legitimation of the established order by establishing distinctions (hierarchies) and legitimating these distinctions'. This is as true for the religious field as any other field, since religion represents a supremely effective legitimizing force in most societies, like in colonial and present-day America, as reflected in the two block quotations immediately above. In colonial Martha's Vineyard, Christian doctrine was thus a form of 'symbolic production' employed in the form of various 'instruments of domination', or as 'weapons of symbolic violence', for it clearly legitimated the radical social inequalities on the island, just as it did for, say, the Spanish in Mexico, the Portuguese in Brazil, and the French in

Saint-Domingue. It also manifested in quite physical violence, at least in the form of corporal punishment, a practice among Puritans that the Wampanoag found 'shocking' (Silverman 2005, 209).

In an insightful discussions of the operative nature of class relations and the reification of social inequalities, Scott (1990, 133) arrives at a similar conclusion: 'As an integral part of their claim to superiority, ruling castes are at pain to elaborate styles of speech, dress, consumption, gesture, carriage, and etiquette that distinguish them as sharply as possible from the lower orders', all with the implicit aim of perpetuating the social order. Scott suggestively refers to such effects of symbolic violence as 'cultural segregation'. The only way for the Wampanoag to overcome such 'cultural segregation' was to largely abandon their religion and culture and adopt those of the English, though hardly with the results for which they had hoped:

> On the one hand, the Vineyard Wampanoags, like most Indians in sustained contact with Euro-Americans, felt outside pressure to take up Christianity and adopt alien practices and values such as male plow agriculture, private property holding, monogamous lifelong marriage, formal education, Judeo-Christian law, a six-day sunrise to sundown work schedule, clothes that cover nearly the entire body, and more. On the other hand, whenever the Wampanoags yielded to the most stringent demands, they learned there was yet another standard that they had failed to meet, which enabled the colonists to justify consigning them to third-class status (Silverman 2005, 14).

Bourdieu contends that in the religious field it is mainly orthodoxy's 'religious specialists' and their ideological allies, namely economic and political elites, who commit collaborative acts of symbolic violence, though they are only able to do so because of the 'complicity' of the victims of such forms of violence in the construction and maintenance of the *doxa* and the *illusio* of the religious field itself. Religious specialists have much to gain (or maintain), after all, by promoting religious orthodoxy, especially since the *legitimierende Macht* afforded by the moral and symbolic hegemony of the Church is often irreplaceably supportive of elites' capitalistic exploits in the economic, cultural and political fields, hence their dominant positions in the meta-field of power. This goes far in explaining the pertinence of their united efforts to restrain heretical religious activity that seriously threatens the status quo. In colonial Martha's Vineyard, for example, 'Christianity and the English had become such indelible parts of the Indians' world that it was difficult to imagine a peaceful future without placating God and easing the colonists' suspicion' (Silverman 2005, 87).

Bourdieu (1971a, 319–20) writes that 'the struggle for the monopoly over the legitimate exercise of religious power over the laity and the administration of the goods of salvation is necessarily organized around the opposition between 1) The Church . . . and 2) The prophet (or heresiarch)'. The prophet, or 'independent entrepreneur of salvation' (ibid., 321), along with his or her following (the heresiarchy), represents the single greatest threat to the Church's monopolistic control over religious capital. Furthermore, the heresiarch's ambition to cater to the laity's religious needs amounts to a real challenge to the entire conglomerate of institutionalized orthodoxy and society's chief benefactors of ecclesial sanction. This actually seemed to become more of a concern to Martha's Vineyard's Congregationalists when other Christian denominations began evangelizing on the island than it ever did during the period when they were the only Christians on the island. In any case, it is thus of paramount importance to the Church and to those with whom it enjoys a clientelic relationship (in the all-encompassing field of power) to defeat or at least contain any emergent heresiarchy. It is especially to this end that the employment of symbolic violence, or religious violence, is most useful to orthodoxy. Most apposite in this regard is Bourdieu's (1987a, 134) observation that the historical periods exhibiting the most significant rises in heretical religious activity are, not coincidentally, also those periods marked by the greatest production of canonical doctrine in Catholic history: 'In order to counter the attacks made by prophets or intellectualist criticism from within the laity, the priesthood has to assume the obligation of codifying . . . doctrine . . . and delimiting what must and what must not be regarded as sacred. In short, it must equip itself with weapons of symbolic struggle that are at once homogenous, coherent and distinctive; it must do this in the sphere of ritual as much as in the sphere of dogma (doctrinal corpus)'.

One would be hard-pressed to find a more powerful slogan for the Church's campaign to monopolize the production and administration of religious capital than its age-old declaration '*Extra Ecclesiam nulla salus*' ('outside the Church there is no salvation'), which is traceable to Origen and Cyprian in the third century. This infamous dictum, which for one and a half millennia was Catholic dogma, has served as the sharpening stone for some of the Church's most destructive weapons of symbolic violence, like excommunication and anathema, as well as the paternalistic supremacism that has generally characterized Christian missions. This doctrine also rendered the entire colonial conquest of the Americas, for all of its brutality and greed, palatable to the European conscience, as, after all, a dispossessed, colonized, marginalized and vanquished Christian Native American or enslaved Christian African was incomparably better off, from the Christian soteriological standpoint, than a free 'pagan' Native American or African. Catholic and Protestant European religious specialists alike demonstrated no waning of diligence in employing ecclesial 'weapons of symbolic violence', like threats of excommunication and damnation, in the European conquest of the New World.

Yet even in such a broader context of struggle, there is a certain rigidity to Bourdieu's two-dimensional, top-heavy, institutionally focused paradigm, as several scholars note (e.g., Dillon 2001, Rey 2004, Verter 2003). As will be further discussed in Chapter 5, Bourdieu's model of the religious field is far from ideally suitable for incisive or extensive analysis or prediction of anomalies like divergent uses of religion by the powerful or successful rebellious use of religion by the dominated. We may turn to one last example from colonial Martha's Vineyard to illustrate this limitation. For Silverman (2005, 276), Martha's Vineyard offers a counter-example to the routine presentation of historians that casts Christianity as the handmaiden of the destruction of Native American freedom and culture:

> Historians frequently use Christianity to stand for the evils of colonization, but on the Vineyard its role as a gateway between the Wampanoag and English communities was indispensable to their coexistence. . . When the sachems [traditional leaders] fell, Wampanoag congregations supplied the prototype for the town meeting governments that replaced them. In the eighteenth and nineteenth centuries, when exogamous marriages were on the rise, churches helped introduce newcomers to Wampanoag ways. Christianity, in short, bound the Wampanoags together and helped sustain them as a people.

Conclusion

For Bourdieu, the extent to which orthodoxy succeeds in inculcating a pliant religious habitus in the laity determines both the measure of control and domination maintained over them and the margin of victory gained in its struggle against the heresiarch.[16] In the first case, if the laity's religious habitus disposes them to recognize as legitimate and effective the unique sacramental powers of orthodoxy's religious specialists, they remain consumers of orthodox forms of religious capital and consequently misrecognize the social order as legitimate. In the second instance, the heresiarch's appeal to agents in the religious field will rise in proportion to the degree of failure in orthodoxy's campaign to inculcate in the laity a religious habitus in accord with the dominant worldview, for renegade religious interests, ones uncontrolled by orthodoxy, develop in the laity and lead them to 'take their business elsewhere'. I intend no pun by this colloquial expression, for it reflects accurately the economic logic at the structural heart of the religious field, as Bourdieu envisions it.

Of course, all is not lost if orthodoxy's religious specialists are not entirely successful in their efforts of religious habitus-inculcation in the laity, for they almost never are. In reality, provided the margin of failure remains unyielding of any religious coup d'etat, orthodoxy still maintains a 'de facto monopoly' over legitimate religious capital administration, which the Congregationalists did up until Baptist Christianity surpassed Puritanism as the most popular religion in Martha's Vineyard by the end of the eighteenth century. Negotiating the diffuse variety of habitus among a diversifying populace of religious consumers, which inevitably results from the Church's catholic expansion, demands, according to the economic logic that structures the field, coloring the product anew (à la Vatican II) to keep consumers interested, without, of course, sacrificing ultimate hegemonic dominance. To wit: 'The nearer the body of religious priests is to holding de facto monopoly of the administration of the goods of salvation in a class divided society, the more divergent, indeed contradictory, are the religious interests to which its preaching and pastoral activities must respond and the more these activities and the agents carrying them out tend to become diversified' (Bourdieu 1987a, 133). Thomas Mayhew, Sr.'s brilliance lied in part in his realization and negotiation of this fundamental reality of the religious field, and thus he quite effectively 'played the role of Christian *powwow*' (Silverman 2005 24). This was surely one key to Christianity's success among the Wampanoag of colonial Martha's Vineyard.

In conclusion, we may extract an historical trajectory of the religious field from Bourdieu's model. In pre-modern societies no adequate degree of division of labor exists to permit the religious field emerge as an autonomous social field. With increasing division of labor, however, conditions are created in which a class of religious specialists emerges as distinct from the laity, whom the religious specialists 'dispossess' of religious capital. Thereby the laity are transformed into consumers and the religious specialists transformed into producers who, furthermore, institutionalize their orthodoxy and call it a Church. Prophets emerge to disrupt the Church's monopolization of the administration of religious capital, however, which is an important dynamic of struggle in the religious field and gives the field its first dimension of religious pluralism. Eventually, further development of religious pluralism (and spiritual pluralism) leads to the gradual dissolving of the borders of the religious field, which Bourdieu (1987b) refers to as the 'dissolution of the religious', as explained in Chapter 3. For Bourdieu (1998a, 125), speaking here (as usual) of the Catholic Church, this means that 'we are moving toward a *Church without a faith-*

ful', one that is 'ever more exclusively female' (Bourdieu 2001, 84, original italics).

By this term, 'dissolution of the religious', Bourdieu does not mean that religion is disappearing, but only that the borders of the religious field are dissolving.[17] This phenomenon is in large part the result of the emergence of alternative forms of the production of the means of healing, wellness and enlightenment, which has historically been largely the provenance of religion, and results in the erasure of the religious field's borders and the reconstitution of religion proper in the broader 'field of symbolic manipulation'. To illustrate this, in Martha's Vineyard, the *pow-wow* and his flock were indeed effectively dispossessed of religious capital, which became monopolized by white Congregationalist pastors. In time, Baptist Christianity emerged as a formidable heresiarch, eventually counting more congregants than Congregationalism itself, as struggle continued to structure Martha's Vineyard's religious field. Nowadays, although Christianity remains the religion of most of the island's residents who do practice religion, there exists a whole range of competitors in the fields of wellness and 'symbolic manipulation' who market what Bourdieu (1987b, 122) calls 'new forms of salvation services', thereby facilitating the 'dissolution of the religious' and the related development of what Peter Berger (2001, 448), citing Robert Wuthnow, calls 'patchwork religion'.[18] And thus today in Martha's Vineyard there are at least two acupuncturists; five chiropractors; two agencies specializing in 'complementary' or 'holistic' medicine; two for hypnotherapy; thirteen for massage, most of which also practice 'alternative' medicine; one 'wellness center'; about a half dozen yoga centers; and a 'Face and Body Sanctuary'. Both the descendants of the English Puritan settlers and the descendants of the Wampanoags they colonized, meanwhile, still have churches of their own today in the Vineyard. There are also three Catholic churches on the island, one Universalist Unitarian denomination, and more than two dozen other places of worship, including a Reform Jewish synagogue, a Mormon Stake, a Christian Scientist church and reading room, three Episcopal churches, a Kingdom Hall of Jehovah's Witnesses, and a Quaker Meetinghouse, a Karma Kagyu Buddhist center, and an interfaith center—all for a year-round island population of some 15,000![19] Oh, and of course there is at least one New Age gift shop on the island, whose website invites visitors to 'Awaken to the Divine' and use their credit cards to purchase 'inspired gifts'.[20]

Summary of Key Elements to Chapter 4

- Religion and Colonialism: Bourdieu's model of the religious field is perhaps best suited for the analysis of religion and social inequalities in colonial and emergent post-colonial societies, like New England in the seventeenth and eighteenth centuries (pp. 83–84);
- Religion and Social Inequality: For Bourdieu, religion's primary social function is the legitimation of social inequality. It performs this function by promoting 'dominant religiosity', which, through 'consecration', sanctions the positions and privileges of the dominant classes in society, and 'dominated religiosity', which, through 'misrecognition', provides the dominated classes with a fundamental means to make sense of their own subordinate positions in society (pp. 84–92);
- Religious Habitus: For Bourdieu, religion succeeds in performing its primary social function by 'inlculcating' both 'dominant religiosity' and 'dominated religiosity' into the religious habitus of its adherents; one's religious habitus is her/his 'matrix of perception' of all things religious and the seat of her/his dispositions toward religious belief and practice (pp. 92–94);
- Religious Capital: Religious institutions and their specialists produce forms of religious capital, like sacraments and the sanction of political and economic power, which are pursued and consumed by the laity. Furthermore, competition in the religious field, as Bourdieu's conceives of it, is chiefly between the Church (orthodoxy) and the heresiarch over the production, control and administration of religious capital (pp. 94–99);
- Symbolic Violence in the Religious Field: Any act of symbolic violence creates or perpetuates distinctions and inequalities between individuals and classes in society. For Bourdieu, the paradigmatic model par excellence of symbolic violence is the Catholic doctrine *'Extra Ecclesiam nulla salus'* ('Outside the Church there is no salvation') (pp. 99–103).

Chapter 5

Using Bourdieu to Interpret Religion: Applications and Limitations

Once he takes upon himself the right, as is sometimes recognized as his, to indicate the limits between classes, regions, and nations, to decide with the authority of science whether or not social classes exist . . . the sociologist assumes or usurps the functions of the archaic king . . . to dictate the boundaries, the limits, that is to say, the sacred (Bourdieu 1982, 12–13).

Applications

Soon after *Outline of a Theory of Practice* first appeared in French in 1972, Pierre Bourdieu began attracting considerable attention in fields beyond sociology, especially education, art and literary criticism, and anthropology. Having already taken interest in his two major articles on religion, which were published just the year prior, scholars of religion, too, began exploring ways to apply Bourdieu's theory of practice to their subject. The first book-length study to emerge in this exploration was Otto Maduro's *Religion and Social Conflicts*, discussed below, which was first published in Spanish in 1979. A second, François-André Isambert's *Le Sens du sacré*, soon followed. Meanwhile, articles citing Bourdieu and covering a variety of topics in religious studies began to appear, first in France and Belgium,[1] in the 1970s (e.g., Liénard and Rousseau 1972; Remy 1972; Colonna 1974; and Grignon 1977) and somewhat later abroad in the 1980s (e.g., Weiler 1983; Kennedy 1984; Devisch and Vervaeck 1985; Vincent 1985; Delteil 1986; Ebertz and Schultheis 1986a, 1986b; and Prakash 1986), covering a fairly wide range of topics, from religious indifference, religious education and religious language, to African divination, Catholic pastoral theology, and popular religion.

   To date, more than a quarter century since *Outline* was translated into English, there have been published far more scholarly applications of Bourdieu to the study or religion than can be effectively summarized in this chapter. Instead, I explain and assess here four of the most extensive of these applications: Maduro's study of religion and social conflict in Latin America; Catherine Bell's innovative theorization of ritual practice; Thomas Csordas's 'cultural phenomenology' of Catholic Charismatic Christianity; and Joan Martin's womanist interpretation of the Christian work ethic of enslaved African-American women. Added to these are intertwined summaries of two of my own Bourdieian interpretations of central aspects of Afro-Atlantic religion, namely charismatic prophecy and syncretism. This chapter ends with consideration of several stated limitations of Bourdieuian theory for understanding religion or various aspects thereof.

Otto Maduro on Religion and Social Conflicts

Otto Maduro's *Religion and Social Conflicts* is the first book-length application of Bourdieuian theory to the study of religion.[2] Here Maduro explains sociologically how religion has contributed to, by legitimizing, the division between the rich and the poor, the socially dominant and the socially dominated, in Latin America's history and present. Unable 'to remain impassive vis-à-vis the millions of human beings in Latin America today who suffer under the yoke of a social organization whose only purpose is to fatten the bank accounts of a minority', thanks in large part to a 'church in Latin America [that] has established such bonds with the powerful that its preaching and activity often serve to prevent persons from making the commitment the gospel seems to demand' (1982, xxv), Maduro finds Bourdieu's model of the religious field well suited for approaching his central objectives. These objectives can be summed up as a systematic attempt to employ the sociology of religion[3] to answer the following three questions (1982, xxvii): 'How and why have relationships between church and society in Latin America come to their present state? What changes are possible in these relationships? How are these changes feasible—how can they be brought about?'

In seeking to overcome some of the limitations in Marxist theory of religion that the sociology of religion had revealed to him, Maduro turns to Bourdieu, among other thinkers, to approach these fundamental questions. Over and above the regular use that he makes of Bourdieuian language (e.g., 'religious fields', 'inculcation'),[4] specifically there are two avenues of analysis down which Maduro travels with Bourdieu: (1) the transformation of the pre-Columbian into the colonial and post-colonial Latin American religious field; and (2) the mutually buttressing relationship between the Catholic Church hierarchy and the political and economic elites in Latin American societies. Concerning the first, Maduro (1982, 53–54, original italics) draws on the first section of Bourdieu's 'Genèse et structure du champ religieux' to explain that:

in the presence of a greater *social division of collective labor*, the possibilities and needs increase for a greater *division of religious functions*. This hypothesis seems adequate to explain the differences we have noted between the two groupings of pre-Columbian communities with regard to their respective religions. . . When . . . the institutionalization of a social division of collective labor is introduced into a community, it becomes much more likely that all its important activities, religion included, will begin to be socially differentiated.

Furthermore, the religious field becomes autonomous from other fields to the degree to which labor in society is increasingly divided, with various forms of capital, including religious capital, thereby becoming unequally distributed in postcolonial Latin American societies.

European colonial conquest of course radically restructured Latin America societies in many ways, like introducing systems of forced labor, which, as Maduro demonstrates (1982, 86), emerged in consort and conspiracy with the establishment of the Catholic Church hierarchy as dominant in the Latin American religious field:

> In Latin America . . . Luso-Hispanic colonialism established a marked social division of labor. Similarly, religious work was gradually established as specialized work, assigned to a body of functionaries (the Catholic clergy), concentrated in urban centers . . . With the appearance of a body of functionaries specializing in religious production, religion was no longer a product arising directly out of the interest of indigenous Latin American communities. Little by little, undifferentiated religious activity . . . gave way to the genesis of a religious field—an articulated complexus of individuals, groups, and institutions specially charged with satisfying the religious interest of the various groups comprising Latin American society.

This 'body of (religious) functionaries' created its own importance through the systematic 'expropriation' of the indigenous people's 'means of religious production'. As a result, '[t]he remaining members of the community will become the *dispossessed* (the 'laity', in a broad sense), forced to have recourse to the clergy in order to satisfy their religious interest' (1982, 90). Maduro (ibid., 91–92) provides an interesting and insightful discussion of some of the mechanisms through with such a 'strategy of expropriation' was implemented in colonial Latin America:

> an emergent clergy can expropriate a traditionally communitarian religious ritual such as the invocation of supernatural forces to obtain rain by recourse to a number of strategies:
>
> * *Disqualification*—designating the traditional rite 'sorcery'.
> * *Conversion*—crediting the occurrence of rain to a religious figure strange to the community but familiar to the emergent clergy.

- *Disparagement*—announcing the exact date when rain should begin and, when drought continues, denouncing the inefficacy of the traditional religious practice.
- *Replacement*—introducing another rite, showier and more emotionally satisfying.
- *Competition*—introducing a new rite, controlled by the emergent clergy, celebrated during and after the rains.
- In extreme cases, violent *persecution* of the traditional rite.

Maduro's second Bourdieuian foray concerns the disturbing tendency in Latin American history for the Catholic hierarchy to be allied with political and economic elites in such a way as to legitimate, or even 'sacralize', the radical social inequalities that continue to plague the region. The titles of the two chapters in which Maduro makes some of his most penetrating use of Bourdieu are as revealing as they are suggestive: 'Incorporation of Religion into the Hegemonic Strategy of Dominant Classes' and 'The Clerical Contribution to the Hegemonic Strategy of the Dominant'. Maduro's (1982, 126) argument that ecclesial complicity in the perpetuation of social inequalities is largely unconscious or unwitting is also reflected in Bourdieu's understanding of the dialectic between habitus and field,[5] and Bourdieu would probably take much delight in the former's careful detailing of the ways in which the Church hierarchy is 'incorporated' into the agenda of the social and economic elites of Latin America, and the ways in which it exercises its power of *legitimierende Macht* for the benefit of the dominant, who require from the Church 'the production of practices and discourses that will legitimize and sacralize this dominance, and point to it as something desired by supernatural and metasocial forces . . . and the desacralization of any struggles against it' (ibid., 123).

Catherine Bell on Ritual

In her highly acclaimed *Ritual Theory, Ritual Practice* (1992), Catherine Bell takes cue from Bourdieu to challenge the very direction of 'ritual studies', a subfield (or offshoot) of the anthropology of religion and religious studies that concentrates on many secular arenas in addition to its original concern with religious ritual. For Bell, here echoing Bourdieu quite resoundingly, ritual studies suffers from its uncritical acceptance that ritual behavior is distinguished from other forms of human behavior, and from its negligence of the political and 'strategic' processes that cause practitioners and observers alike to recognize (or misrecognize) ritual as distinguished. As such, the study of ritual 'loses sight of what may be the more useful questions that can be brought to bear on ritual activities of various kinds: Under what circumstances are such activities distinguished from other forms of activity? How and why are they distinguished?' For Bell

(1992, 70), to answer these questions is 'to break free from the en-
trenched tendency to define ritual as a distinct and autonomous set of
activities', which requires a shift in focus from ritual itself to 'ritualization',
or to that:

> way of acting that is designed and orchestrated to distinguish and privilege what
> is being done in comparison to other, usually more quotidian, activities. As such,
> ritualization is a matter of various culturally specific strategies for setting some
> activities off from others, for creating and privileging a qualitative distinction
> between the 'sacred' and the 'profane', and for ascribing such distinctions to
> realities thought to transcend the powers of human actors (ibid., 74).

Thus consistent with the overarching aim of Bourdieu's theory of practice to understand how distinction in society is reproduced, Bell develops
'an approach to ritual activities that is less encumbered by assumptions
about thinking and acting and more disclosing of the strategies by which
ritualized activities do what they do' (ibid., 4). Such assumptions are problematic because they operate according to a 'logic based on the opposition of thought and action' (ibid., 6). This is where Bourdieu's notion of
'practice' can empower ritual studies and move its discourse beyond the
limitations dictated by these assumptions, because '[a]s a term designed
to represent the synthetic unity of consciousness and social being within
human activity, "practice" appears to be a powerful tool with which to
embrace or transcend all analogous dichotomies' (ibid., 76). Bourdieu's
application of the notion of practice, as Bell (ibid., 78) effectively explains, consists in 'a dialectical relationships between a structured environment . . . and the structured dispositions engendered in people which
lead them to reproduce the environment even in a transmuted form', or
in the dialectical relationship between field and habitus. And although
Bell finds Bourdieu's notion of habitus to be 'awkward' and 'unclear', it is
precisely in this relationship where Bell (ibid., 80) locates her notion of
'rationalization':

> Habitus is an awkward but explicit formulation of the real insight within Bourdieu's
> work on practice, namely the need 'to confront the act itself'. With regard to
> myth, for example, he argues that we should approach a myth neither as an
> object (a completed event laid out neatly for analysis) nor in terms of some
> mythopoetic subjectivity, but as the very act of myth-making. It is possible to
> confront the act in this way, he writes, only by addressing the principle that
> generates, organizes, and unifies all practices . . .

Both 'myth-making' and 'ritual-making' constitute forms of what
Bourdieu refers to as 'world-making', processes that produce and repro-
duce the social world and the way that it is perceived. Bell follows
Bourdieu's (2000a, 16) insistence that such processes be subjected to

How do we take up residence in our body? We do as our society tells us.

112   Bourdieu on Religion

critical sociological inquiry in the sense that they 'have to be related to the economic and social conditions that make them possible'. In this manner does Bell (1992, 74) construct her notion of ritualization 'to draw attention to the way in which certain social actions strategically distinguish themselves in relation to other actions'.

Bell is also quite taken by the corporal implications of Bourdieu's theory of practice. One's habitus is necessarily an embodied habitus (and one's body a 'socially informed body'), and the structures of the social world, including of course the structures of ritual, result from, and are reproduced by, '"a dialectic of objectification and embodiment" that makes it *the locus* for the coordination of all levels of bodily, social, and cosmological experience' (ibid., 97). Applying Bourdieu's habitus/field dialectic as a paradigm for understanding ritual—or, better yet, for understanding ritualization—Bell provides the key insight that participants in ritual and observers of ritual alike all have 'ritualized bodies', which both (re)produce and are (re)produced by the process of ritualization 'through the interaction of the body with a structured and structuring environment' (1992, 98):

> Adapting Bourdieu's discussion of practice, we can speak of the natural logic of ritual, a logic embodied in the physical movements of the body and thereby lodged beyond the grasp of consciousness and articulation. The principles underlying this logic can be made explicit only with great difficulty; they are rarely in themselves the object of scrutiny or contention. And yet, suggests Bourdieu, nothing less than a whole cosmology is instilled with the words 'Stand up straight!' (1992, 99).[6]

Thomas Csordas on Embodiment and Charismatic Christianity

Thomas Csordas is one of the leading anthropologists of religion in the field today, primarily for his innovative 'cultural phenomenology' of the Catholic Charismatic Renewal, which is concerned with 'synthesizing the immediacy of embodied experience with the multiplicity of cultural meaning in which we are always and inevitably immersed' (1994, vii). The Charismatic Renewal is a relatively recent development in Roman Catholicism that is essentially comprised of Pentecostal spirituality and ritual; i.e., faith healing, speaking in tongues, exorcisms, and baptismal renewal in the Holy Sprit, all of which is theorized in sophisticated fashion in three of Csordas's books: *The Sacred Self: A Cultural Phenomenology of Charismatic Healing*; *Language, Charisma, and Creativity: Ritual Life in the Catholic Charismatic Renewal*;[7] and *Mind/Body/Healing*. In developing his theory of embodiment in Charismatic ritual and practice, Csordas finds great utility in Bourdieu's 'dialectical structuralism', which is unsurprising because Bourdieu and Csordas are each driven to overcome certain longstanding dualities that have marked (or marred) both Western philosophy and social theory. Each, moreover, is fundamentally influenced by Merleau-Ponty's phenomenology in his grounding of human experience in the body. For Csordas (2002, 59)—here clearly echoing both Merleau-Ponty and Bourdieu—'the paradigm of embodiment has as a principal characteristic the collapse of dualities between mind and body, subject and object'. Csordas (ibid., 60) constructs his own paradigm largely on the pillars of Merleau-Ponty's elaboration of 'embodiment in the problematic of *perception*', and Bourdieu's location of 'embodiment in the anthropological discourse of *practice*':

> The collapsing of dualities in embodiment requires that the body as a methodological figure must itself be nondualistic, that is, not distinct from or in interaction with an opposed principle of mind. Thus, for Merleau-Ponty the body is a 'setting in relation to the world', and consciousness is the body projecting itself into the world; for Bourdieu the socially informed body is the 'principle generating and unifying all practices', and consciousness is a form of strategic calculation fused with a system of objective potentialities.

In similar fashion to Bell, Csordas (ibid., 63) finds Bourdieu's notion of habitus particularly helpful for the analysis of religious ritual and practice 'because it focuses on the psychologically internalized content of the behavioral environment' (e.g., Bourdieu's 'whole cosmology instilled with the words "Stand up straight!"'), and for its consistent 'groundedness in the body'.[8] Participation in Charismatic ritual is, for Csordas, so effective for believers—effective even in the realm of bio-physical healing—because of the operative and resonating presence of *both* beliefs and *bodily* emotions as dispositions in their collective *embodied* habitus: 'The group leaders' enumeration of the physical accompaniments of divine power that some participants would experience (heaviness, heat, tingling) recapitulates a repertoire acquired from their own experience and from reports of participants at similar events. These somatic images are being inculcated as *techniques du corps* that will embody dispositions characteristic of the religious milieu' (ibid., 70).

Usually the effect of the laying on of hands during faith healing, falling is one such *technique du corps* that is common in Charismatic healing rituals: 'The act of falling is spontaneously coordinated in such a way that, following Bourdieu, it can be described as a disposition within the ritual habitus' (Csordas 1994, 233). Likewise, manifestations of demons in exorcistic rites are 'examples of an embodied process'—'original acts of communication that nevertheless take a limited number of common forms because they emerge from a shared habitus' (Csordas 2002, 66). The manifestation of demonic spirits in such rituals is often accompanied by a dramatic scream, the propensity for which is also, for Csordas (ibid., 68), elemental to the Charismatic religious habitus because it is 'a deeply ingrained somatic component of the experience and symbolism of evil'. In Charismatic ritual, the scream 'is subsequently identified as the sign of the spirit . . . [that] exemplifies the "arbitrary necessity" (Bourdieu 1977) of evil in the Charismatic Christian habitus'. Csordas (2002, 76) underlines that the scream is both the projection of an embodied disposition within this habitus and a bodily act, which can also be said about what is perhaps the quintessential Charismatic experience of glossolalia, or speaking in tongues:

> [S]peaking in tongues is a ritual statement that the speakers inhabit a sacred world, since the gift of ritual language is a gift from God. The stripping away of the semantic dimension in glossolalia is not an absence, but rather the drawing back of a discursive curtain to reveal the grounding of language in natural life, as a bodily act. Glossolalia reveals language as incarnate, and this existential fact is homologous with the religious significance of the Word made Flesh, the unity of human and divine.

In Csordas's cultural-phenomenological interpretation, the image of God in flesh and the image of God giving the gift of tongues are embodied images that dwell in the perceptive function of the Charismatic habitus. And so, when a believer perceives a co-congregant speaking in tongues, she or he understands this to be a manifestation of divinity and not the gibberish of a madman. Thus the habitus is both the generator of this form of ritual behavior in the speaker and the matrix of perception in the hearer that makes sense of something that would otherwise be senseless. Bourdieu would certainly be pleased with Csordas's (2002, 72) interpretation of the fundamental function of such images in the following impressive passage:

> Through these embodied images, dispositions of the habitus are manifest in ritual behavior. Because they are shared at a level beneath awareness, they are inevitably misrecognized, and the principle of their production is identified with God instead of the socially informed body. This conclusion is to be distinguished from Durkheim's functionalist abstraction of the sacred as self-affirmation of social morality and solidarity, as much as it must be distinguished from an incarnational acceptance that 'God' inhabits the socially informed body. Instead, it suggests that the lived body is an irreducible principle, the existential ground of culture and the sacred (2002, 72).

A sociologist who has also done extensive research on the Catholic Charismatic Renewal in North America, Meredith McGuire (1990, 284–85) asserts that the social-scientific study of religion in general is 'impoverished' by its longstanding inconsideration of the body, an inconsideration 'in which things of the spirit have been radically split from material things, and in which mind is considered separate from body'. For this reason, McGuire (1995, 342) deems Csordas's work to be 'an outstanding contribution to the literature' because it 'argues cogently that embodiment and bodily experience are definitive aspects of human consciousness and subjectivity' (ibid., 341), which Csordas is enabled to do largely through application of Bourdieu's notions of habitus and practice.[9] More concretely, Csordas 'links body practices (e.g., posture, breathing patterns, ritual movement) to self-processes (e.g., imagination, memory, emotion), showing how healing effectiveness is possible . . . [and thus] suggests the ways that religious practice may effect real transformations—bodily, emotional, spiritual—of a person's self' (ibid.).

Joan Martin on the Christian Work Ethic of Enslaved Women in the United States

Womanist theology may be characterized as an emergent academic field that foregrounds and critically engages, both deconstructively and reconstructively, the historical and contemporary experiences of African-American women, and places them in conversation with mainstream Christian theology. Though sharing in the struggle against racism that characterizes Black theology and the critique of patriarchy central to feminist theology in general, womanist theology departs from the former because of its perceivable male chauvinism and the latter because of its production and control by white theologians. As Linda Thomas (1998, 4) explains, '[w]omanist theology's goals are to interrogate the social construction of black womanhood in relation to the African-American community . . . to unearth the ethnographic sources within the African-American community to reconstruct knowledge and overcome subordination'. Given such an anti-subordination agenda, Bourdieu's theory of practice has much analytical potential for womanist inquiry, as impressively demonstrated by Joan Martin in *More Than Chains and Toil: The Christian Ethic of Enslaved Women*. Martin's book is a womanist theological and historical-sociological interpretation of the Christian work ethic of enslaved African-American women from their own perspective. Oriented theoretically in large part by Bourdieu, Martin (2000, 105) makes important contributions to several fields of study by demonstrating 'that enslaved women had a work ethic in terms of their lives' purpose and that this ethic was, in part, the vehicle through which they acted as moral agents'.

With considerable profit, Martin employs the central concepts of Bourdieu's theory of practice, namely habitus, practice and field, in her investigation of the work ethic of enslaved women of color in the United States. Her theoretical orientation is especially effective in its deft attention to the relational, positional and structural insistence of Bourdieu's field theory, which thus guides inquiry into:

the normative, formative principles of operation in the social world and how people act in an everyday and taken-for-granted manner—in this instance the everyday world of slave holders and enslaved women. For Bourdieu, the point is to understand (among other things) how objective structures, individuals, and groups within them function in relation to concrete class and status positions through forms of capital—economic, symbolic, cultural—in the 'fields' of inter-related social space (2000, 56).

In this vein Bourdieu's theory of practice is germane to Martin's investigation of 'the intersection of the objective relations of slavery' and 'the social world of enslaved women'. Most importantly, we can begin to understand this 'social world' from the perspective of these women when we take seriously, as Bourdieu would recommend and as Martin does, their own *strategies, interests and improvisations*. And so, for example, the dispositions that are elemental to enslaved women's habitus, far from being merely passively incorporated traits, are the means by which their work ethic is constructed and sustained: 'Translated into skills learned in the doing, dispositions can become intergenerational practices' (2000, 60).

In her analysis of slave narratives, Martin makes similarly fruitful use of Bourdieu's notions of field and habitus. But to overcome what she perceives (2000, 73) to be 'Bourdieu's aversion to a role of conscious intention', she conjoins these notions with James Scott's notion of 'hidden transcript',[10] paying particular attention to the function of dispositions in the creation of autonomy in enslaved feminine discourse:

> To take seriously the slave narrative and thus the practices of enslaved women as hidden transcripts adds depth to Bourdieu's theoretical model in relation to the theoretical tools of practice, disposition, and *habitus*. . . Like practices themselves, the hidden transcript encompasses more than words of 'the speech act' spoken to or about the slave master or mistress. It captures a range of practices that are inclusive of skills and competencies, like clandestine organization of the religious life . . . or other forms of countersocialization in the enslaved community (2000, 70).

Most importantly, for Martin (2000, 75), this fusion of Bourdieu and Scott allows for an understanding of 'the strategies of the enslaved not simply as reactions to domination, but as building social spaces relatively free from, and alternative to, life under domination'.

In effect, Martin demonstrates that the religiously structured symbolic violence underlying the institution of slavery in the US ultimately failed to inculcate into enslaved women's habitus the misrecognition of the social order as divinely sanctioned, for 'the ex-slaves' testimony clearly demonstrates that slaves did not believe that slavery was the will of God' (2000, 81). As reflected in slave narratives, their theology in fact largely conceived of the Supreme as a 'God of freedom and not slavery' (ibid., 82),

Isn't it necessary to add Scott to Bourdieu in order to qualify the idea of misrecognition as this over-generalized statement

and represented a 'cultural site of empowerment and the religious site of ritual (empowering) prayer to God, bringing together enslaved ancestors and the Christian God' (ibid., 83). Essentially, the liberative and empowering dispositions of *both* a traditional African religious habitus and a Christian habitus were thus fused in enslaved women (and men), despite all efforts of the slave regime to inculcate in them the disposition to misrecognize as just, and to thereby accept, 'their place' in the social order. In such a way did their 'feel for the game' include a clear sense that the rules of the game were extremely unjust, and that they could—and in fact they did—construct 'hidden transcripts' and resist in often subtle and complex ways. By combining the positional/relational orientation of Bourdieu's theory of practice and Scott's notion of 'hidden transcripts', Martin sheds refreshing light on enslaved 'blackwomen's self-understanding of the work *unchained* from slavery's meaning, yet *arising out of those very chains'*, thereby 'remind[ing] the reader of the interplay of the logic of practice structuring those chains' (ibid., 80).

Terry Rey on Charisma and Syncretism in Afro-Atlantic Religion[11]

In separate analyses (Rey 1998; 2005a), I focus upon a 'heresiarch' who led an insurgent movement against the French slave regime during the early stage of the Haitian Revolution (1791–1792),[12] a 'man' named Romaine-la-Prophétesse, to explore the issues, respectively, of prophetic charisma and syncretism in Afro-Atlantic religion. Each analysis is theoretically oriented by Bourdieu's theory of practice. In the first case I raise a question that is as seemingly obvious as it is important, and one that curiously is largely ignored in the literature: Where does religious syncretism occur? Hybridity in symbolism, mythology, ritual and deities have been the chief foci of scholars of religious syncretism, when in reality these are but some of its outward signs or products. The process of religious syncretism itself, however, is not trenchantly explained by merely pointing to and describing such things. In the second case I adopt Bourdieu's relational model of charisma to argue that Romaine-la-Prophétesse was either Kongolese or that his prophetic charisma was attuned to a distinctively Kongolese religious habitus.

Religious syncretism, I propose, is primarily an integrative epistemological and somatic process that cannot be fully understood without fixing careful attention on the place where it occurs. That place is precisely what Bourdieu calls the religious habitus, or 'the matrix of perception' through which a person filters all religious experiences and stimuli. Moreover, depending on the dispositions that in large part comprise one's religious habitus, new religious experiences and stimuli may or may not

be interpreted in positive ways that in turn lead to inter-religious improvisation and the incorporative process of religious syncretism. Bourdieu's
notion of religious habitus can thus help us more fully understand the
integrative and interrelated forces of popular theology and somatic im-
pressions and emotions in the development of syncretism in Afro-Catholic religion and, in particular, the prophetic movement led by Romaine-la-
Prophétesse. Following the tenets of revisionist historical scholarship of
the African diaspora (Lovejoy 1997), analysis of these subjects should
begin in Africa.[13]

Early in the eighteenth century the Virgin Mary appeared in the Kingdom of the Kongo, not far from the mouth of the great River Congo, to
proclaim that 'Jesus was angry with the Kongolese and that they must ask
his mercy. To do this, it was necessary to say the Hail Mary three times,
following it with three calls for mercy' (Thornton 1997, 105). Word of
these messages spread rapidly, and soon thousands of Kongolese people,
now several generations deep in their Catholic history,[14] were engaging
in this ritual. This sparked extraordinary religio-political fervor among them,
which was also profoundly shaped by the series of civil wars then racking
the one-time large and powerful kingdom. All that was needed to create
a classic example of a millenarian movement was a charismatic leader,
which was provided when 'a Kongolese woman [Dona Beatriz Kimpa
Vita] possessed by Saint Anthony led a mass movement to restore the
Kingdom of Kongo' (Thornton 1997, 1).

The style and content of Beatriz's theology and prophecy reveal a
fundamental characteristic of the Kongolese religious habitus that goes far
in explaining both Afro-Catholic religious syncretism in general and, subsequently (and transatlantic-ly), the charisma of Romaine-la-Prophétesse
in particular. The inclusive spirit of this habitus led Beatriz and her followers to take considerable licence in adopting and contorting Catholic doctrines, myths and symbols, precisely the kind of licentious improvisation
that has so indelibly marked New World African-derived religions like
Vodou, Santería and Candomblé. For example, Beatriz burned crosses,
claimed that her pregnancy was an immaculate conception, and declared
that Christ had been born in the Kongo. Such theological and symbolic
radicalism was simply beyond what the Portuguese clergy and their elite
Kongolese patrons were willing to tolerate, however, and so they burned
Beatriz at the stake for heresy in 1706.

By the middle of the eighteenth century, people from the Kongo region of Central Africa tragically comprised the majority of enslaved Africans imported to the French colony of Saint-Domingue, the western third
of the island of Hispaniola that would become the independent Republic
of Haiti in 1804. At the outbreak of the Haitian Revolution in 1791, there

were more than 500,000 slaves in Saint-Domingue, fully half of whom were African-born and African-socialized. And of this half, furthermore, more than half were from Central Africa, which means that by then there were well over 100,000 Kongolese in the colony. It is of tremendous significance that these people were from a Central African culture that had already been heavily influenced by Catholicism for a quarter-millennium, and that they were thus possessed of a collective religious habitus that esteemed *both* Catholic saints and the spirits and ancestors of traditional African religion as being powerful supernatural intermediaries who regularly intervene in the lives of the living.

Charismatic individuals like Romaine-la-Prophétesse are credited with combining religious prophecy and political ideology to inspire world history's only successful national slave revolt (Mennesson-Rigaud 1958; Rey 1998). Careful examination of Romaine's prophecy reveals the operative nature of the Kongolese religious habitus in the nascence of Haitian Vodou, a religion that truly began to crystallize during the Revolution. Furthermore, application of Bourdieu's relational model of charisma reveals certainly a heavily Kongolese dimension to his movement, while suggesting that either Romaine was himself either Kongolese or at least that he crafted his message and its delivery to resonate with the Kongolese religious habitus of his followers:

> The renegade slaves, especially the Kongolese majority among them, were thus socially predisposed to respond positively to Romaine's prophecy in all of its Marian and royalist overtones. Romaine's religious power, then, was not the product of nature, but rather 'the product of a transaction' between the 'religious agent', Romaine, and 'the lay people', in which their religious interests were reflected and their religious needs satisfied (Rey 1998, 356).[15]

Calling himself both the 'godson of the Virgin Mary' and a king, Romaine amassed a following of several thousand escaped slaves in a mountain redoubt near the port city of Leogane, whom he inspired to carry out violent raids of plantations throughout the region from December 1791 to March 1792. The nature of Romaine's prophecy and ritual performance were remarkably similar to those of Beatriz, as reflected in the following examples: he said Mass before an inverted cross, while holding a saber in one hand, and he placed his head inside of the tabernacle of his church to retrieve the Virgin's handwritten message (Rey 1998, 352). In doing so, the Virgin's godson appropriated Catholic symbolism and myth in ways that were perfectly resonant with Kongolese prophetic tradition, for, as John Thornton notes (1993, 189), 'Kongolese ideologues had reworked Christian concepts in similar ways for years'.

Once coupled with his self-identification as the godson of the Virgin Mary, Romaine's choice of the feminine title '*la Prophétesse*'[16] also reflects the disposition toward Afro-Catholic syncretism that is integral to the Kongolese religious habitus. From the outset, Kongolese appropriation of Catholicism combined the legitimating authority of Catholic saints with the traditional Kongolese leadership roles of the *ngunza* (prophet) and the *nganga* (healer). Dona Beatriz Kimpa Vita was herself a *nganga marinda* (a healer of social discord) whose proclamations and charisma were sanctioned by her self-identification with St. Anthony (Thornton 1997, 54). Like Beatriz, Romaine was esteemed by his followers, many of whom were in fact Kongolese, as a *ngunza*. Furthermore, like Beatriz's claim to be the incarnation of a *male* saint, Romaine's claim to be a 'prophetess' (as opposed to a 'prophet') inverted his gender. This would have made perfect sense to his Kongolese followers, for, as James Sweet (1996, 193) demonstrates, by the sixteenth century in West Central Africa, the spiritual power of transgendered male prophets was well established and 'universally known': 'the feminization of these men, as measured by their social and sexual roles as females, rendered them vulnerable to the spirit world. . .' Again, either because he was himself possessed of a Kongolese religious habitus, or because he crafted his prophecy to resonate with the religious habitus of his Kongolese followers, Romaine took the feminine title '*la prophétesse*' as a reflection of a feminized passivity that made him readily penetrable by the spirit world. This transgendered state made his mediumship both possible and understandable to his largely Central African flock, thereby enabling and enhancing his charisma, charisma understood here in Bourdieu's relational terms of a dialectic that involves prophet, message and hearer. The syncretic dimension in the examples of both Beatriz and Romaine of course lies in their use of Catholic saints to effect such traditionally Kongolese ways of self-transgendering to enhance one's capacity for spirit possession and charismatic prophecy.

Limitations

Maduro, Bell, Csordas and Martin, among others,[17] employ Bourdieuian theory to interpret religion quite fruitfully, but not so enthusiastically as to partake in the alleged 'heady rush to utilize Bourdieu's vogue categories of "practice" and "habitus"' (Coakley 2000, 8). Far from being 'heady' or hasty, their readings of Bourdieu also reveal several limitations to his theory of practice for the study of religion. It is in keeping with the 'reflexivity'[18] that Bourdieu demands of sociology that we should carefully consider several of these limitations, beginning with reflection on the kind of 'aversion to a role of conscious intention' that Martin (2000, 73), for example, finds in Bourdieu's theory of practice—an aversion that effectively obstructs, she claims, any meaningful depth of understanding of the 'alternate visions' or 'the fantasy life' of subaltern groups and/or individuals.

As already noted, however, Martin (2000, 72) overcomes this perceived limitation by fusing Scott's notion of 'hidden transcripts' to Bourdieu's dialectic of habitus and field:

> Scott's most important contributions and corrections to Bourdieu's theory of practice include his discussions of false consciousness and his rejection of the Neo-Marxist notion of ideological hegemony. He believes that the dominated have alternate ways of seeing the contradictions in the established order and have the capacity to critique them. Slave narratives reveal Scott's claim to be true. . . Bourdieu contends that within structure, *habitus*, and power, the functions of the established order limit alternative representations, recognition of classifications and forms of power. Thus, agents' chances of neutralizing those effects . . . can be done only through compliance with those very dimensions in order to use them to their own ends.[19]

It would of course be painfully ironic if Martin were totally correct in her portrayal of Bourdieu's supposed denial of subaltern agency, or his implication that the subordinated sectors of society are incapable of the kind of indigenous assertiveness to alter social realities that is generally called 'resistance'—painfully ironic both because Martin herself uses Bourdieu (albeit fused with Scott) in essence to reveal precisely the subaltern agency of her subjects, and for everything implied in the title of one of Bourdieu's later, more politically engaged books, *Acts of Resistance: Against the Tyranny of the Market*, which Bourdieu wrote (1998b, vii) 'as contributions to movements and moments of resistance' out of a hope to 'provide useful weapons to all those who are striving to resist the scourge of neo-liberalism'.

Therefore, I must suggest that Martin's criticism, for all of its echoes in the wider academy's negotiation of Bourdieu, might not be entirely valid. To recall from Chapter 3, Bourdieu (1958b, 54) found that in spite of the rigid gender hierarchies of rural society in Algeria, Mozabite Muslim women were nonetheless able to create spaces of autonomy in the very culture and religion that generally cast them as inferior to men—'hidden transcripts', as it were, and as I called them in Chapter 3. The fact that Bourdieu's interpretation here parallels Martin's own study in remarkable ways raises the question as to whether Martin (2000, 69) has not overstated her claim that 'Bourdieu inadequately addresses the power of subordinated individuals and groups to resist and subvert the dominant objective structures'.[20] It should also be recalled from Chapter 3 that Bourdieu saw Islam as the sole hope of resistance for Mozabite culture against the scourge of colonialism and modernity. During his fieldwork in

Algeria, furthermore, in the midst of the Algerian War of Independence, Bourdieu befriended at least one Catholic priest *who was an active member of the armed Algerian resistance* (ALN—*Armée de Libération Nationale*), and he recounts a gripping tale of personally driving this priest to safe haven while French soldiers were approaching his rural monastery to take him in to custody (Bourdieu 2004, 66–68).

But Martin is certainly not alone—far from it, in fact—in finding in Bourdieu a kind of stucturalist determinism that would seem to portray the dominated as virtually and structurally un-free and thus unable to rise up, resist, and act to change the very social order that enables their oppression. Scott (1990, 75), for one, finds Bourdieu to exemplify precisely this kind of 'minimal notion of ideological resistance [which] has become almost an orthodoxy one encounters again and again in the literature on such issues'. More specifically as pertains to the religious field, meanwhile, Hugh Urban (2003, 354), in his trenchant analysis of the ecstatic Hindu/Muslim Bāul sect of Bengal, concludes that 'the Bāul offer a powerful challenge to Bourdieu's work, demonstrating that there is perhaps far more room for subversion or critique of the dominant "social marketplace" than his model of society and culture seems to allow'. And finally, early in Pierre Carles's highly successful 2001 video documentary *La Sociologie est un Sport de Combat—Pierre Bourdieu* ('Sociology is a Martial Art—Pierre Bourdieu'), a young woman approaches Bourdieu enthusiastically in the streets of Paris both to praise him for his work and to assail him, in an admiring way, for having revealed to her that she is 'not free'. Later in the film, furthermore, Bourdieu seems caught off guard by a Spanish journalist who asks him, 'What is the key to happiness?' His response is most revealing both in its content and the hesitating manner in which he articulates it: 'To do what we can with *the modicum of freedom that we have* to change the world' [my emphasis].[21] However limited that the subaltern may be for structural reasons—though not quite as entirely as Martin (or Scott or Urban, for that matter) reads Bourdieu to mean—one *must* act (and one *can* act because, for Bourdieu, 'everything is *not* in a state of constant inertia') to confront the 'vast problem' of social inequality.[22]

Nick Crossley (2001, 112) discusses the issue of 'Bourdieu's relative inattention to the possibility of resistance', which is one of the most hotly debated questions in what we might call 'Borudieuian studies', in a most helpful way:

> I would concede that Bourdieu has more to say about 'reproduction' than about 'transformation', but this is only a matter of emphasis. Bourdieu does and always has made reference to struggle and conflict in his work. He argues, for example, that the various 'unconscious' expectations, assumptions and beliefs, the *doxa*,

which hold the *status quo* in place are the outcomes of a historical process, and have often been preceded by struggle . . . Legitimation and stability are not inevitable therefore, but are rather the contingent and observable effect of a dying down of struggle and perhaps, in some cases, a forgetting of it from historical memory.

In effect, when prophets succeed they become the priests of the new orthodoxy, just as when revolutions succeed revolutionaries soon enough morph into elites, and just as whenever the meek actually do inherit the earth, one can expect that they won't remain meek for much longer!

Perhaps the strongest refutation of assertions that Bourdieu's theory of practice is incapable of conceptualizing resistance in the religious field (or in any field) would be one focusing on Bourdieu's critical discussions of the revolutionary praxis of prophecy. 'Prophetic explanations', after all, amount to 'a discourse of rupture and of critique' that aims at 'contesting the authority of those holding a monopoly over the legitimate exercise of symbolic power' (1971b, 15–16). Bourdieu (1987a, 130–31, original italics) goes on to cite Marcel Mauss in this regard: 'famines and wars give rise to prophets and heresies: violent clashes have far-reaching effects on . . . populations. . . ; *innovation and revolution may be the work of groups*, subgroups, sects or individuals acting through and for groups'. His italicization of part of this passage is revealing, for lest we think that Bourdieu's prophet is but another kind of elite who arbitrarily dictates the rules of the game (or of the subaltern *doxa*), as if by fiat, in such a way that negates the possibility of any creative lay contribution, we should recall that charismatic prophecy is only effective if its message resonates with the understandings and interests of the laity. 'The prophet', furthermore, 'is the one who can contribute to realizing the coincidence of the revolution with itself by operating the symbolic revolution that is called political revolution' (Bourdieu 1991a, 37).

It is to be noted that Bourdieu's discussions of prophecy themselves have not escaped criticism. As Urban suggests (2003, 363), 'for Bourdieu, the prophetic call to revolution is always a flawed or failed one'. Jacques Berlinerblau (2001, 348, n. 104), furthermore, criticizes Bourdieu's very understanding of prophecy as being flawed by certain historical inaccuracies: 'Without justifying the association, Bourdieu consistently equates the prophet with the heretic (in the Hebrew bible, however, we hear of prophets who seem to defend the orthodoxy/monarchy against antagonistic prophets such as Jeremiah, e.g., Jer 28, 26-10). His prophet/heretic is everywhere at odds with the church (i.e., 'trustee and guardian of an orthodoxy') and its priestly hierarchy'. These points are well taken.

In a similar vein, I (Rey 2004) find some degree of inadequacy in the 'strongly dichotomous' (Dillon 2001, 414) structure of Bourdieu's model

of the religious field, which seems to limit the social forces in this particular field to two: 'Church' and 'heresiarch', or more broadly, as Roger
Friedland (1999, 305) puts it, 'Bourdieu reduces all field relations to the
power binary of dominant and dominated'. There may of course be a
plurality of heresiarchs against whom the Church's 'specialists' militate,
and Bourdieu was surely recognizant of this, so the two-dimensionality of
Bourdieu's construction of the religious field is relative. Still, it remains
rigidly dualistic in the sense that Bourdieu limits the Church's alliances in
the field of power (which is broader than and encompasses the religious
field itself) to ones with political and economic elites—alliances that are
mutually beneficial constructions and maintenances of the *doxa*, which
perpetuates the status quo. In order to maintain its ascendant position in
the field of power, moreover, the Church must eliminate or suppress the
heresiarchy, as explained previously in Chapter 4. However, Bourdieu's
model of the religious field cannot help explain occasions, however rare
or anomalous, where political and economic elites court and co-opt the
sanction and blessing of the heresiarch,[23] sometimes in shocking defiance of the *doxa* and the Church itself. For example:

> One of modern history's most ruthless dictators, François Duvalier, ruled Haiti
> from 1957 until his death in 1974. Excommunicated by the Catholic Church
> (*l'Eglise*) in 1962, Duvalier cultivated his association with Vodou (*l'herésiarch*) to
> consolidate his power—recruiting Vodou priests into his notorious legions of
> thugs known as the Tonton Macoutes and appearing in public to resemble Gede,
> the main Vodou spirit of death. Much as Duvalier succeeded in leveling the
> economic playing field by creating a black bourgeoisie to counter Haiti's tradi-
> tional mulatto bourgeoisie, so too did he level the religious playing field by
> making Vodou Haiti's most powerful administrator of religious capital, at least for
> a while. His success cannot be explained by Bourdieu's dichotomous paradigm,
> although struggle clearly *did* remain the main structural determinant of the
> religious field during François Duvalier's reign (Rey 2004, 340–41).[24]

Yet even if Bourdieu's analysis of religion could help explain such anomalies as Duvalier's appropriation of the heresiarchy toward solidifying his
reign of terror in Haiti, it would still not transcend its top-heaviness, by
which I mean its over-emphasis on the imposition of worldview by religious specialists (orthodox or heterodox) on the laity, whose consumption
thereof serves primarily and almost exclusively to legitimate their place in
the social order. Not unjustifiably, Danìele Hervieu-Léger (2000, 110–11)
thus argues that Bourdieu's discussions of religion amount to a form of
reductionism that 'rules out from the start any chance of allowing religion
to have any reality outside the institutional structure where group and
class interests are converted into religious interests'. Consequently, the
creative agency of the laity, or of the 'system of meaning produced by

groups of men and women', is rendered mute in Bourdieu's analysis, in large part because for Bourdieu 'the Catholic model of relations between professionals and non-professionals provides the permanent reference':

> The questions raised by Bourdieu's presentation of the religious field are indeed helpful and potent in considering the struggle for control of the legitimate tradition within the Christian faith. They are less readily applicable in the case of monotheistic religions, such as Judaism or Islam, in which the contrast between professional and non-professionals is less formalized. But they have little practical value in assessing the religious ingredient in social phenomena that have little surviving connection to . . . traditional religions as strictly understood. And they are of little assistance in analyzing trends in secular modernity that show the production and circulation of religious-symbolic assets to be moving relentlessly away from institutional control (ibid.).

Key

Cristián Parker and Michele Dillon, respectively, share Hervieu-Léger's concern that Bourdieu's theory of religion is problematic in its over-emphasis upon religious institutions and their specialists as the sole producers of religious capital and of worldview. For Parker (1996, 239), Bourdieu's 'theory is in error . . . when it generalizes its conception of the religious field as a simple "market" of salvation goods. It fails to understand that the "consumers" of those goods are actors as well—in their fashion—and that as collective actors, they too are collective producers of their own goods of symbolic consumption', or of 'popular' goods. Or, as Dillon (2001, 412), puts it, the Bourdieuian model of the religious field is prohibited by its 'bias . . . toward a structural, institutional approach to the production of ideology that underplays the relative autonomy and cultural agency of ordinary people. Such top-down approaches to ideological production understate the ways in which people actively construct meaning in their everyday practices'. For example, in many Latin American countries where popular Catholicism is Mario-centric, so much of the Virgin's symbolic power—say, for example, the cult of Our Lady of Guadalupe in Mexico (Lafaye 1976), or the cult of Our Lady of Perpetual Help in Haiti (Rey 1999)—is in fact the product of the laity and not the Church hierarchy. In Parker's view, Bourdieu's theory is thus predisposed to give inadequate consideration to this and other kinds of 'religious discourse and practice of the people standing in contradistinction to cultivated "knowledge"'. Erwan Dianteill (2004, 82) echoes these criticisms as well, while also noting a resultant geographic dimension to them: 'while focusing on Catholicism, and in particular on French Catholicism, which was the state religion until the twentieth century, Bourdieu assuredly minimized the importance of the question of religious pluralism that cannot be ignored in North America'.[25]

Key

To be sure, there is much soundness to the mirrored criticisms made by Hervieu-Léger Parker, Dianteill, Dillon, and others (e.g., Robertson 1992 and Verter 2003), which should thus be taken seriously. However, Hervieu-Léger's charge that for Bourdieu 'the Catholic model of relations between professionals and non-professionals provides the permanent reference', and Parker's assertion that Bourdieu 'fails to understand' that the laity are 'actors' in the process of the production of religious goods, are not entirely fair. As we have seen, in Bourdieu's earliest considerations of religion he took popular Islam in rural Algeria as his subject in an analysis 'from below' that in no way relied on any 'Catholic model'; and he clearly affirmed the creative agency of the rural 'laity' in the production of religious goods as being at least as determinant of the value of these goods as the orchestration or imposition by any institution or religious specialist. Neither Hervieu-Léger, Parker, nor Dillon considers Bourdieu's early discussions of Mozabite Islam, and so their otherwise important indications of limitations in Bourdieu for the study of religion should be seen in the light of their own limitations.[26]

For different reasons, David Swartz and Roger Friedland find Bourdieu's emphasis on the function of power in oppositional conflicts between dominant and dominated social groups to impede his theory of practice from sound analysis of, respectively, single congregations and religious nationalism in the contemporary world. As Swartz points out (1996, 83), 'a popular form of study that Bourdieu's field framework would *not* encourage would be the case of congregations, denominations, or religious leaders. The field analytic perspective calls for situating particular entities, whether denominations or congregations, within a broader framework of struggle over the significance of religion'. For Friedland (1999, 301), meanwhile, Bourdieu's theory of practice tends to 'deculturalize power' in such a way as to render religious nationalism incomprehensible: 'While Bourdieu historically locates a new source of class power and legitimacy in cultural capital, credentialed and consumed, culture remains a medium for power, not its content. Power operates through culture, but is not itself cultural' (1999, 305).

The criticisms leveled by Swartz and Friedland are very well informed and quite intelligently developed, and thus we should welcome them critically both as cautions and suggestions: cautions against any 'heady' forays into Bourdieuian interpretation of religion, and suggestions for modifying Bourdieu's theory of practice for an even sounder interpretation of religion. Even if, as Swartz argues, congregations are too singularly grouped for Bourdieu's theory of practice to effectively theorize; or, even if religious nationalism is socially unifying in such a way that, for Friedland, distinctions between sub-groups of dominant and dominated are effec-

[handwritten annotations in top margin: "globalization ↓", "the post - nation state", "power of", "of the capital", "markets", "to", "consecrate"]

tively effaced by national unity, it remains the case that individual congregants often reside in their respective congregations because they find these congregations' offerings of *capital* attractive and thus they pursue, consume and attend. Likewise, American religious nationalism (or any other kind, for that matter) can only be effective if the nation state (as something like Bourdieu's notion of *l'Eglise*) effectively *inculcates* in its people the *misrecognition* that, say, President George W. Bush does indeed reflect their interests every time he says 'God bless America'.

That roughly 95 per cent of Americans believe in God of course gives President Bush's words great potential for resonance and reception among his people. It is also testimony to the stunning failure of the secularization thesis in the sociology of religion, one that Bourdieu seemingly does not entirely reject, as Steven Engler (2003, 446, 455) explains:

> His view that religion is anachronistic, that it was left behind by modernization, misses its continuing, and even increasing, importance. . . His exclusive emphasis on the state as the primary agent of consecration begs important questions of globalization processes above the level of the state and localized reactions and fragmentations below it. In the face of these developments, as the growth of Pentecostalism and the hardening of fundamentalisms in religious traditions around the world suggest, religion is more important as a site of consecration than Bourdieu acknowledges.

[handwritten annotations in right margin: "Key", "nice"]

Bourdieu's discussions of religion do give the clear impression that he envisions a decline in religion's importance in modern societies, where, as discussed in Chapters 3 and 4, the boundaries of the religious field are 'dissolving' as traditional religious institutions face increasing competition in the broader fields of power, healing and consecration. In this regard, as concerns religion in the West (and especially in the abundantly and pluralistically religious USA), I can certainly agree with Engler's criticism. I would caution, however, against extending this critique to the developing world, for Bourdieu clearly affirms the power of religious 'fundamentalism' there as an almost inevitable feature of the modern world:

> If resistance to the economic and political imperialism of western countries, and especially of the U.S.A., has taken the form of religious fundamentalism, it is because those countries affected by this imperialism have no other mobilizable or mobilizing cultural resource. . . [O]ne must not forget . . . that the economic and social structures that contributed to the production of colonial and neo-colonial domination did not favor the modernization of the religious message, and that western countries and their secret services worked ceaselessly to nip at the bud [*étoufer dans l'ouef*] any and all progressive cultural and political movements—and they continue to do so today. The drama of the wretched of the earth . . . is a tragic historical irony (Bourdieu, with Schultheis and Schosser 2001).

Conclusion

Shortly after it appeared in English translation, Bourdieu's *Outline of a Theory of Practice* received brief mention in the *Journal of Religion* (Anonymous 1979, 130), where it is suggested that 'the most significant feature of his work for the historian of religion is the constant meditation on the epistemology of the anthropological informant and his speech (chaps. 1 and 3), which provides a powerful critique against the systematic formalizations which have played an important role in both anthropological and history of religions literature influenced by the French sociological school'. Now thirty years later, a review of the literature reveals that this aspect of his work has yet to have any significant influence in religious studies or the sociology of religion. Instead, Bourdieuian theory has thus far proven most useful to scholars of religion in three primary areas: religion and social class; religion and the body; and religion and perception.

Concerning religion and social class, being the first extensive application of Bourdieuian theory to any area of religious studies, Maduro's *Religion and Social Conflicts* establishes important groundwork, especially for scholars interested in understanding the role of religion in colonial and emergent postcolonial societies. Carefully drawing upon Bourdieu's most direct statements on the nature of the religious field, Maduro demonstrates how the arrival of a colonizing force (like the Spanish and Portuguese in the Americas) under sanction of its religious specialists (like Catholic missionaries) creates a radically unequal system of the division of labor, including religious labor, and the concomitant and likewise radically unequal distribution of capital, both material and symbolic, across society. The maintenance and perpetuation of the emergent unjust social order, in Maduro's case in Latin America, relies in significant part on its fundamental sanction by the Catholic Church hierarchy.[27]

From Bourdieu's teeming quiver of 'thinking tools', scholars of religion have, to date, made the greatest use of his notions of habitus and practice. This is not at all surprising regarding practice, as for as long as religious studies has existed as an academic field it has concerned itself as much with 'religious *practice*' as anything else, in fact using the term 'practice', often somewhat uncritically, arguably to a greater extent than any other field in the humanities or social sciences. Regarding habitus, meanwhile, scholars of religion have found this notion to be most serviceable because it represents perhaps the most convincing place to locate belief; it is as if, thanks to Bourdieu, we can finally say that religious belief has a home. This home is the habitus, which is as much bodily as mentally constituted. In adopting the notions of habitus and practice, and tracing their dialectical relations and functions as Bourdieu represents them,

Bell and Csordas each demonstrate, in their respective analyses of ritual and Catholic Charismatic practice, that Bourdieu's work offers much analytical power to scholars seeking to understand the central place of the human body in religious experience and practice. So much of what we observe in religious practice is, per Bell and Csordas, the manifestation of dispositions that are embodied in the religious habitus of the practitioner, which is one of the most important insights to emerge thus far out of the Bourdieuian interpretation of religion.

In one sense, Martin's womanist interpretation of the Christian work ethic of enslaved women in the United States combines the chief concerns of Maduro with those of Bell and Csordas, for there is no deeper scar in the history of the social conflict of colonialism in the Americas than slavery, while the work ethic of enslaved African and African-American women that she examines is one that Martin rightly locates in their habitus. Despite the slave regime's efforts to inculcate in its victims' habitus the misrecognition of the social order as just, or to establish 'the naturalization of its own arbitrariness', the slave regime in the US itself 'misrecognized' entirely the 'perdurance' of the African religious habitus of slaves, which enabled enslaved women to creatively maintain dispositions toward resistance in their Christianized religious habitus. In identifying a similar fusion of African and Christian dispositions in the religious habitus of Kongolese slaves in colonial Saint-Domingue, meanwhile, I find Bourdieu's notion of habitus to be likewise persuasively suggestive in my research into the charisma of Romaine-la-Prophétesse and, more generally, the nature of religious syncretism in the Afro-Atlantic world.

Ultimately, all of the approaches to using Bourdieu for the study of religion that I have outlined in this chapter, whatever their respective subjects, methodologies, or argumentations, converge in their collective application of Bourdieu for understanding various dimensions of *perception* in religious experience: Maduro's Church, indeed like Bourdieu's *Eglise*, strives to shape the laity's *perception* of its symbolic production as orthodox and hence worthy, and that of the heresiarch as unworthy; Bell sees the field of ritual studies as impoverished for ignoring the ways in which we come to *perceive* of ritual as somehow distinguished from other forms of human behavior; Csordas uncovers the bodily dispositions in the Charismatic Catholic habitus that allow Charismatics to *perceive* of screams, unintelligible speech, and falling as manifestations of divinity; Martin finds in slave narratives evidence of a fusion of African and Christian dispositions in the habitus of enslaved women in the United States to *perceive* of the social order in ways contrary to the 'public transcript'; while I have found great utility in the notion of habitus, as 'the matrix of *perception*' to understand prophecy and syncretism in Afro-Atlantic religion.

For all of the tremendous worth of Bourdieuian theory for religious studies, however, there are discernible limitations, as we have seen. The most serious of these limitations vis-à-vis the religious field is the perceivably rigid structuralism in Bourdieu's theory of practice that can seem to render lay agency quite anemic because the laity are doomed by the structures of the field to misrecognize the social order as inevitable, and therefore doomed to act (and believe and practice) in ways that contribute to this order's very reproduction. Scholars of religion are here echoing longstanding criticisms in an array of academic fields (e.g., DiMaggio 1979; Jenkins 1982; Comaroff 1985) of Bourdieu's alleged ultimate failure to truly overcome the kind of structuralist determinism for which he assails Lévi-Strauss.[28] The irony—or perhaps the paradox—in this regard is that Bourdieu conceived of sociology as a means to empower the subjugated to resist social oppression. This irony is not lost on Urban (2003, 382), who feels that this simply amounts to 'a fundamental tension and an unresolved contradiction in Bourdieu's work' at large: 'on one side, there is a rather cynical view of human nature as inherently self-interested and motivated by the pursuit of profit, that is, a seemingly "capitalist" view that reproduces the economic determinisms that he professes to repudiate. Yet, on the other side, there is the hope for a more universal social concern, transcending individual interests and seeking some larger ideal of collective happiness'.[29]

Bourdieu was of course acutely aware of the widespread charges of structuralist determinism that are made against his theory of practice, charges that he refuted on numerous occasions (e.g., Bourdieu and Wacquant 1992, 131–37). Toward the end of *Pascalian Meditations*, as powerful and beautiful a book as he ever wrote, Bourdieu (2000a, 234–35, emphasis added) revisits this issue in a subsection instructively entitled 'A Margin of Freedom', which recalls the concept of 'conditional freedom' that he had developed exactly a quarter-century earlier in *Outline of a Theory of Practice*:

> [E]ven the most subversive symbolic actions, if they are not to condemn themselves to failure, must reckon with dispositions, and with the limitations these impose on innovative imagination and action. They *can succeed* only to the extent that—acting as symbolic triggers capable of legitimating and ratifying senses of unease and diffused discontents, socially instituted desires that are more or less confused, by making them explicit and public—they manage to reactivate dispositions which previous processes of inculcation have deposited in people's bodies.

Somewhere within all of us there thus lurks a spirit of resistance, lying for the most part dormant and 'confused' under layers upon layers of misrecognition that dupe us into submission to the social order in all of its inequalities and injustices. Until of course a prophet (hopefully one who has read Bourdieu!) comes along to 'reactivate' it.

Summary of Key Elements to Chapter 5

Applications of Bourdieu to the Study of Religion:

- Otto Maduro on religion and social conflicts: Maduro demonstrates how Bourdieu's theory of the genesis and structure of the religious field can be employed toward understanding the relationship between religion and sociopolitical inequality in Latin American history (pp. 108–10).
- Catherine Bell on ritual: Bell takes cue from Bourdieu in developing her original notion of 'ritualization', the process by which ritual behaviors become distinct from non-ritual forms of behavior. Bell also uses Bourdieu's notions of practice and habitus toward advancing the field of ritual studies (pp. 110–12).
- Thomas Csordas on embodiment and Charismatic Christianity: Synthesizing Merleau-Ponty's work on embodiment and perception and Bourdieu's work on embodiment and practice, Csordas produces his innovative 'cultural phenomenlology' for the interpretation of ritual and belief in Charismatic Catholic practice. Like Bell, Csordas profits considerably from Bourdieu's notions of habitus and practice (pp. 112–15).
- Joan Martin on the Christian work ethic of enslaved women in America: In her womanist analysis of slave narratives, Martin fuses Bourdieu's notions of habitus and practice with James Scott's concept of 'hidden transcript' to reveal the Christian work ethic of enslaved African-American women in the United States (pp. 115–17).
- Terry Rey on charisma and syncretism in Afro-Atlantic religion: Rey argues that Bourdieuian analysis can help shed light on the function of prophetic charisma and the nature of religious syncretism in Afro-Atlantic religion, especially by focusing on the nature of relevant African religious habitus and their perceptions of and dispositions toward, respectively, prophetic discourse and Catholic symbolism, ritual, and beliefs, i.e., forms of religious capital (pp. 117–20).

Critiques of Bourdieuian Theory for the Study of Religion:

- Ignores the agency of subaltern classes to find in religion power for resistance to social domination (pp. 120–23);
- Possesses an historically unsound understanding of prophecy (pp. 123–24);
- Too binary, to the exclusion of creative popular religious capital production; i.e., the laity are reduced to mere consumers in the religious field (pp. 124–26);
- Overemphasizes institutional over popular religion (pp. 126–27);
- Unsuitable for the analysis of single congregations and religious nationalism (pp. 124–26).

Conclusion

Whereas heresy . . . and all forms of critical prophecy tend to open up the future, orthodoxy, the discourse of the maintenance of the symbolic order, works . . . in a sense to stop time, or history . . . by announcing the end of history, a reassuring inversion of all millenarian utopias (Bourdieu 2000a, 235).

'The church does not impose. It doesn't force anyone to accept the message of the gospel'. So proclaimed Pope Benedict XVI on September 28, 2006. The pontiff was in full damage-control mode that day, confronted with the tumultuous and global reaction to a speech that he had delivered about two weeks prior. Muslims around the world were understandably outraged when Benedict quoted fourteenth-century Byzantine emperor Manuel II Paleologus: 'Show me just what Muhammad brought that was new, and there you will find things only evil and inhuman, such as his command to spread by the sword the faith that he preached'. The overarching objective of Benedict's speech, to promote inter-religious dialogue and renounce religious violence, was irretrievably lost in this poorly chosen citation. The pope's arguably fallible lapse in judgment reflects the same two forms of denial that are implicit to his claim that the Catholic church 'does not impose': (1) denial of a history in which the Catholic church certainly did, for centuries, impose its doctrine upon millions of colonized and/or enslaved peoples, just as it did provide the sanction that aided European powers to impose themselves and their *doxa* on the very same peoples; and (2) denial of the imposition of doctrines on its own laity that are arbitrarily produced by its episcopal councils, as overseen by a Congregation for the Doctrine of Faith, and euphemized, as Bourdieu would say, as 'revelation' or 'magesterium', all toward establishing, preserving and spreading abroad a de facto Catholic monopoly over the European religious field.

For more than a millennium in Europe, the Catholic Church enjoyed such a monopoly over the religious field. As we've seen, this historical example, interpreted through a creative synthesis of some of the most influential ideas in the history of Western philosophical and classical sociology, provides the paradigmatic foundation for not only Bourdieu's theory of religion but of his social theory at large. The Church's monopoly, furthermore, was achieved and reproduced by cornering the market of the production and administration of religious capital. It did this by effectively imposing itself on the world by, in Bourdieuian terms, successfully inculcating into the habitus of millions of people over generations both a worldview and the (mis)recognition that forms of religious capital produced by the Church are the true goods of salvation, whereas those produced by the heresiarch are diabolical and thus illegitimate. This also required the Church to keep its own religious specialists in line, something at which Benedict himself excelled while, under his predecessor John Paul II, presiding for seventeen years over the Congregation of the Doctrine of Faith, the Vatican body responsible for imposing orthodoxy. During this tenure, then known as Cardinal Ratzinger, the German pontiff-in-waiting earned the nickname 'Kardinal Panzer' for, among many other things, punishing some of the Church's most influential contemporary theologians: Hans Küng, for questioning the doctrine of papal fallibility; Leonardo Boff, for ecclesiological 'deviations'; and Charles Curran, for questioning the Church's position on birth control. Pope Benedict should thus understand better than anyone that the Church *does* impose, though certainly in our age it does so with much less effect than during the centuries when it enjoyed a monopoly over the European religious field, and much less than when in the fifteenth century it sanctioned the enslavement of Africans and the conquest of Native American peoples. As Bourdieu would certainly argue, the Catholic Church indeed imposed a worldview on millions of these people.

Two of modern history's watershed moments overlapped in such a way that resulted in momentous consequences for the nature of religion in Latin America. Just as the Protestant Reformation was dismantling the Catholic Church's monopoly over the European religious field, the Iberian conquest of Latin America was pushing forth with increasing vigor. R. Andrew Chesnut (2003, 17–18) insightfully writes about the subsequent Catholic monopoly of an entire continental religious marketplace:

> The Iberian conquest and colonization of the New World in the sixteenth century gave the Roman Catholic Church a new lease on life. As a result of the Protestant Reformation, the church had lost its millennial monopoly on religious production in Western Europe . . . As Protestantism claimed Geneva and London, the alliance between the Iberian crowns and the Vatican guaranteed Catholicism's religious control over the indigenous peoples and African slaves, as well as Portuguese and Spanish colonists from Sao Paulo to San Francisco. . . [I]t was able to corner the religious market in South, Central, and a significant part of North America for at least three centuries and well beyond in many areas.

Chesnut here provides an excellent example of the analytical power of microeconomic theory for the historical and especially the sociological investigation of religion, which over the last quarter-century or so has become the dominant theoretical approach in the sociology of religion, though not without inciting some rather fierce criticism.[1]

Theoretically oriented by the work of Peter Berger, Rodney Stark and Roger Finke, Chesnut explains the recent tremendous success of 'pneumacentric'[2] forms of religion in Latin America, chiefly Pentecostalism (both Protestant and Catholic) and African-derived religions (like Candomblé, Santería and Vodou), in microeconomic terms: the success of these particular 'religious firms' has depended upon their 'product, marketing, sales representatives, and organizational structure' (Chesnut 2003, 152). In the model that Chesnut and his mentors propose, further-more, the laity are perceived of as 'religious consumers'. While first read-ing Chesnut's excellent book, I kept wondering why he, like Berger, Stark and Finke before him, does not incorporate Bourdieuian theory, espe-cially for its wealth of economic metaphors that have proved so fruitful to scholarly interpretation of an increasingly wide array of social fields.[3] One clear reason eventually came to mind: Chesnut is interested in analyzing the relatively new 'free market economy' of the Latin American religious field, whereas Bourdieu's model of the religious field is more suitable for analysis of the kind of monopolistic religious economy, which is very well reflected in Otto Maduro's work, as summarized in the previous chapter. Indeed, as Erwan Dianteill (2004, 82) argues, because 'Bourdieu assur-edly minimized the importance of the question of religious pluralism', his model of the religious field is less suitable for the analysis of free market religious economies like the kind that interests Chesnut.[4]

It may very well be that proponents of the microeconomic interpreta-tion of religion, or of 'the new paradigm' (Warner 1993, 2002), have not engaged Bourdieu because they share Dianteill's assessment and thus consider him to be emblematic of what R. Stephen Warner (2002, 2) identifies as 'the old paradigm metanarrative of religion', one rooted in the very medieval Catholic model that so influenced Bourdieu's model of the religious field: 'There was only one provider of religious meaning and religious services, only one place to approach God and only one institu-tion to confer legitimacy on rites of passage. Since the church was a protected monopoly, assent was assured by the fact that there were no ideological alternatives, and the church's viewpoint, it is said, was un-questionably taken for granted'. It could be, therefore, that Bourdieu is almost entirely absent from the massive literature in the sociology of religion relative to 'rational choice theory'[5] because rational choice theo-rists consider his model of the religious field to be something of a relic of the 'old paradigm'.[6]

Or, perhaps Bourdieu's own explicit criticisms of rational choice theory make him 'off-limits' to proponents of the new paradigm. Fundamental to such criticisms is Bourdieu's opposition to the thorough subjectivity and freedom of individual choice upon which the new paradigm is predicated, a point that is well made by Jean-Pierre Bastian (2006) and Roland Robertson (1992). As discussed in Chapter 3, Bourdieu developed his pivotal notion of habitus in part to overcome the kinds of subjectivist assumptions that underlie rational choice theory and the new paradigm: 'Thus, against the scholastic illusion which tends to see every action as springing from an intentional aim, and against the socially most powerful theories of the day which, like neomarginalist economics, accept that philosophy of action without the slightest questioning, the theory of habitus has the primordial function of stressing that the principle of our actions is more often practical sense than rational calculation' (Bourdieu 2000a, 63–64). Put otherwise, 'most actions are objectively economic without being subjectively economic, without being the product of rational economic calculation' (Bourdieu 1990b, 90–91). Robertson (1992, 151) helpfully suggests how Bourdieu's theory of practice, despite some measure of structuralist rigidity that many scholars have assailed, can help counter the 'complete absence of constraint on consumers' in rational choice theory of religion. Such a Bourdieuian adjustment guides inquiry into how 'choices are formed by circumstances' (ibid., 155), being neither freely individualist and subjective nor the unalloyed products of circumstance and social structure, though for Bourdieu the latter are resoundingly dominant over the former in the production of religious practice, or any form of practice, for that matter.

Like Robertson, Bradford Verter (2003, 150) feels that '[t]heorizing religion with Bourdieu also suggests ways of rethinking the economic approach to religion championed by rational choice theorists'. Taking Bourdieu's notion of religious capital and de-institutionalizing it in such a way that both softens the rather mechanistic supply-and-demand logic of rational choice theory and 'grants an agency to the layperson that Bourdieu denied' (ibid., 170), Verter makes a very important contribution to Bourdieuian theory of religion in developing his notion of 'spiritual capital'. There is much potential here to overcome the most common criticism of Bourdieu's model of the religious field (that it over-emphasizes institutions at the expense of individual agency [e.g., Hervieu-Léger 2000]), insofar as Verter suggests a means by which we can appreciate that in the religious field the production of capital, in the words of Michele Dillon (2001, 412), 'occurs in multiple interpretive sites, and as such, the meanings and lived practices of religion may be relatively independent of official church discourses or of the meanings imputed to them by distant observers'. Likewise employing Bourdieu to enhance rational choice theory of religion, Bastian (2006, 77) argues for placing the entire discussion of religious markets in a broader Bourdieuian analysis of fields toward allowing one to better 'explain in particular the interaction of different religious organizations with the State as well as their struggles over a hegemony whose purpose is to define religious legitimacy'. Or, as Jörg Stoltz (2006a, 8) puts it, rational choice theory of religion would benefit from a forthright engagement of Bourdieu toward overcoming its present inability 'to explain the quest of religious groups to gain social legitimacy or religious power'.

It is most encouraging that an increasing number of scholars of religion are taking Bourdieu seriously and profitably employing his ideas, whether by adopting elements of his theory of practice or by exploring ways to overcome limitations or drawbacks in Bourdieu's writings on religion. In some cases, as with Verter (2003), the correctives are found within Bourdieu's larger body of work itself, while in others, as with Joan Martin's (2000) engagement of James Scott (1990), discussed in Chapter 5, and Hugh Urban's (2003) engagement of Michel de Certeau (1984), correctives are found in the work of other social theorists. It is indeed the case, as noted by Otto Maduro in this book's Preface, that 'things now seem to be veering in a different direction' in the sense that a towering figure of contemporary Western thought, after decades of relative disinterest, especially in the United States, is finally attracting critical attention in the study of religion.

Usually scholars of religion treat Bourdieu's theory of practice like a toolbox, picking up one or two 'thinking tools' as appropriate for the interpretive task at hand. Maduro (1982), for instance, concentrates on the religious field, while Catherine Bell (1992) and Thomas Csordas (1994, 2001, 2002) pick up Bourdieu's notions of habitus and practice while leaving the other tools, like capital and *illusio*, in the box; such selectivity is to be advocated, though it is always a good idea to read Bourdieu's writings on religion against the backdrop of his larger body of work. Whatever facets of Bourdieuian theory that they do employ, both in their theoretical embraces and their criticisms of Bourdieu, such scholars as these are pushing the proverbial envelope forward, which is very much in keeping with the 'reflexive sociology' that Bourdieu promoted: 'to think with Bourdieu', writes Loïc Wacquant (in Bourdieu and Wacquant 1992, xiv), 'is of necessity an invitation to think beyond Bourdieu, and against him whenever required'.

Thus moving beyond and against, taken together, criticisms of both rational choice theory of religion and Bourdieuian theory of religion are to be welcomed by anyone who, like me, finds disconcerting their perceivably a *priori* dismissal of both the sacred and the believer's *spiritual* (as opposed to *rational*) engagement thereof, and by their over-emphasis of self interest to the negation of the 'other interest' (Urban 2003, 382) that religion is capable of inspiring: 'a more universal concern, transcending individual interests and seeking some larger idea of collective happiness'. Some readers of either rational choice theory of religion and/or Bourdieu's treatment of religion will surely reach the conclusion that religion from the perspective of the seeker engulfed in mystery is, in the portrayals of both/either, almost altogether unrecognizable. Take, for instance, the following example from one of the most widely cited proponents of the former: 'Religious commodities are not physical goods like cars or computers that can be manufactured, packaged and sold in stores. Nor are they services like haircuts or banking that we have others do for us', writes Laurence Iannoccone (1992, 125). So far, so good—but wait!: 'Rather, they fall into a third category that economists call "household commodities"—valued goods and services that families and individuals produce for their own consumption'. So, religion is kinda like waffles made from scratch or the sweater that Grandma knits for Jimmy? And from Bourdieu (1998a, 126, emphasis added), take this example: 'Through a sort of inversion of ends and means, the defense of private teaching appears to be a defense of the indispensable means for accomplishing the Church's spiritual (pastoral, apostolic) function, while it seeks *first* to assure the Church the positions, the "Catholic" jobs which are the *primary condition of its perpetuation* and which the teaching activities are used to justify'. So, the whole point of Catholicism is to provide jobs for Pope Benedict and the priests and nuns below him? The dangers of the reductionism, or oversimplification, in each case speak for themselves.

But, to conclude in a resoundingly positive reaffirmation that there is so much of value in Bourdieuian theory for the study of religion, as I hope that this book has shown, I would like to suggest that one key to overcoming such reductionisms lies in Bourdieu's notion of habitus. In thinking with Bourdieu against rational choice theory of religion, toward advancing the sociological theory of religion, it is important to conceive of Bourdieu's signature concept of habitus 'as an individual or a socialized biological body, or as the social, biologically individuated through incarnation in a body' that is 'collective and transindividual' (Bourdieu 2000a, 157). This is plentifully suggestive of newly nuanced ways to approach some of the most fundamental questions that one can ask about religion, sociologically or otherwise: Why do people believe in things that they cannot see? Or, why are people religious in the first place? What explains an individual's 'choice' of one church or religion over all others? What explains fidelity, and what explains conversion? Where rational choice

theory over-emphasizes rational calculation in explaining religious practice, habitus restores the force of the emotional and the somatic, providing trenchant ways to formulate more holistic answers to such questions.[7]
Perhaps it is best to leave the final word to poetry: this crucial dimension
of Bourdieu's notion of habitus and its fruitful implications for the study of
religion are quite beautifully reflected by Chinua Achebe's (1994, 147,
emphasis added) portrayal of one of his African character's conversion to
Christianity in *Things Fall Apart*: 'It was not the logic of the trinity that
captivated him. He did not understand it. It was the poetry of the new
religion, *something felt in the marrow*'.

Notes

Introduction

1 Throughout this book all translations from French are mine.

2 Bourdieu (1990b, 15) is aware of this liberating effect of his sociology, its perceivably deterministic bent notwithstanding: 'This being the case, how can it escape notice that by expressing the social determinants of different forms of practice, especially intellectual practice, the sociologist gives us the chance of acquiring a certain freedom from these determinants?'

3 Derek Robbins (1991, 2) puts this very nicely: 'The conventional "subject" labels that might be applied to his writings are all inadequate, and this is no accident. He has made contributions in the fields of anthropology, sociology, socio-linguistics, philosophy, economics, sociology of knowledge, sociology of science, sociology of education, art history, literary criticism, and so on, but he has tried to prevent his work from reinforcing the social oppression of organized Anthropology, Sociology, Philosophy as enshrined in teaching establishments. This explains why his work resists cataloguing and why assistants in book shops have to search for his texts in different departments, guessing, perhaps, whether *La Distinction* would be likely to be found in Cultural Studies, Sociology, or Art and Aesthetics.' Bourdieu, incidentally, with Loïc Wacquant, cast aspersions on 'Cultural Studies' as a fashionable fabrication of American academia that is 'a mongrel domain' (Bourdieu and Wacquant 2005, 186).

4 Reed-Danahay (2005, 43) surmises that the neglect of religion in most of Bourdieu's empirical work on France 'indicates a lack of reflexivity on his part'. I believe, furthermore, that it is clearly detrimental to his work. I think, for example, (and I cannot imagine many people disagreeing with me here) that any study of marriage in a traditionally Catholic society (even one like France that is today marked by secularization) that does not consider the religious dimensions of the institution is impoverished thereby, and the same can be said about the study of obituaries: While it may or may not be the case, as Bridget Fowler (2004, 149) claims, that 'Bourdieu is the trailblazer in the sociological analysis of obituaries', his inattention to religion in his discussion of obituaries in *The State Nobility* (Bourdieu 2000c) is at best a missed opportunity. Bourdieu studied each of these subjects without raising the slightest question as to, for instance, whether the doomed bachelors of Béarn felt deprived of a sacrament, or, say, of what percentage of the obituaries announce religious funerals, and what it all might mean.

5 This is not to say that Bourdieuian theory cannot be useful for the objective analysis of the positive side of religion. In fact, I know of no other thinker whose work

provides, for example, such a compelling epistemology for the understanding of human belief and practice, which are each obviously so central to religion, *however understood*.

6 I gratefully acknowledge help in translating this passage from German from my good friends Gereon Kopf, Claudia Schippert and Alfons Teipen. It is interesting to note that Weber himself, rather famously, purposely avoided constructing any explicit definition of religion of his own. The 'Weberian definition' to which Bourdieu alludes is thus one that is implicit in Weber's impressive sociological interpretations of religion.

7 See, for example, Schäfer 2004, Smith 2004, and Tanner 2005 and 2006–2007.

8 Deborah Reed-Danahay (2005, 43) suggests that Bourdieu's frequent 'uses of religion as a metaphor . . . were veiled criticisms of the church'.

9 I have not seen the original in German of the *Der Spiegel* text whence derives this quotation but only its English translation on the Internet by Michael K. Palamarek, entitled 'The Depoliticization of Genoa: An Interview with Pierre Bourdieu', which I read on January 18, 2007 at http://www.yorku.ca/jspot/5/pbourdieu.htm.

10 In English 'Bourdieuian', 'Bourdieuan' and 'Bourdeiusian' are each used as adjectives, though I have not yet come across any of these terms being used for a 'disciple' of Bourdieu, nor have I encountered the English equivalent of *'Bourdieusologue'* ('Bourdieusiologist'), which at least one scholar (Green 2004, 180) has used in francophone academia; the term 'Boudieuconomics', meanwhile, already has some currency in Anglophone scholarship (e.g., Svendsen and Svendsen 2003). As for which English equivalent of *'Bourdieusien'* is to be preferred, if the website google.com is any indication, it would be, by a slight margin, 'Bourdieuian' (977 items), followed by 'Bourdieuan' (943 items) and 'Bourdieusian' (883 items). By stark contrast, the term 'Bourdieuist' generates only four items on Google, and of these only two are in English, while 'Bourdieusan' generates thirteen, all but two in English. In Spanish, meanwhile, *'Bourdieuano'* retrieves 212 items. http://www.google.com, accessed December 18, 2006.

11 Bourdieu's (1971a, 1971b) two most important essays on religion, in fact, have been published together as a book in German (Bourdieu 2000b).

Chapter 1

1 'Habitus' is perhaps the most important concept in Bourdieuian theory, and therefore it will receive much fuller explanation later in this book. Suffice it to say here that an individual's habitus is, put simply, both her internal mechanism of perception and her generator of dispositions.

2 The term *'une grande famille'* in French can mean either 'a large family' or 'an important family'. In this case, the latter is meant.

3 Coincidentally, Lycée de Pau counts Isadore Ducasse (1846–1870), who wrote under the pseudonym Comte de Lautréamont, among its graduates. Author of *Chants de Maldoror*, written in 1868–69, Ducasse is considered the father of the surrealist movement of French literature.

4 Dianteill's generalization cannot be extended to the study of sociology in other parts of the francophone world, at least not to Belgium, where an important tradition of

sociology was being developed around the same time at the Catholic University of Louvain. As Luc Van Campenhoudt (2005, 403–404) explains: 'For young Catholics born just after the Second World War, the choice to study sociology was strongly marked by religious convictions. Sociology represented a transposition of the love of one's neighbor. A large segment of the sociologists of this generation had also considered the priesthood, generally without great perseverance. The typical sociology student was rather to the left, a third-world-ist, or a labor activist. Sociology was not an end in itself but a way to serve and to change the world'.

5 As Maria Chiavola Birnbaum (1993, 19) explains, 'Antonio Gramsci may best be understood if one remembers that he was a Sardinian dwarf, and a hunchback. His bodily sense of difference gave him an immediate consciousness of subordinate cultures and the marginality of others'.

6 Bourdieu translated selected chapters from Weber for his students in the late 1950s, as there were then no French translations available, and in 1967 he translated Erwin Panofsky's *Gothic Architecture and Scholasticism* into French (Panofsky 1967), an effort that was crucial to his intellectual development because here, in his addendum to his translation of Panofsky, Bourdieu first introduces his own adaptation of the notion of habitus, as explained in Chapter 2.

7 Bourdieu 1953. Among the greatest of the seventeenth-century philosophers of the Rationalist school, Leibniz's *Animadversiones* maps out a model for the analysis of organic bodies.

8 Judging from hyper-Bourdieu, a website devoted to Bourdieu that contains an extensive bibliography, it appears that Bourdieu actually did begin to write a doctoral dissertation, though it was left 'unfinished'. Its title, tentatively at any rate, was to be 'Structures temporelles de la vie affective' ('Temporal Structures of the Affective Life'). http://hyperbourdieu.jku.at. Last accessed January 4, 2007.

9 Bourdieu in fact remained deeply engaged with philosophy throughout his life: 'Hardly a day goes by when I do not read or reread philosophical works . . . I am constantly at work with philosophers and putting them to work' (in Bourdieu and Wacquant 1992, 158).

10 A diagram that sounds a great deal like what Bourdieu here describes can be found in Bourdieu 1971b, though it is omitted from the English translation thereof (Bourdieu 1987a). It is maintained in the German translation (Bourdieu 2000b).

11 *Liber* was published independently until 1990, 'when it became a supplement of *Actes*' (Grenfell 2004, 154).

12 Such negative comments about Bourdieu by his collaborators are by no means universal, it must be said. For example, Jean-Claude Passeron (2003, 18), who worked as closely with him as anyone, called Bourdieu 'a charmer', while Hans Haacke (2005, 186) found him to be 'generous and friendly' (albeit 'animated by a contagious combativeness'). Others, meanwhile, have lauded Bourdieu for his patience and kindness (e.g., Jenkins 1992; Robbins 1991; Swartz 1997), 'his warmth, his energy and his sense of humor' (Mahar 1990, 28), and for being 'ironic, amused, and amusing, and much less dogmatic when speaking than comes across in his writing style' (Reed-Danahay 2005, 9).

13 Bourdieu also received the Erving Goffman Prize from the University of California Berkeley in 1996, the Ernst Bloch Prize from the city of Ludwigshafen, Germany in 1997, and the Huxley Memorial Prize from the Royal Anthropological Institute in 2000.

Huxley laureates include a veritable 'who's who' among luminaries in the history of anthropology, including E.B. Tylor, James Frazer, A.R. Radcliffe-Brown, Marcel Mauss, E.E. Evans-Pritchard, Claude Lévi-Strauss, Mary Douglas and Clifford Geertz. He also received honorary doctorates from the Free University of Berlin in 1998, the Johannes Wolfgang Goethe University in Frankfurt in 1996, and the University of Athens in 1996. In 1972–73, furthermore, he was Visiting Member at the Institute for Advanced Studies (Princeton), and in 2001 he was named Corresponding Fellow of the British Academy. But the honor that probably would have meant more to him than any of these was the naming of the local nursery/elementary school in his native Denguin '*Groupe Scolaire Pierre Bourdieu*', upon his death in 2002 (Mairie de Denguin, n.d.).

14 'Sartre truly invented and incarnated the figure of the *total intellectual*, the thinker-writer, metaphysician-novelist and artist-philosopher who brings to the political struggles of the time all the authority and abilities combined in his person' (Bourdieu 1996, 209, original italics).

15 Briefly stated, 'anomie' is a term that Durkheim coined to designate the effect on individuals in societies whose norms are in a state of turmoil or collapse. Out of states of anomie, forms of deviant behavior can be expected to emerge.

16 This long essay was republished in Bourdieu 2002.

17 These books are translated into English, respectively, as Bourdieu and Passeron 1977 and 1979.

18 Certainly one of the 'gains' that Bourdieu preserves from structuralism is from its 'linguistic model', as Murray Milner (1994, 5) explains: 'in the relationship between the speech of individuals and the structures of a language, the latter is both the result of the former and the medium of subsequent speech'. Structuralist linguisitis thus provides a fundamental model for Bourdieu's negotiation of the central sociological issue of agency/structure.

19 Hegel taught that all history is the dialectical progression of a supreme Mind/Spirit (*Geist*) toward its self realization. Marx adopted Hegel's notion that history does indeed progress in dialectical fashion, though he explicitly denied the existence of *Geist*, and hence Marx's philosophy is categorized as 'dialectical materialism', as distinct from Hegel's 'dialectical idealism'.

20 Bourdieu would, of course, *contra* Pascal, add religion itself to such 'worldly consolations'.

21 In *The Logic of Practice* (1990a, 48–49), Bourdieu includes a long quotation from Pascal's *Pensées*, which begins: 'For we must make no mistake about ourselves: we are as much automaton as mind'.

22 Among other important influences on Bourdieu than those enumerated here, one may list Aristotle, Austin, Benveniste, Cassirer, Chomsky, Descartes, Dewey, Elias, Freud, Goffman, Habermas, Halbwachs, Hegel, Hume, Husserl, Kant, Leibniz, Lewin, Panofsky, Piaget, Plato, Rawls, Saussure, Schutz, Spinoza and Wittgenstein.

Chapter 2

1 Certain passages in this chapter, much revised here, previously appeared in Rey 2004, reproduced here with the permission of Elsevier, Ltd.

2 Though an engagement of debates over practice and others that involve criticism of key elements of Bourdieuian theory are beyond the scope of my project, it should be noted here that the concept as used by Bourdieu and others has been assailed as being 'deeply elusive' by, for one, Stephen Turner (1994, 2), whose *The Social Theory of Practices* provides a helpful critical discussion of the concept.

3 I am here merely pointing out a semantic and by no means logical exception, for Bourdieu clearly would allow that fields may be thought of as 'playing fields', and he uses sporting or gaming analogies quite often in his work (e.g., n. 5, below).

4 Portes and Landolt (2000, 531) feel that this 'fungible' nature of capital—its transferability across social fields—is 'Bourdieu's key insight'.

5 I italicize the word 'inclines' here to suggest that criticisms of Bourdieu's notion of habitus as being deterministic are perhaps misguided because they miss some of the brilliant subtlety of the concept, which is quite nicely reflected in Bourdieu's use of sporting metaphors: 'It's clear that the problem should not be discussed in terms of spontaneity and constraint, freedom and necessity, individual and society. The habitus as the feel for the game is the social embodied and turned into second nature. Nothing is simultaneously freer and more constrained than the action of the good player. He quite naturally materializes at just the place the ball is about to fall, as if the ball were in command of him—but by that very fact he is in command of the ball. The habitus, as society written into the body, into the biological individual, enables the infinite number of acts of the game—written into the game as possibilities and objective demands—to be produced' (Bourdieu 1998b, 63).

nice

6 As Omar Lizardo (2004) demonstrates, Bourdieu's articulation of the notion of habitus is also indebted to Lévi-Strauss and to the developmental psychology of Jean Piaget. Piaget's influence on Bourdieu regarding habitus is also discussed trenchantly in Bronckart and Schurmans (2001).

7 Generally considered to have originated with the French social theorist Auguste Comte (1798–1857), positivism, put briefly, is based on the notion that only empirically (scientifically) verifiable facts can be considered true, thus rejecting a *priori* all forms of inquiry into things that cannot be physically perceived, like habitus and symbolic violence, and love and God, for that matter.

8 There is no index in Panofsky's English original.

9 For further interesting discussion of Panofsky's influence on Bourdieu, see Lechte 2004.

10 Beate Krais (1993, 170) argues that an agent's habitus is also inevitably a 'gendered habitus, an identity which has incorporated the existing division of labor between the genders', and that thus conceiving a sociological understanding of sexual domination, 'the theory of Pierre Bourdieu is of utmost relevance'. Similarly, James H. Sweet (2005) speaks in suggestive ways of a 'racialized habitus' in an interesting essay on the history of anti-black racism.

11 For a very good overview of this influence, see Beasley-Murray (2000).

12 This point is well put by Jeff Browitt (2004, 2): 'Bourdieu expands Marx's idea of "economic capital" to encompass all forms of power that enable individuals, groups, or classes to cement or reproduce their position in the social hierarchy. Thus he speaks of "cultural capital" . . . "social capital" . . . and "symbolic capital" . . . which represent forms of power and domination . . . The exercise of power requires justification (legitimation) and this is achieved, according to Bourdieu, by "symbolic capital"'.

13 As Schultheis (forthcoming, n. 1) explains: 'It should be remembered that Bourdieu in his concept of capital, as used in "religious", "cultural" or "symbolic capital", clearly adopts Weber's concept of "salvation goods"'.

14 However rarely, capital may also be an instrument of resistance, especially if and when the prophet gains the proverbial upper hand in the struggle over the control of capital in any given field.

15 For DiMaggio (1979, 1468), the proliferation of forms of capital in Bourdieu's work is problematic: 'Capitals proliferate: in addition to economic, cultural, and symbolic capital, we have linguistic capital, academic capital, scholastic capital, credential cultural capital, capitals of authority and of consecration, university, scientific, and artistic capital. No doubt there are others . . . As the number of capitals increases, the metaphorical currency undergoes inflation and its value declines accordingly'.

16 Beasley-Murray (2000, 100) points out that Bourdieu's notion of cultural capital 'has found remarkable success, and has probably been taken up and disseminated more than any other item in his critical terminology; *habitus*, for instance, has scarcely demonstrated such wide appeal'. Interestingly, however, in Bourdieuian analyses of religion, habitus has held more appeal to scholars than most notions of capital, as alluded to in Chapter 5.

17 I do not mean to imply here that holders of large stores of economic capital are also automatically holders of large stores of cultural capital, as this is sometimes clearly not the case, for, as Brubaker (2004, 51) reminds us with an example that for me hits acutely close to home: '… professors, rich in cultural capital, are (relatively) poor in economic capital, while executives and professionals, rich in economic capital, are (relatively) poor in cultural capital'.

Chapter 3

1 Where Bourdieu does offer something like a definition of religion, as cited in my Introduction, he simply draws upon one that is only implicit in Weber's work, which he finds 'satisfying' (Bourdieu, Schultheis and Pfeuffer 2000, 123). Schultheis (forthcoming) suggests that Bourdieu's leaving religion undefined is both purposive and fruitful. It is more likely that Bourdieu did not bother defining religion because his assumptions about the subject rendered, for him, such an enterprise unimportant. Reed-Danahay (2005, 43) suggests, meanwhile, that Bourdieu was 'unwilling or unable' to broach the subject in any way that might require a careful consideration of just how religion should be defined.

2 To date, there are literally dozens of scholarly articles on religion that employ Bourdieuian theory in some prominent way, and the number of entire MA theses, doctoral dissertations, and books, several of which are featured in Chapter 5, of the kind is also on the rise.

3 Although Bradford Verter (2004, 183) is correct in challenging claims that Bourdieu wrote little about religion, his estimation that 'he did write about a dozen and a half short pieces on religion' is slightly exaggerated.

4 For Sartre (1984, 86–112), one acts in bad faith when self-deceived to believe that one is anything other than 'doomed to be free'. Bad faith is the denial of existentialism's catchphrase, 'Existence before Essence'; in other words, there is nothing essential to anything in or about human existence, and any belief to the contrary is exemplary of bad faith.

5 In fact, as Bourdieu later recalls (2004, 56), he was still in the French army when he began studying sociology and writing *Sociologie de l'Algérie* (1958b).

6 These considerations of Islam as a source of resistance to cultural dissolution in the colonial context, and of syncretism between indigenous Algerian tradition and Islam, were surely the backdrop against which Bourdieu read, around the same time, Roger Bastide's (1960) influential *Les religions africaines au Brésil: Vers une sociologie des interpénétrations de civilizations*. Bourdieu reviewed Bastide's landmark book for the very first issue of *L'Homme*, which was founded by Lévi-Strauss and which would soon become France's premier academic journal of anthropology. He clearly identifies with Bastide in the sense that Bastide was, like Bourdieu, attempting 'to analyze . . . a society engaged in a process of destruction and reinterpretation' (Bourdieu 1960, 114). Bourdieu's review of Bastide is highly favorable, identifying as 'Bastide's greatest merit' his demonstration that any consideration of contact cultures must take critically into account 'the question of the threatened civilization's struggle with its [own] past'.

7 '*Expression corporelle*' (lit. 'corporal expression') is a practice combining concentration and the examination of muscles to explore one's emotions, based in part on Mind-Body Centering, 'a somatic education and therapy modality . . .' (www.bmcassoc.org; accessed August 15, 2006).

8 Here is reflected one of the most significant limitations in Bourdieu's view of religion, one to which several scholars alluded, some of whose positions are summarized in Chapter 5. By over-focusing his attention on the Church hierarchy and greatly reducing his consideration of pilgrimage to the hierarchy's financial concerns, Bourdieu ignores entirely the motivations of pilgrims themselves, just as he denies any possibility of sincerely religious motivations among the clerical organizers of pilgrimage. The result is a very cynical and truncated portrayal of this important form of religious practice.

9 Relative to the notion of Buddhist monks as mercenaries, for an interesting study of the militaristic role of Zen Buddhism in Japanese culture, see Victoria 1998.

10 The eight errors are: 'in person presiding'; 'in place'; 'in time'; 'in tempo'; 'in behaviours'; 'in language'; 'in dress'; and 'in sacraments' (Bourdieu 1991c, 108).

11 In *The Holy Family, or Critique of Critical Criticism*, Marx and Engels mark their departure from the 'family' of Hegelian philosophers to which Marx once belonged. Among the book's most interesting contents is a brilliant synopsis of French materialism and its contributions to the development of socialist thought.

12 Because 'he was in fact worried about understanding a world that was foreign to him', according to Monique de Saint Martin (2003, 72), who co-authored this essay with him, Bourdieu actually did very little fieldwork for this study (ibid., 71).

13 The essay contains, for instance, interesting discussions about marriage, the family, and theological vocations, to name a few.

14 Although Lash locates Bourdieu's critical engagement with Weber 'in the early 1970s', in fact it began more than ten years earlier.

15 The term *karism* is employed, for instance, in 1 Corinthians 12:4–11, 'Now there are these diversities of gifts (*karisms*), but the same Spirit . . . For to one is given by the Spirit, the word of wisdom; to another the word of knowledge by the same Spirit . . . To another diverse kinds of tongues; to another the interpretation of tongues'.

16 When he died, Bourdieu left unfinished an extended revision of 'Genesis and Structure of the Religious Field' that was to carry the title 'Maxwell's Devil, Structure and Genesis of the Religious Field', and 'will likely appear in a posthumous volume on field theory' (Loïc Wacquant, personal communication, November 13, 2006). The forthcoming essay in question is cited in Bourdieu and Wacquant 1992, 234, n. 24, while references to 'Maxwell's Devil' can be found in Bourdieu 1992 and Bourdieu 1998a, and perhaps elsewhere.

Chapter 4

1 The term 'heresiarch' is used interchangeably by Bourdieu (1991a, 23) with the term 'prophet'. It literally means leader of a heretical movement. By extension, such a movement may be called a 'heresiarchy'. To further clarify my use of the latter term, a heresiarch is to a heresiarchy as a monarch is to a monarchy. The terms 'Church' and 'heresiarch', like the related terms that Bourdieu adopted from Weber (e.g., priest, prophet, sorcerer), should be understood in a generalized paradigmatic sense to expand the use of Bourdieu's model beyond the analysis of the European Catholic model that so influenced his thinking of religion. For an excellent example of this, see Urban 2003.

2 This chapter is a thoroughly revised adaptation of Rey 2004. A few passages remain the same and are republished here with the generous permission of Elsevier, Ltd., the publisher of the journal *Religion*, where my earlier essay was published. The present incarnation differs perhaps most significantly in taking colonial Martha's Vineyard as its substantive example, whereas my earlier article, which is briefly discussed in Chapter 5, used Haitian religious history as its substantive example for explaining Bourdieu's theory of religion. I deem this change to be especially useful for many of the likely readers of this book who are either American or English and will thus have greater familiarity with the New English case than with Haitian religious history. Furthermore, it may be suggested that the case under analysis here establishes foundations for the central racial, class and religious distinctions (or ethos) that characterize the United States of America to this day, though testing this hypothesis through Bourdieuian analysis is beyond the scope of this book. An earlier version of this chapter, finally, was read by my graduate seminar in 'Religion, Race, and Ethnicity' at Temple University in the fall semester of 2006; I am grateful to my students for their helpful feedback.

3 Urban (2003, 355) is of the opinion that Bourdieu's writings on religion are actually among the weakest in his entire oeuvre: 'Bourdieu rarely addresses the question of religion directly, and in the few cases where he does . . . he presents some of his least sophisticated and most reductionist analyses. Hence many have concluded that Bourdieu's discussion of religion is among the least useful aspects of his work'. Urban does not indicate who these 'many' detractors are, however, and Bourdieu actually wrote more about religion than Urban seems to have realized when preparing his

otherwise excellent essay, a point of criticism that is also made by Bradford Verter (2004, 183) and echoed by Andrew McKinnon (2006, 183, n. 5).

4 Weber's influence on Bourdieu in this regard is to be noted, for here Bourdieu clearly takes from Weber the focus on religious needs and the market of symbolic goods (which in the religious field take the form of 'the goods of salvation') that emerges to meet such needs, as discussed previously in Chapters 1 and 2.

5 I use the term 'denomination' here as inclusive of indigenous Native American religion.

6 Bourdieu adopts the term 'goods of salvation' (*Heilsgut*) from Weber. As Jörg Stoltz (2006a, 18) points out, although Weber does not explicitly define the *Heilsgut*, one important sense (and this is the sense in which Bourdieu uses the term) in which Weber uses the term is that such products 'can be strived for, supplied and consumed. Instead of salvation goods, Weber also uses the terms "salvation goals" (*Heilsziele*), "salvation means" (*Heilsmittel*) and "promises of the religions" (*Verneissungen der Religionen*)'.

7 Lest we are led to think that by using sporting metaphors Bourdieu intended to imply that 'games' are fun, it is worth speculating that had he ever read the following passage by George Orwell (1950, 153) he would have said, 'Bingo!': 'Serious sport has nothing to do with fair play. It is bound up with hatred, jealousy, boastfulness, disregard of all rules and sadistic pleasure in witnessing violence. In other words, it is war minus the shooting'. But if Orwell may have disliked sports (I'm not sure that he did in fact), Bourdieu himself played rugby in his youth and was an avid tennis player.

8 The translations of these terms are in the original English translation and are faithful to how Bourdieu first translated them from German into French.

9 As David Silverman has pointed out to me, upon graciously commenting on an earlier draft of this chapter, it is important to note that the Puritan 'de facto monopoly' was not an 'English' achievement *per se*, despite its initiation by the English. It is better understood, he notes, as being the result of a 'process of religious translation' that was 'necessarily broadly participatory, necessarily integrative of traditional Wampanoag and Christian religious ideas, and necessarily dependent on Wampanoags themselves explaining and disseminating Christian messages. By the mid to late seventeenth century, Wampanoags were the primary Christian missionaries and preachers on the Vineyard, Nantucket, and Cape Cod. They had a strong influence over their own message and, as I argue, they helped to create a distinctly indigenous Christianity' (personal correspondence, March 12, 2007). I am deeply grateful to Professor Silverman for his invaluable feedback. His main point here is not only invaluable as a corrective but as a reflection of some of the limitations of Bourdieu's model of the religious field, which will be further discussed in Chapter 5.

10 This is not to imply, however, that the laity thus possess greater power in the religious field than the Church, because in reality their religious needs are, for Bourdieu, themselves largely shaped by the Church for the Church's interests. 'The priest says, "Outside the Church there is no salvation". Well of course, because his job depends on it' (in Carles 2001).

11 For examples of a similar elucidation of the function of religious charisma in Melanesia and Haiti respectively, see Worsley 1957 and Rey 1998, the latter of which is briefly discussed in Chapter 5.

12 'Though "spirituality" is notoriously ill defined, when used in opposition to "religion" (as in the lamentably common locution, 'I'm not religious, but I'm spiritual'), it generally connotes an extrainstitutional, resolutely individualistic, and often highly eclectic personal theology self-consciously resistant to dogma (Bellah et al. 1985; Roof 1993, 1999; Wuthnow 1998). Thus, if religious capital is conceived à la Bourdieu as something that is produced and accumulated within a hierocratic institutional framework, spiritual capital may be regarded as a more widely diffused commodity, governed by more complex patterns of production, distribution, exchange, and consumption' (Verter 2003, 157–58).

13 This is not always the case, however. See Chapter 2, n. 16.

14 '[T]he unique concentration of human behavior on activities leading to salvation may require the participation within the world (or more precisely: within the institutions of the world but in opposition to them) of the religious individual's idiosyncratically sacred religious mood and his qualifications as the elect instrument of god. This is "inner-worldly asceticism"' (Weber 1963, 166).

15 Weber (1963, 108) explains that the theodicy of compensation is 'envisaged in various ways but always involving rewards for one's own good deeds and punishment for the unrighteousness of others'. It is, furthermore, 'the most widely diffused form of mass religion all over the world'.

16 I do not meant to imply by this statement that orthodoxy's religious specialists are any less driven to do what they do by misrecognition than are members of the laity, or that they are any more calculating and reflective than the laity. Religious specialists act not primarily out of a conscious and deliberate plan to maintain or gain power over the religious field. Because, for Bourdieu, the field is structured and actors, clerical and lay alike, are positioned therein in such ways that they see religious capital as inherently or naturally worthy, they misrecognize what they do as being 'the done thing'; hence they partake not out of rational calculation but out of a 'practical sense', which shapes their 'practice' and thereby contributes to the reproduction of the field and the broader social order. On this, see also Chapter 5, n. 5.

17 'It should be noted that the "dissolution of the religious" does not mean, for the sociologist, a regression towards an undifferentiated state of symbolic activity', explains Erwan Dianteill (2004, 78). 'The symbolic activity at the margins of the religious field, which fosters a certain confusion concerning its limits, does not, however, signify its disappearance' (ibid., 78–79).

18 'In one study after another in America, not only by Wuthnow but by others (notably Wade Clark Roof and Nancy Ammerman), one finds people who put together an individualized religion, taking bits and pieces from different traditions, and coming up with a religious profile that does not fit easily into any of the organized denominations. Many of them assert that they are not "religious" at all, but are pursuing a quest for "spirituality". Very similar data came up in European research' (Berger 2001, 448).

19 Lists of religious or spiritual institutions in today's 'field of symbolic manipulation' in Martha's Vineyard are available at http://www.citysearch.com and http://www.about.com (accessed February 8, 2007).

20 http://www.shopsanctuary.com, accessed February 11, 2007.

Chapter 5

1 Swartz (1996, 71, n. 1) asserts that '[w]hile Bourdieu dominates the sociology of culture in France, he has had little impact on the post-World War II generation of French sociologists of religion. . . Nonetheless, one can see growing signs of his influence on the post-'60s generation of French sociology of religion scholarship . . . Bourdieu's influence on the sociology of religion has been more striking outside of France'. It may be suggested that Swartz's assessment is not entirely accurate in the sense that Hervieu-Léger is more critical of Bourdieu than she is influenced by him. Meanwhile, Maduro did his doctorate at a Francophone university in Belgium, *l'Université Catholique de Louvain*, and he counts the Belgian social scientists François Houtart and Jean Remy, along with the French anthropologist Maurice Godelier, among his chief influences.

2 There are earlier articles by other scholars that apply Bourdieuian theory to some aspect of the study of religion (Liénard and Rousseau 1972; Remy 1972; Colonna 1974; and Grignon 1977), though I deem Maduro's work as more deserving of discussion here as the first book-length study that draws extensively on Bourdieu's theory of practice, and because it remains as clear a reflection as any other of how Bourdieu envisioned the sociology of religion.

3 Maduro (1982, 19, original italics) defines sociology of religion in terms with which Bourdieu would certainly agree: 'the sociology of religion is the study of religions as phenomena that are socially *produced*, socially *situated* and *limited*, socially *oriented* and *structured*, and have an influence upon the society in which they find themselves. And therefore in order to do sociology of religion it is necessary to render oneself capable (however provisionally and fictitiously—that is, purely methodologically) of putting one's own religious beliefs and preferences in parentheses, in suspension'. Maduro, in essence, is here affirming the fundamental importance of what Peter Berger (1967, 100) calls 'methodological atheism' to the sociological study of religion.

4 Although Maduro quite extensively employs the Bourdieuian notion of field, nowhere does he incorporate the notions of 'habitus' or 'doxa', which could each have been of great utility to his analysis.

5 In an earlier draft of this chapter, I had written, 'Though Maduro's argument (1982, 126) that ecclesial complicity in the perpetuations of social inequalities is largely unconscious or unwitting might strike Bourdieu as letting the Church of the hook too easily . . .'. Otto Maduro kindly read that version of this chapter and disputed this claim (personal correspondence, December 13, 2006), explaining that he did 'not think Bourdieu would have thought otherwise!' Upon further reflection and carefully revisiting Bourdieu's writings on religion, I came to the conclusion that Maduro is in fact correct and that I was mistaken, for Bourdieu (1998a, 118) argues clearly that misrecognition is elemental to the religious field not only in the laity but also in the clergy: 'Clerics themselves also have an ambiguous economic status, as they live in misrecognition: they are poor (they receive the guaranteed minimum wage), but their poverty is only apparent (they receive all sorts of gifts) and is elective (their resources come in the form of offerings, gifts; they are dependent on their clientele). This structure suits a double habitus, endowed with the genius of euphemism, of ambiguous practices and discourse,

of double meanings without a double game'. I am most grateful for Professor Maduro's invaluable feedback.

6 Bell (1992, 99, 176) twice sites this compelling passage from Bourdieu's *Outline of a Theory of Practice* (1977, 94): 'The principles em-bodied in this way [i.e., 'the fundamental principles of the arbitrary content of culture'] are placed beyond the grasp of consciousness, and hence cannot be touched by voluntary, deliberate transformation, cannot even be made explicit; nothing seems more ineffable, more incommunicable, more inimitable, and therefore more precious, that the values given body, *made* body by the transubstantiation achieved by the hidden persuasion of an implicit pedagogy, capable of instilling a whole cosmology, an ethic, a metaphysic, a political philosophy, through injunctions as insignificant as "stand up straight" or "don't hold your knife in your left hand"'.

7 Notably, the second section of *Language, Charisma, and Creativity*, which is itself comprised of two chapters, is entitled 'Habitus and Practice'.

8 el-Sayed el-Aswad (2002, 91–92) makes similar use of Bourdieu's notion of corporal-hexis (without using the term itself) in theorizing popular cosmology in contemporary rural Egypt.

9 It is interesting to note that Csordas does not make any significant use of Bourdieu's notion of capital, despite his extensive use of the notions of habitus and practice.

10 Scott (1990, xii) defines 'hidden transcript' as 'a critique of power [among subordinated groups] spoken behind the back of the dominant'.

11 Parts of this subsection are derived from Rey 2005 though translated from the French by me and slightly revised. Reprinted by permission of Sage Publications Ltd from Terry Rey, 'Habitus et hybridité: une interpretation du syncrétisme dans la religion afro-catholique d'après Bourdieu', *Social Compass* 52.4: 453–62 (copyright Sage Publications, 2005).

12 Traditionally, the beginning of the Haitian Revolution is fixed as August 14, 1791, the date on which Boukman Dutty conducted a Vodou ceremony that rallied slaves to rise up against white plantation owners in the French colony of Saint-Domingue. Final victory over the French was achieved late in 1803, and the Republic of Haiti declared independent on January 1, 1804.

13 'A revisionist interpretation of the dispersal of enslaved Africans in the era of the trans-Atlantic slave trade . . . concentrates on the role of Africa in the genesis and ongoing history of the diaspora. This revisionist approach emphasizes the continuities in African history and the extension of that history into the diaspora' (Lovejoy 1997, 1).

14 Catholicism was introduced in the Kongo Kingdom by the Portuguese toward the end of the fifteenth century, and it rapidly spread from the elite to the masses. See Thornton 1997.

15 'The prophet's power rests upon the force of the group he can mobilize. This depends on his ability to give symbolic expression—in an exemplary form of conduct and/or in a (quasi-) systematic discourse—to the specifically religious interests of lay people occupying a determinate position in the social structure' (Bourdieu 1987a, 129).

16 In French, the word *'prophétesse'* means 'prophetess', while *'prophète'* means 'prophet'.

17 Other impressive applications of Bourdieu to the study of religion include Berlinerblau 1999; Dawson 2006; Dianteill 2004; Dillon 2001; Ebertz and Schultheis

1986a and 1986b; Engler 2003; Isambert 1982, Milner 1994; Schäfer 2004; Stone 2001; Swartz 1996; Tanner 2005; Urban 2003; and Verter 2003.

18 'If there is a single feature that makes Bourdieu stand out in the landscape of contemporary social theory, it is his singular obsession with reflexivity . . . Bourdieu has continually turned the instruments of science upon himself' (Wacquant 1992, 36).

19 Hugh Urban (2003, 380–81) makes a similar move to Martin in this regard by employing Michel de Certeau's concept of 'tactics of consumption', as developed in de Certeau 1984.

20 In *More than Chains and Toil*, Martin does not cite Bourdieu's early work on Algeria.

21 Remarkably, Bourdieu here resoundingly echoes Mother Theresa, one of his most influential religious contemporaries: 'We ourselves feel that what we are doing is just a drop in the ocean. But the ocean would be less because of that missing drop. I do not agree with the big way of doing things' (Mother Theresa 1997, 137).

22 Bourdieu (1977, 76) negotiates the issue of determinism in quite dense and complex argumentation where his position is that the dialectical structuralism of human society 'can grant only a conditional freedom' to not only the subjugated but to all human agents.

23 For much the same reason, Bourdieu's model of the religious field would have difficulty explaining the inverse phenomenon of Liberation theology and the now-fading success of base church communities in Latin America, for both were constituted in large part by the Church attuning itself anew to the interests of the dominated.

24 Franz Schultheis (forthcoming) disagrees with me on this position, arguing that such a claim that Bourdieu's model of the religious field is 'too rigid' 'is greatly relativated [*sic*], if not dispelled completely, by an apt tribute to the theoretical, methodological and empirical merits of this approach'. I think, though, that those of us writing about religion who find rigidity in Bourdieu, find it in Bourdieu's explicit model of the religious field, not so much in 'Bourdieu's field theory' at large. Far from being a merely semantic point of difference, this argument is importantly suggestive of how limitations in Bourdieu's *explicit* theorization of religion can be overcome by applying elements of Bourdieu's broader theory of practice. For excellent examples of this, see Swartz 1996 and Verter 2003.

25 Verter (2003) makes essentially the same criticism, while also offering one of the most insightful correctives in this regard by developing the notion of 'spiritual capital', which is explained briefly in my Conclusion.

26 Hervieu-Léger's charge that Bourdieu's discussions of religion are 'of little assistance in analyzing trends in secular modernity that show the production and circulation of religious-symbolic assets to be moving relentlessly away from institutional control', likewise, seems to ignore the fact that this very issue is one of the main considerations of Bourdieu's essay 'La dissolution du religieux' (1987b). Unlike Hervieu-Léger and Parker, Dillon (2001, 413) does at least cite Bourdieu's work on Algeria, but only as it pertains to the issue of gift exchange.

27 For a similar application of Bourdieu to the role of religion in the colonial encounter, one that regrettably I developed without referencing Maduro's important work, see Rey 1996 and 1999.

28 There is much disagreement on this point in interpretations of Bourdieu. Craig Calhoun (1993, 75), for one, argues that such critics 'have overstated the extent to which Bourdieu's account focused on reproduction at the expense of openings to the possibilities for action to create a new and different world—for example, to revolutionary struggle. Bourdieu's emphasis on reproduction did not foreclose contrary action, though neither did it introduce any notion of systematic pressures for such action'.

29 Verter (2004, 190, n. 9) explicitly disagrees with Urban on this count, claiming that instead of being a contradiction in Bourdieu's work, any perceived 'tension' between determinism and resistance in Bourdieu 'is due to a difference between his scholarship and his activism'. The entire debate over Bourdieu and resistance, Verter (ibid., 185) further argues, is itself somewhat misguided—or at least somewhat un-Bourdieuian—because 'social power in Bourdieu's Hobbesian world is too complex and dynamic to allow for such vulgar categories as oppression and resistance'. In response to Verter, Urban (2005, 167, n. 2) correctly points out that Verter himself, in his 2003 article, 'makes several of the exact same criticisms' of Bourdieu's theory of religion as limited, and thus Urban understandably wonders 'why Verter takes such issue with my article'.

Conclusion

1 One of the leading critics of rational choice theory of religion, Steve Bruce (1999, 1) argues that it amounts to 'the malign influence of a small clique of US sociologists of religion' whose demonstrable flaws are 'beyond redemption' (Bruce 2002, 182). For a useful summary of other criticism of rational choice theory of religion, see Adhar 2006.

2 'I consider pneumatic religion to be any faith-based organization that puts direct communication with the Spirit or spirits at the center of its belief system' (Chesnut 2003, 5).

3 Although Bourdieu does not appear in Chesnut's detailed (10 percent of the entire book) index, Bourdieu's 'Genesis and Structure of the Religious Field' does appear in his bibliography. Jörg Stoltz (2006b), furthermore, understandably finds curious the general lack of engagement of Weber in microeconomic theory of religion, or of rational choice theory of religion—curious especially because Weber is the pioneer in the use of economics to analyze religion and because of his otherwise awesome influence on the sociology of religion.

4 I am actually not in as complete agreement with Dianteill here as this sentence implies. Whereas the dismantling of a monopoly in a given religious field certainly means that Bourdieu's model of the religious field loses some of its effect, pluralistic religious fields nevertheless remain characterized by struggle, and at their hearts they remain fields of struggle in which competing institutions seek to inculcate in the laity the recognition of their—and not their competitors'—religious capital as legitimate.

5 Put simply by William Sims Bainbridge (2002, 65), 'rational choice theory is forward-looking, modeling individual action as the result of calculations about future costs and rewards'. Rational choice theory, or market theory, as applied to religion would answer affirmatively to the following questions posed by Ted Jelen (2002, vii): 'Can individual decisions concerning whether or where to attend church, to contribute

time or money to religious organizations, or to forgo certain temporal activities be described or explained as a special case of economic theory? Can religious choices be understood as responding to the same laws of supply and demand as other forms of consumer behavior?' There are degrees of strictness in rational choice theory of religion, it should be noted, while Warner (2002, 5, original italics) reminds us that 'the new paradigm is not *defined* by economic imagery; nor is it identical to rational choice theory', even if economic metaphors are pervasive in new paradigm applications.

6 This is admittedly speculative on my part, for proponents of the new paradigm do not explain why they, sociologists most of them, largely ignore one of the most important sociologists of their era in Bourdieu. Neither of Warner's important essays (1993; 2002), for example, includes any reference to Bourdieu, nor does any single contributor to a volume in which several of them appear (Jelen 2002). This is not to suggest that they are thereby impoverished in any significant way, however, but only to raise a point of curiosity, at least.

7 My observation here echoes one made by scholars in other realms of inquiry, as noted by Noble and Watkins (2003, 520): 'Bourdieu's development of the notion of habitus has proved a rich vein for cultural theory. Habitus has been useful, with the growing interest in the processes of embodiment, in countering the cognitive and representational bias in much cultural analysis, and in providing a basis for avoiding the dualisms—of mind and body, structure and agency—that trouble social theory'.

Concise Glossary of Key Terms

Capital – any form of a socially produced possession (possession understood here to mean either *an object belonging to* or *an acquired trait or authority residing in*) or resource, either material or symbolic, that amounts to power to maintain or improve one's status in society.

Collusio – the collective and tacitly affirmed understanding of 'the done thing' among any particular social group.

Cultural capital – any form of culturally produced possession (possession understood here to mean either as *an object belonging to* or *an acquired trait or authority residing in*) or resource, either material or symbolic, that represents power to distinguish oneself as 'sophisticated' or 'cultured', such as rarefied articulation, designer clothing, or knowledge of art history.

Doxa – the collective understanding across groups in any given society of all that is 'doable' and 'thinkable' in the social world.

Field – any sub-space of society in which individuals occupy positions in relation to one another in a struggle over the production, control and consumption of forms of capital specific to that sub-space; alternatively conceivable as 'market'.

Genetic structuralism/generative structuralism – term used by Bourdieu to characterize his work, meaning sociological inquiry that seeks centrally to understand how social structures 'generate' a person, who is turn is conditioned to 'generate' and/or reproduce the very same social structures in a dialectical fashion. Alternatively, Bourdieu employs the terms 'costructivist structuralism' and 'structuralist constructivism' to mean essentially the same thing.

Habitus – the fundamental dimension of the individual as a social being that is at one and the same time the 'matrix of perception' and the seat and generator of dispositions.

Heresiarch – a religious specialist who is labeled a heretic by orthodoxy and who produces and markets independent forms of religious capital in an effort to gain adherents and power in the religious field; e.g., a prophet.

Illusio – the belief of any individual or status group that selected fields have value and that the forms of capital 'at stake' in said fields are worthy of pursuit; or, the belief that the 'games' that comprise society are worth playing.

Misrecognition – the affirmation of the value or naturalness of any kind of social capital or social distinction as being something more than arbitrary, i.e., as being 'natural' and thus 'legitimate'.

Phenomenology – school of modern Western philosophy influenced by the work of Husserl, Heidegger and Merleau-Ponty (Bourdieu's teacher), among others. Phenomenology is centrally characterized by the concern to describe the intuitive experience of phenomenon; e.g., what is essential about the way in which human beings perceive of and experience the world is the starting point of phenomenology.

Practical sense – one's implicit understanding of how the social world functions and how one is to negotiate it; practical sense is as much a somatic as cognitive form of understanding.

Practice – human action and human behavior; basically what people do in society.

Religious capital – forms of socially and/or culturally produced capital (possession understood either as *an object belonging to* or a *trait or authority inherent to*) pertaining to the religious field, like sacraments and 'salvation goods' and the authority to administer them. For Bourdieu, religious capital is produced by religious specialists, like priests and prophets, and consumed by the laity; consumption understood here not so much as *buying* but as *buying into*.

Religious field – the social space in which religion most centrally takes place; a sub-space of society that is a network of relations between individual and institutional agents in various positions relative to the production, administration and control of forms of religious capital; alternatively conceivable as 'religious market'.

Religious habitus – that fundamental dimension of the individual as a social being in the religious field that is at one and the same time the 'matrix of perception' of religious symbols, teachings and practices, and the seat and generator of dispositions toward them.

Structuralism – also referred to by Bourdieu as 'objectivism', a form of social theory strongly influenced by French anthropologist Claude Lévi-Strauss in which human beings are extensively shaped by the structures of the social world, which are the ultimate determination of their identities and actions.

Symbolic capital – any form of capital, as defined above, that is not material; e.g., cultural capital, religious capital, etc.

Symbolic power – any form of power, or fungible resource, that issues from symbolic capital, as defined above; e.g., the power of the Catholic Church to excommunicate believers and the power of a university to grant academic degrees, etc.

Symbolic violence – generally covert or unrecognized (misrecognized) aspects of a struggle of the power to impose or inculcate into people the acceptance of a particular worldview or of the social order as natural and/ or legitimate; usually generated by dominant social sectors with the unwitting complicity of the dominated.

Bibliography

Selected Texts by Pierre Bourdieu

Bourdieu, Pierre (1958b) *Sociologie de l'Algérie*. Paris: Presses Universitaires de France. Bourdieu's first book is a brief but insightful sociological interpretation of Algerian society in transition, with particular focus upon several ethnic groups in rural milieus. Especially of note is the early influence of Max Weber on Bourdieu's interpretation of Algerian Islam.

——(1971a) 'Genèse et structure du champ religieux', *Revue française de sociologie* 12.2: 295–334. English translation: Bourdieu, Pierre (1991a) 'Genesis and Structure of the Religious Field'. Trans. Jenny B. Burnside, Craig Calhoun and Leah Florence, *Comparative Social Research* 13: 1–44. Arguably Bourdieu's single most important and influential essay on religion, this article first focuses on religious history as it is influenced by the history of the division of labor in society, then maps out the various structures and forces that shape the religious field; i.e., religious capital, religious habitus, struggle, Church, heresiarch. The influences of Marx, Durkheim and Weber are predominant in this essay.

——(1971b) 'Une interprétation de la théorie de la religion selon Max Weber', *Archives européenne de sociologie* 12.1: 3–21. English translation: Bourdieu, Pierre (1987a) 'Legitimation and Structured Interests in Weber's Sociology of Religion'. Trans. Chris Turner, in Scott Lash and Sam Whimster (eds.), *Max Weber, Rationality, and Modernity*. London: Allen and Unwin, 119–36. Bourdieu praises Weber's sociology of religion for its 'healthy materialism' and for its application of economic logic and paradigms to the sociological interpretation of religion. Bourdieu also criticizes Weber's model of charisma for ignoring the social structures that determine the success or lack thereof of prophecy, namely the relationship between the charismatic message and the religious habitus of its recipients.

——(1977) *Outline of a Theory of Practice*. Trans. Richard Nice. Cambridge, UK: Cambridge University Press. One of Bourdieu's most important and influential works, *Outline* uses data from Bourdieu's earlier fieldwork in Algeria to construct and illustrate the key features of Bourdieu's social theory, namely habitus, capital, and practice. Although there is much written in this book about ritual, their situation in a broader category of religion is not a concern of Bourdieu's here.

——and Monique de Saint Martin (1982) 'La sainte famille: L'épiscopat français dans le champ du pouvoir', *Actes de la recherche en sciences sociales* 44/45: 2–53. Bourdieu's most extensive empirical investigation into a religious subject, this long and dense article analyzes the demographic backgrounds and trajectories of the French Catholic bishops, based on extensive statistical data produced by five other fieldworkers.

——(1984) *Distinction: A Social Critique of the Judgment of Taste*. Trans. Richard Nice. London: Routledge and Kegan Paul. First published in French in 1979, and ranked by the International Sociological Association as the sixth most influential social-scientific book of the twentieth century, *Distinction* created an uproar in France for its diligent and detailed argument that culture is no less a site of class struggle than economics, and that cultural tastes are little more than '[r]eproduction strategies' employed consciously or unconsciously by individuals and families to secure or improve their positions of social status.

——(1987b) 'La dissolution du religieux', *Choses dites*. Paris: Éditions de Minuit. Short essay in which Bourdieu outlines the ways in which the religious field is changing in the contemporary world, due mainly, he argues, to the emergence of 'alternative' forms of healing and wellness in the field of 'symbolic manipulation', in which is situatuated the religious field, whose boundaries are thus disappearing.

——(1987c) 'Sociologues de la croyance et croyances de sociologues', *Choses dites*. Paris: Éditions de Minuit. Address delivered before the Association Française de Sociologie Religieuse in which Bourdieu asserts that a genuinely objective sociology of religion is difficult to conceive of and virtually impossible in the case where the sociologist is an adherent of the tradition under study.

——(1990a) *The Logic of Practice*. Trans. Richard Nice. Stanford, CA: Stanford University Press. A theoretical exegisis that uses Bourdieu's data from his fieldwork in Algeria to further develop his theory of practice, whose foundation was laid in *Outline of a Theory of Practice* several years prior; one of Bourdieu's most important books.

——(2000b) *Das religiöse Feld: Texte zur Ökonomie des Heilsgeshehens*. Trans. Andreas Pfeuffer. Konstanz, Germany: Universitätsverlag Konstanz. German translation of Bourdieu's 1971 essays on religion, along with an extensive commentary by the book's German editors and their important interview with Bourdieu focusing on religion.

Selected Texts by Others on Bourdieu and Religion

Bell, Catherine (1992) *Ritual Theory, Ritual Practice*. Oxford and New York: Oxford University Press. Groundbreaking monograph in ritual studies that argues, following Bourdieu, that the study of ritual is limited because it neglects consideration of the broader social and political forces that create distinctions between ritual and non-ritual behavior.

Csordas, Thomas J. (2002) *Body/Mind/Healing*. New York: Palgrave. A selection of essays from Csordas's anthropological work that, oriented by Bourdieu and Merleau-Ponty, develops a sophisticated 'cultural phenomenology' to analyze the bodily dimensions of healing in various religious contexts, like the Catholic Charismatic Renewal and Hopi shamanistic tradition.

Dianteill, Erwan (2004) 'Pierre Bourdieu and the Sociology of Religion: A Central and Peripheral Concern', in David L. Swartz and Vera L. Zolberg (eds.), *After Bourdieu: Influence, Critique, Elaboration*. Dordrecht, The Netherlands: Kluwer Academic Press, 65–85. Introductory essay that discusses the intellectual influences on Bourdieu's thinking on religion and the influence of Max Weber's sociology of religion on Bourdieu's social theory at large.

Dillon, Michele (2001) 'Pierre Bourdieu, Religion, and Cultural Production', *Cultural Studies – Critical Methodologies* 1.4: 411–29. Introductory summary of several of Bourdieu's writings on religion and an insightful demonstration of both the usefulness and limitations of their theoretical content for the analysis of the popular push in the Catholic Church for the ordination of women.

Engler, Steven (2003) 'Modern Times: Religion, Consecration and the State in Bourdieu', *Cultural Studies* 17.3–4: 445–67. A critical discussion of the religious foundations of Bourdieu's understanding of the State, with focus upon the transfer of the key notion of 'consecration' from religion to the modern nation state.

Isambert, François-André (1982) *Le Sens du sacré: Fete et religion populaire*. Paris: Éditions de Minuit. One of the rare texts about religion to be originally published under the 'Sens Commun' series that Bourdieu edited from 1964–1992, Isambert employs Bourdieu's discussion of 'euphemization' in modern Catholicism to explore the contours and contested meanings of 'the sacred', per Durkheim, and its sociological ramifications in popular Catholic feast celebrations.

Maduro, Otto (1982) *Religion and Social Conflicts*. Maryknoll, NY: Orbis. First book-length study to appear that uses Bourdieu centrally in the analysis of a religious topic. Maduro uses Bourdieu's 1971 articles to construct a sociological paradigm for the analysis of the history and structure of the religious field in Latin America. This remains the best model for the Bourdieuian analysis of the relationship between religion and social and political power.

Martin, Joan M. (2000) *More than Chains and Toil: A Christian Work Ethic of Enslaved Women*. Louisville, KY: Westminster John Knox Press. Historical analysis of slave narratives in sociological context, oriented centrally by Bourdieu's notions of habitus and practice, Martin's book is a compelling womanist reconstruction of the Christian work ethic of enslaved women of color in the United States.

Milner, Murray (1994) *Status and Sacredness: A General Theory of Status Relations and an Analysis of Indian Culture*. New York: Oxford University Press. Drawing centrally upon Bourdieu's notion of 'symbolic capital', this book is a well-argued discussion of the relationship between notions of sacredness and social status or caste in India. It is especially insightful in its effort to move beyond some of the drawbacks of both theories of practice and rational choice theory in the study of religion.

Rey, Terry (2004) 'Marketing the Goods of Salvation: Bourdieu on Religion', *Religion* 34.4: 331–43. Essay designed to introduce the basic concepts and dynamics in Bourdieu's social theory for the study of religion, with especial emphasis on his 1971 essays. Demonstrates the applicability of Bourdieu's theory through substantive analyses of key features in Haitian religious history and culture.

Schäfer, Heinrich (2004) *Praxis – Theologie – Religion. Grundlinien einer Theologie- und Religionstheorie im Anschluss an Pierre Bourdieu*. Frankfurt am Main: Verlag Otto Lembeck. Extensive and well-developed model that uses Bourdieu's theory of practice to formulate both a theory of religion and a prescription for understanding 'religious practice and theological production' in our increasingly culturally interconnected world.

Stone, Lora (2001) '"Misrecognition of the Limits": Bourdieu's Religious Capital and Social Transformation', *Journal for Cultural and Religious Theory* 3.1: 1–37. Careful exploration of Bourdieu's notion of 'religious capital' in the context of his larger body of work, in conversation with political process models, which seeks to demonstrate the function of religious capital in the genesis and operations of social movements. As with Dillon (noted above), the substantive example for illustration here is the women's ordination movement in the Catholic Church

Swartz, David (1996) 'Bridging the Study of Culture and Religion: Pierre Bourdieu's Political Economy of Power', *Sociology of Religion* 57.1: 71–85. Important introductory essay that outlines key components of Bourdieu's theory of practice and suggests their utility for the sociology of religion at large, with particular attention paid to the Bouridieuian notion of 'field'.

Tanner, Kathryn (2005) *Economy of Grace*. Minneapolis, MN: Fortress Press. Focusing on the Christian concept of grace and related notions of unconditional giving, Tanner develops a theology of economics as an alternative model of economics to the global capitalistic model that dominates the postmodern world. Like Milner, Tanner seeks to move beyond limitations in both field theory and rational choice theory for understanding the relationship between religion and symbolic and material power.

Urban, Hugh B. (2003) 'Sacred Capital: Pierre Bourdieu and the Study of Religion', *Method and Theory in the Study of Religion* 15: 354–89. A rich discussion of the economic logic of Bourdieu's theory of religion against the author's ethnographic fieldwork among the ecstatic Hindu-Muslim Bāul sect; Urban reveals the great worth of Bourdieuian theory for the study of religion, while also exposing certain limitations, suggesting that the 'other interest' that religion often inspires is counter to the uni-dimensional 'self-interest' that predominates in Bourdieuian theory.

Verter, Bradford (2003) 'Spiritual Capital: Theorizing Religion with Bourdieu against Bourdieu', *Sociological Theory* 21.2: 150–74. An excellently crafted application of Bourdieuian theory of culture to overcome some limitations in Bourdieu's model of the religious field, especially the institutional bias of the notion of 'religious capital'. It advocates as a corrective the notion of 'spiritual capital' (a de-institutionalized form of religious capital that may be the product of the laity) and helpfully places Bourdieuian theory in conversation with rational choice theory of religion.

Works Cited

Achebe, Chinua (1994) *Things Fall Apart*. New York: Anchor Books.

Adhar, Rex (2006) 'The Idea of "Religious Markets"', *International Journal of Law in Context* 2.1: 49–65.

Akinnaso, Festus Niyi (1995) 'Bourdieu and the Diviner. Knowledge and Symbolic Power in Yoruba Divination', in Wendy James (ed.), *The Pursuit of Certainty: Religious and Cultural Formations*. London and New York: Routledge, 234–57.

Anonymous (1979) 'Pierre Bourdieu, *Outline of a Theory of Practice*', book note, *The Journal of Religion* 59.1: 130.

Aron, Raymond (1957) *La tragédie algérienne*. Paris: Plon.

——(1990) *Memoirs*. Trans. George Holoch. New York and London: Holmes and Meier.

Bainbridge, William Sims (2002) 'A Prophet's Reward: Dynamics of Religious Exchange', in Ted G. Jelen (ed.), *Sacred Markets, Sacred Canopies: Essays on Religious Markets and Religious Pluralism*. Lanham, MD: Rowan & Littlefield, 63–89.

Bastian, Jean-Pierre (2006) 'La nouvelle économie religieuse de l'Amérique latine', *Social Compass* 53.1: 65–80.

Bastide, Roger (1960) *Les religions africaines au Brésil: Vers une sociologie des interpénétraions de civilizations*. Paris: Presses Universitaires de France.

Beasley-Murray, Jon (2000) 'Value and Capital in Bourdieu and Marx', in Nicholas Brown and Imre Szeman (eds.), *Pierre Bourdieu: Fieldwork in Culture*. Lanham, MD: Rowman and Littlefield, 100–119.

Bège, Jean-François (2004) *Les Béarnais en politique: Portrait et antecdote*. Pau: Cairn.

Bell, Catherine (1992) *Ritual Theory, Ritual Practice*. Oxford and New York: Oxford University Press.

Bellah, Robert (1967) 'Civil Religion in America', in Donald R. Cutler (ed.), *The Religious Situation*. Boston: Beacon Press, 331–56.

Bellah, Robert N., Richard Madsen, William M. Sullivan, Ann Swidler and Stephen M. Tipton (1985) *Habits of the Heart: Individualism and Commitment in American Life*. Berkeley, CA: University of California Press.

Berger, Peter (1967) *The Sacred Canopy: Elements of a Sociological Theory of Religion*. Garden City, NY: Doubleday.

——(2001) 'Reflections on the Sociology of Religion Today', *Sociology of Religion* 62.4: 443–54.

Berlinerblau, Jacques (1999) 'Ideology, Pierre Bourdieu's doxa, and the Hebrew Bible', *Semeia* 87: 193–214.

——(2001) 'Toward a Sociology of Heresy, Orthodoxy, and *Doxa*', *History of Religions* 40.4: 327–51.

Birnbaum, Maria Chiavola (1993) *Black Madonnas: Feminism, Religion, and Politics in Italy*. Boston: Northeastern University Press.

Boltanski, Luc (2003) 'Usages faibles, usages forts de l'habitus', in Pierre Encrevé and Rose-Marie Lagrave (eds), *Travailler avec Bourdieu*. Paris: Éditions Flammarion, 153–61.

Boschetti, Anna (2005) 'Des deux Marx aux deux Bourdieu: critique d'un mythe malveillant', in Gérard Mauger (ed.), *Rencontres avec Pierre Bourdieu*. Paris: Éditions du Croquant, 121–41.

Bourdieu, Pierre (1953) 'Leibnitii animadversiones in partem generalem principiorem Cartesianorum. Traduite du latin et comentée'. Thèse du 2me cycle pour le diplôme d'études supérieures. Paris: École Normale Supérieure.

——(1958a) 'Tartuffe ou le drame de la foi et de la mauvaise foi', *Revue de la Méditerranée* 4/5 (92/93): 453–58.

——(1958b) *Sociologie de l'Algérie*. Paris: Presses Universitaires de France.

——(1960) Review of *Les religions africaines au Brésil: Vers une sociologie des interpénétrations de civilizations* by Roger Bastide, *L'Homme* 1.1: 114–16.

——(1962) 'Célibat et condition paysanne', *Études rurales* 5–6: 32–136.

——(1963) *Travail et travailleurs en Algérie*. Paris: Mouton.

——(1967) 'Postface', in Erwin Panofsky, *Architecture gothique et pensée scholastique*. Trans. Pierre Bourdieu. Paris: Éditions de Minuit, 135–67.

——(1971a) 'Genèse et structure du champ religieux', *Revue française de sociologie* 12.2: 295–334.

——(1971b) 'Une interprétation de la théorie de la religion selon Max Weber', *Archives européenne de sociologie* 12.1: 3–21.

——(1977) *Outline of a Theory of Practice*. Trans. Richard Nice. Cambridge, UK: Cambridge University Press.

——(1979) *Algeria 1960*. Trans. Richard Nice. Cambridge: Cambridge University Press.

——(1980) 'The Production of Belief: Contribution to an Economy of Symbolic Goods'. Trans. Richard Nice, in Richard Collins (ed.), *Media, Culture, and Society: A Critical Reader*. London: Sage Publications, 261–93.

——(1982) *Leçon sur la leçon*. Paris: Éditions de Minuit.

——(1984) *Distinction: A Social Critique of the Judgment of Taste*. Trans. Richard Nice. London: Routledge and Kegan Paul.

——(1985a) 'The Market of Symbolic Goods'. Trans. Rupert Swyer, *Poetics* 14: 13–44.

——(1985b) 'The Social Space and the Genesis of Groups'. Trans. Richard Nice, *Theory and Society* 14.6: 723–44.

——(1986a) 'L'Illusion bibliographique', *Actes de la Recherche en Sciences Sociales* 62/63: 69–72.

——(1986b) 'The Forms of Capital'. Trans. Richard Nice, in John Richardson (ed.), *Handbook of Theory and Research for the Sociology of Education*. New York: Greenwood Press, 241–58.

——(1987a) 'Legitimation and Structured Interests in Weber's Sociology of Religion'. Trans. Chris Turner, in Scott Lash and Sam Whimster (eds.), *Max Weber, Rationality, and Modernity*. London: Allen and Unwin, 119–36.

——(1987b) 'La dissolution du religieux', *Choses dites*. Paris: Éditions de Minuit, 117–23.

——(1987c) 'Sociologues de la croyance et croyances de sociologues', *Choses dites*. Paris: Éditions de Minuit, 106–111.

——(1990a) *The Logic of Practice*. Trans. Richard Nice. Stanford, CA: Stanford University Press.

——(1990b) *In Other Words: Essays Towards a Reflexive Sociology*. Trans. Matthew Adamson. Stanford, CA: Stanford University Press.

——(1991a) 'Genesis and Structure of the Religious Field'. Trans. Jenny B. Burnside, Craig Calhoun and Leah Florence, *Comparative Social Research* 13: 1–44.

——(1991b) 'The Peculiar History of Scientific Reason', *Sociological Forum* 6.1: 3–26.

——(1991c) 'Authorized Language: The Social Conditions for the Effectiveness of Ritual Discourse', in Pierre Bourdieu, *Language and Symbolic Power*. Cambridge, MA: Harvard University Press, 107–116.

——(1991d) *Language and Symbolic Power*. Cambridge, MA: Harvard University Press.

——(1992) 'Rites as Acts of Institution'. Trans. Roger Just, in J.G. Peristiany and Julian Pitt-Rivers (eds.), *Honor and Grace in Anthropology*. New York: Cambridge University Press, 79–89.

——(1994a) 'Pieté religieuse et devotion artistique. Fidèles et amateurs d'art à Santa Maria Novella', *Actes de la recherché en sciences sociales* 105: 71–74.

——(1994b) *Sociology in Question*. Trans. Richard Nice. London: Sage Publications.

——(1994c) 'Le corps et le sacré', *Actes de la recherché en sciences sociales* 104: 2.

——(1994d) *Raisons pratiques*. Paris: Éditions du Seuil.

——(1996) *The Rules of Art: Genesis and Structure of the Literary Field*. Trans. Susan Emanuel. London: Polity Press.

——(1998a) *Practical Reason: On the Theory of Action*. Stanford, CA: Stanford University Press.

——(1998b) *Acts of Resistance: Against the Tyranny of the Market*. Trans. Richard Nice. New York: The New Press.

——(2000a) *Pascalian Meditations*. Trans. Richard Nice. Stanford, CA: Stanford University Press.

——(2000b) *Das religiöse Feld: Texte zur Ökonomie des Heilsgeshehens*. Trans. Andreas Pfeuffer. Konstanz, Germany: Universitätsverlag Konstanz.

——(2000c) *The State Nobility: Elite Schools in the Field of Power*. Trans. Lauretta C. Clough. Cambridge, UK: Polity Press.

——(2001) *Masculine Domination*. Trans. Richard Nice. Stanford, CA: Stanford University Press.

——(2002) *Le bal des célibataires: Crise de la société paysanne en Béarn*. Paris: Éditions du Seuil.

——(2003a) *Firing Back: Against the Tyranny of the Market*. Trans. Richard Nice. New York: New Press.

——(2003b) *Images d'Algérie: Une affinité elective*. Paris: Actes du Sud.

——(2004) *Esquisse pour une auto-analyse*. Paris: Raisons d'agir.

Bourdieu, Pierre and Abdelmayek Sayad (1964) *Le déracinement: La crise de l'agriculture traditionelle en Algérie*. Paris: Éditions de Minuit.

Bourdieu, Pierre and Alain Darbel (1969) *L'Amour de l'art. Les musées d'art européens et leur public*. Paris: Éditions de Minuit.

Bourdieu, Pierre and Jean-Claude Passeron (1977) *Reproduction in Education, Society and Culture*. Trans. Richard Nice. London: Sage Publications.

——(1979) *The Inheritors: French Students and their Relation to Culture*. Trans. Richard Nice. Chicago: University of Chicago Press.

Bourdieu, Pierre, Gershom Scholem and Jean Bollack (1980) 'L'Idendité juive', *Actes de la recherché en sciences socials* 35: 63–72.

Bourdieu, Pierre and Monique de Saint Martin (1982) 'La sainte famille: L'épiscopat français dans le champ du pouvoir', *Actes de la recherche en sciences sociales* 44/45: 2–53.

Bourdieu, Pierre and Loïc J.D. Wacquant (1992) *An Invitation to Reflexive Sociology*. Chicago: University of Chicago Press.

Bourdieu, Pierre and Loïc Wacquant (2005) 'The Cunning of Imperialist Reason', in Loïc Wacquant (ed.), *Pierre Bourdieu and Democratic Politics*. Cambridge, UK and Malden, MA: Polity Press, 178–98.

Bourdieu, Pierre et al. (1993) *La misère du monde*. Paris: Éditions du Seuil.

Bourdieu, Pierre et al. (1999) *The Weight of the World: Social Suffering in Contemporary Society*. Trans. Priscilla Parkhurst Ferguson et al. Stanford, CA: Stanford University Press.

Bourdieu, Pierre, with Franz Schultheis and Andreas Pfeuffer (2000) 'Mit Weber gegen Weber', in Pierre Bourdieu, *Das religiöse Feld: Texte zur Ökonomie des Heilsgeshehens*. Trans. Andreas Pfeuffer. Konstanz, Germany: Universitätsverlag Konstanz, 111–29.

Bourdieu, Pierre, with Roman Leick (2001) 'Politik ist entpolitisiert', *Der Spiegel* 29: 120.

Bourdieu, Pierre, with Franz Schultheis and Anna Schosser (2001) 'Sprechende Turbane: Pierre Bourdieu über Islam und kollektive Intellektuelle', *Frankfurter Rundschau*, November 21.

Bronckart, Jean-Paul and Marie-Noëlle Schurmans (2001) 'Pierre Bourdieu – Jean Piaget: Habitus, schemes et construction du psychologie', in Bernard Lahre (ed.), *Le travail sociologique de Pierre Bourdieu*. Paris: La Découverte, 153–75.

Browitt, Jeff (2004) 'Pierre Bourdieu: Homo Sociologicus', in Jeff Browitt and Brian Nelson (eds.), *Practising Theory: Pierre Bourdieu and the Field of Cultural Production*. Cranbury, NJ: University Press of Delaware, 1–12.

Brubaker, Rogers (1993) 'Social Theory as Habitus', in Craig Calhoun, Edward LiPuma and Moishe Postone (eds.), *Bourdieu: Critical Perspectives*. Chicago: University of Chicago Press, 212–34.

——(2004) 'Rethinking Classical Theory: The Sociological Vision of Pierre Bourdieu', in David L. Swartz and Vera L. Zolberg (eds.), *After Bourdieu: Influence, Critique, Elaboration*. Dordrecht, The Netherlands: Kluwer Academic Publishers, 25–64.

Bruce, Steve (1999) *Choice and Religion*. New York: Oxford University Press.

——(2002) 'The Poverty of Economism or the Social Limits of Maximizing', in Ted G. Jelen (ed.), *Sacred Markets, Sacred Canopies*. Lanham, MD: Rowman and Littlefield, 167–85.

Calhoun, Craig (1993) 'Habitus, Field, and Capital: The Question of Historical Specificity', in Craig Calhoun, Edward LiPuma and Moishe Postone (eds.), *Bourdieu: Critical Perspectives*. Chicago: University of Chicago Press, 61–88.

Carles, Pierre (2001) *La sociologie est un sport de combat – Pierre Bourdieu*. Video documentary. Montpellier: C-P Productions.

Castel, Robert (2003) 'Conclusion: Pierre Bourdieu et la dureté du monde', in Pierre Encrevé and Rose-Marie Lagrave (eds.), *Travailler avec Bourdieu*. Paris: Éditions Flammarion, 347–56.

Centre Généalogique des Pyrénées Atlantiques (2006). 'Les Cagots', http://cgpa64.free.fr/cagots/index.htm. Accessed January 22, 2007.

Chesnut, R. Andrew (2003) *Competitive Spirits: Latin America's New Religious Economy*. New York: Oxford University Press.

Coakley, Sarah (2000) 'Introduction: Religion and the Body', in Sarah Coakley (ed.), *Religion and the Body*. New York: Cambridge University Press, 1–14.

Colonna, Fanny (1974) 'Cultural Resistance and Religious Legitimacy in Colonial Algeria', *Economy and Society* 3: 233–52.

Comaroff, Jean (1985) *Body of Power, Spirit of Resistance: The History and Culture of a South African People*. Chicago: University of Chicago Press.

Crossley, Nick (2001) *The Social Body: Habit, Identity and Desire*. London and Thousand Oaks, CA: Sage Publications.

Csordas, Thomas J. (1994) *The Sacred Self: A Cultural Phenomenology of Charismatic Healing*. Berkeley, CA, Los Angeles, and London: University of California Press.

——(2001) *Language, Charisma, and Creativity: Ritual Life in the Catholic Charismatic Renewal*. New York: Palgrave.

——(2002) *Body/Mind/Healing*. New York: Palgrave.

Dawson, Andrew (2006) 'East is East, Except When It's West: The Easternization Thesis and the Western Habitus', *Journal of Religion and Society* 8: 1–13.

de Certeau, Michel (1984) *The Practice of Everyday Life*. Trans. Steven Rendall. Berkeley, CA: University of California Press.

de Saint Martin, Monique (2003) 'Une inflexible domination?', in Pierre Encrevé and Rose-Marie Lagrave (eds.), *Travailler avec Bourdieu*. Paris: Éditions Flammarion, 323–31.

Delteil, Gérard (1986) 'Les actes pastoraux: Vestiges d'une chrétieneté our diaconie du sens?' *Études théologiques et religieuses* 61.1: 83–89.

Devisch, Renaat and Bart Vervaeck (1985) 'Auto-production, production, et reproduction. Divination et politique chez les yaka du Zaire', *Social Compass* 32.1: 111–31.

Dianteill, Erwan (2004) 'Pierre Bourdieu and the Sociology of Religion: A Central and Peripheral Concern', in David L. Swartz and Vera L. Zolberg (eds.), *After Bourdieu: Influence, Critique, Elaboration*. Dordrecht, The Netherlands: Kluwer Academic Press, 65–85.

Dillon, Michele (2001) 'Pierre Bourdieu, Religion, and Cultural Production', *Cultural Studies – Critical Methodologies* 1.4: 411–29.

DiMaggio, Paul (1979) 'Review Essay: On Pierre Bourdieu', *American Journal of Sociology* 84.6: 1460–1474.

Dobbelaere, Karel (1987) 'Some Trends in European Sociology of Religion: The Secularization Debate', *Sociological Analysis* 48.2: 107–137.

Dubuisson, Daniel (2003) *The Western Construction of Religion: Myths, Knowledge, and Ideology*. Trans. William Sayers. Baltimore, MD: The Johns Hopkins University Press.

Durkheim, Emile (1915) *The Elementary Forms of the Religious Life*. Trans. Joseph Ward Swain. New York: The Free Press.

——(1982) *The Rules of Sociological Method*. Trans. W.D. Halls. New York: The Free Press.

Ebertz, Michael N. and Franz Schultheis (1986a) 'Populare Religiosität in der modernen Gesellschaft. Kontinuität, Pluralität, Visibilität', *Österreichische Zeitschrift für Soziologie* 3: 62–79.

——(1986b) 'Populare Religiosität', in Michael N. Ebertz and Franz Schultheis (eds), *Volksfrömmigkeit in Europa. Beiträge zur Soziologie popularer Religiosität aus 14 Ländern*, Munich: Kaiser Verlag, 11–52.

el-Aswad, el-Sayed (2002) *Religion and Folk Cosmology: Scenarios of the Visible and the Invisible in Rural Egypt*. Westport, CT and London: Praeger.

Engler, Steven (2003) 'Modern Times: Religion, Consecration and the State in Bourdieu', *Cultural Studies* 17.3–4: 445–67.

Ernaux, Annie, with Isabelle Charpentier (2005) 'La literature est une arme de combat', in Gérard Mauger (ed.), *Rencontres avec Pierre Bourdieu*. Paris: Éditions du Croquant, 159–75.

Foster, Stephen W. (1986) 'Reading Pierre Bourdieu', *Cultural Anthropology* 1.1: 103–110.

Fowler, Bridget (1997) *Pierre Bourdieu and Cultural Theory*. London: Sage Publications.

——(2000) 'Introduction', in Bridget Fowler (ed.), *Reading Bourdieu on Society and Culture*. Oxford: Blackwell, 1–22.

——(2004) 'Mapping the Obituary: Notes for a Bourdieusian Interpretation', *Sociological Review Monograph Series*. Oxford: Blackwell, 148–71.

Friedland, Roger (1999) 'When God Walks in History: The Institutional Politics of Religious Nationalism', *International Sociology* 14.3: 301–319.

Friedmann, Daniel (1979) 'Le champ actuel de guerisseurs: Propriétés sociales: Production du 'don' capitale thérapeutiqe illigetime'. Thèse du 3ème cycle, Université de Paris V.

Fritsch, Phillippe (2005) 'Contre le toténisme intellectuel', in Gérard Mauger (ed.), *Rencontres avec Pierre Bourdieu*. Paris: Éditions du Croquant, 81–100.

Garnham, Nicholas and Raymond Williams (1980) 'Pierre Bourdieu and the Sociology of Culture: An Introduction', *The Sociological Review* 34.2: 423–33.

Gebara, Ivone and Clara María Bingemer (1989) *Mary: Mother of God, Mother of the Poor*. Trans Phillip Berryman. Maryknoll, NY: Orbis.

Goity, Bernard (n.d.) 'Apercus sur l'histoire du Diocèse de Bayonne', http://www.diocese-bayonne.com/2_histoire/goity/histoirediocese_goity.html. Accessed November 4, 2006.

Green, Nancy L. (2004) 'Réflexions d'une outsider', in Pierre Encravé and Rose Marie Lagrave (eds.), *Travailler avec Bourdieu*. Paris: Éditions Flammarion, 175–81.

Grenfell, Michael (2004) *Pierre Bourdieu: Agent Provocateur*. London and New York: Continuum.

Grignon, Claude (1977) 'Sur les relations entre les transformations du champ religieux et les transformations de l'espace politique', *Actes de la recherche en sciences sociales* 16: 3–34.

Guillroy, John (1993) *Cultural Capital: The Problem of Literary Canon Formation*. Chicago: University of Chicago Press.

Haacke, Hans (2005) 'Pierre Bourdieu au service du public', in Gérard Mauger (ed.), *Rencontres avec Pierre Bourdieu*. Paris: Éditions du Croquant, 185–87.

Hervieu-Léger, Danièle (2000) *Religion as a Chain of Memory*. Trans. Simon Lee. New Brunswick, NJ: Rutgers University Press.

Iannoccone, Laurence R. (1992) 'Religious Markets and the Economics of Religion', *Social Compass* 39.1: 123–31.

Isambert, François-André (1982) *Le Sens du sacré: Fête et religion populaire*. Paris: Éditions de Minuit.

Jelen, Ted G. (2002) 'Preface', in Ted G. Jelen (ed.), *Sacred Markets, Sacred Canopies: Essays on Religious Markets and Religious Pluralism*. Lanham, MD: Rowan & Littlefield, vii–viii.

Jenkins, Richard (1982) 'Pierre Bourdieu and the Reproduction of Determinism', *Sociology* 23.4: 639–45.

——(1992) *Pierre Bourdieu*. London: Routledge.

Kennedy, William B. (1984) 'Education for a Just and Peaceful World', *Religious Education* 79: 550–57.

Krais, Beatte (1993) 'Gendered and Symbolic Violence: Female Oppression in the Light of Bourdieu's Theory of Social Practice', in Craig Calhoun, Edward LiPuma and Moishe Postone (eds.), *Bourdieu: Critical Perspectives*. Chicago: University of Chicago Press, 156–77.

Kühle, Lene (2002) 'Globalisation and Bourdieu and New Religions', conference paper, New Religions and Globalization: Theoretical and Methodological Perspectives, Research Network on New Religions, Ebeltoft, Denmark, September 26.

——(2004) 'Bourdieu, Religion and Integration', conference paper, Nordic Migration Conference, Aalborg University, November 11.

Lafaye, Jacques (1976) *Quetzacóatl and Guadalupe: The Formation of Mexican National Consciousness, 1531–1813*. Chicago: University of Chicago Press.

Lahire, Bernard (2001a) 'Présentation: Pour une sociologie à l'état vif', in Bernard Lahre (ed.), *Le travail sociologique de Pierre Bourdieu: Dettes et critiques*. Paris: La Découverte, 5–20.

——(2001b) 'Champ, hors-champs, contrechamp', in Bernard Lahre (ed.), *Le travail sociologique de Pierre Bourdieu: Dettes et critiques*. Paris: La Découverte, 23–57.

——(2005) 'Prolongements. Les traditions scientifiques comme conditions de toute innovation', in Gérard Mauger (ed.), *Rencontres avec Pierre Bourdieu*. Paris: Éditions du Croquant, 291–304.

Lallot, Jean (2005) 'Pablo', in Gérard Mauger (ed.), *Rencontres avec Pierre Bourdieu*. Paris: Éditions du Croquant, 25–30.

Lambert, Yves (1982) 'Limerzel, catholicisme et société en Bretagne 1900–1982'. Thèse du 3ème cycle, Université de Paris V.

Lanzmann, Claude and Robert Redeker (1998) 'Les méfaits d'un rationalisme simplificateur', *Le Monde*, September 18.

Lash, Scott (1993) 'Pierre Bourdieu: Cultural Economy and Social Change', in Craig Calhoun, Edward LiPuma and Moishe Postone (eds.), *Bourdieu: Critical Perspectives*. Chicago: University of Chicago Press, 193–211.

Lash, Scott and Sam Whister (1987) 'Introduction', in Scott Lash and Sam Whister (eds.), *Max Weber, Rationality and Modernity*. London: Allen and Unwin, 1–31.

Lechte, John (2004) 'The Beauty of Bourdieu', in Jeff Browitt and Brian Nelson (eds.), *Practising Theory: Pierre Bourdieu and the Field of Cultural Production*. Cranbury, NJ: University Press of Delaware, 65–73.

Lee, Alison (2005) 'When is a Text?' *Proceedings of the International Conference on Critical Discourse Analysis: Theory into Research*, 350–59.

Lelong, R.P. (1972) *Le dossier noir de la communion solonelle*. Paris: Mame.

Lévi-Strauss, Claude (1973) *Tristes tropiques*. Trans. John and Doreen Weightman. New York: Atheneum.

Liénard, G. and André Rousseau (1972) 'Conflit symbolique et conflit social dans le champ religieux. Propositions théorique et analyse d'un conflit suscité par l'Action Catholique Ouvriére dans le nord de la France', *Social Compass* 19.2: 263–90.

Lizardo, Omar (2004) 'The Cognitive Origins of Bourdieu's *Habitus*', *Journal for the Theory of Social Behavior* 34.4: 375–401.

Lovejoy, Paul E. (1997) 'The African Diaspora: Revisionist Interpretations of Ethnicity, Culture and Religion under Slavery', *Studies in the World history of Slavery, Abolition and Emancipation* 2.1: 1–21.

MacAskill, Ewen (2005) 'George Bush: "God told me to end the tyranny in Iraq"', *The Guardian*, October 7, http://www.guardian.co.uk/international/story/0,1586883,00.html, accessed May 20, 2007.

Maduro, Otto (1977) 'New Marxist Approaches to the Relative Autonomy of Religion', *Sociological Analysis* 38.4: 359–67.

——(1982) *Religion and Social Conflicts*. Maryknoll, NY: Orbis.

Mahar, Cheleen (1990) 'Pierre Bourdieu: The Intellectual Project', in Richard Harkes, Cheleen Mahar and Chris Wilkes (eds.), *An Introduction to the Work of Pierre Bourdieu: The Practice of Theory*. London: Macmillan, 26–57.

Mahar, Cheleen, Richard Harker and Chris Wilkes (1990) 'The Basic Theoretical Position', in Richard Harkes, Cheleen Mahar and Chris Wilkes (eds.), *An Introduction to the Work of Pierre Bourdieu: The Practice of Theory*. London: Macmillan, 1–25.

Mairie de Denguin (n.d.) 'Cite officiel de la Mairie de Denguin commune de Miey de Béarn', http://www.denguin.fr. Accessed January 22, 2007.

Martin, Joan M. (2000) *More than Chains and Toil: A Christian Work Ethic of Enslaved Women*. Louisville, KY: Westminster John Knox Press.

Marx, Karl and Friedrich Engels (1956) *The Holy Family, or Critique of Critical Critique*. Trans. Richard Dixon. Pyonyang, North Korea: Foreign Languages Publishing House.

——(1964) *On Religion*. Atlanta, GA: Scholars Press.

——(1976) *The German Ideology*. Trans. S.W. Ryazanskaya Moscow: Progress Publishers.

——(2002) *The Communist Manifesto*. Trans. Samuel Moore. London and New York: Penguin.

Mauger, Gérard (2005) 'Résistance à la sociologie de Pierre Bourdieu', in Louis Pinto, Gisèle Sapiro and Patrick Champagne (eds.), *Pierre Bourdieu, sociologue*. Paris: Fayard, 369–91.

Mauss, Marcel (1967) *The Gift: Forms and Functions of Exchange in Archaic Societies*. Trans. Ian Cunnison. New York: Norton.

McGuire, Meredith B. (1990) 'Religion and the Body: Rematerializing the Human Body in the Social Sciences of Religion', *Journal for the Scientific Study of Religion* 29.3: 283–96.

——(1995) Review of *The Sacred Self*, by Thomas J. Csordas, *Sociology of Religion* 56.3: 341–42.

McKinnon, Andrew M. (2006) 'Ritual Re-Description as Passport Control: A Rejoinder to Fitzgerald after Bourdieu', *Method and Theory in the Study of Religion* 18.2: 179–88.

Mennesson-Rigaud, Odette (1958). 'Le rôle du vaudou dans l'indépendance d'Haïti', *Présence africaine* 17–18: 43–67.

Merleau-Ponty, Maurice (1955) *Les aventures de la dialectique*. Paris: Gallimard.

——(1962) *Phenomenology of Perception*. Trans. Colin Smith. London: Routledge & Kegan Paul.

Milner, Murray (1994) *Status and Sacredness: A General Theory of Status Relations and an Analysis of Indian Culture*. New York: Oxford University Press.

Monod, Jean-Claude (2002) 'Une politique du symbolique?', in Bernard Lahire (ed.), *Le travail sociologique de Pierre Bourdieu: Dettes et critiques*. Paris: La Découverte, 231–54.

Morgan, David (2005) *The Sacred Gaze: Religious Visual Culture in Theory and Practice*. Berkeley and Los Angeles, CA: University of California Press.

Mother Theresa (1997) *The Joy in Loving: A Guide to Daily Living*. Hamondsworth: Penguin Books.

Nice, Richard (1977) 'Translator's foreword', in Pierre Bourdieu, *Outline of a Theory of Practice*. Cambridge, UK: Cambridge University Press, vii–viii.

Noble, Greg and Megan Watkins (2003) 'So, How Did Bourdieu Learn to Play Tennis? Habitus, Consciousness and Habituation', *Cultural Studies* 17.3: 520–38.

Orwell, George (1950) *Shooting an Elephant*. New York: Harcourt, Brace & Co.

Panofksy, Erwin (1957) *Gothic Architecture and Scholasticism: An Inquiry into the Arts, Philosophy, and Religion in the Middle Ages*. New York: Meridian.

——(1967) *Architecture gothique et pensée scholastique*. Trans. Pierre Bourdieu. Paris: Éditions de Minuit.

Parker, Cristián (1996) *Popular Religion and Modernization in Latin America*. Trans. Robert R. Barr. Maryknoll, NY: Orbis Books.

Parsons, Talcott (1963) 'Introduction', in Max Weber, *The Sociology of Religion*. Boston: Beacon Press, xix–lxvii.

Pascal, Blaise (1995) *Pensées*. Trans. A.J. Krailsheimer. New York: Penguin Classics.

Passeron, Jean-Claude (2003) 'Mort d'un ami, disparition d'un penseur', in Pierre Encrevé and Rose-Marie Lagrave (eds.), *Travailler avec Bourdieu*. Paris: Éditions Flammarion, 17–90.

Portes, Alejandro and Patricia Landolt (2000) 'Social Capital: Promises and Pitfalls of its Role in Development', *Journal of Latin American Studies* 32: 529–47.

Postone, Moishe, Edward LiPuma and Craig Calhoun (1993) 'Introduction: Pierre Bourdieu and Social Theory', in Craig Calhoun, Edward LiPuma and Moishe Postone (eds.), *Bourdieu: Critical Perspectives*. Chicago: University of Chicago Press, 1–13.

Prakash, Gyan (1986) 'Reproducing Inequality: Spirit Cults and Labor Relations in Colonial Eastern India', *Modern Asian Studies* 20.2: 209–230.

Reed-Danahay, Deborah (2005) *Locating Bourdieu*. Bloomington, IN: Indiana University Press.

Remy, Jean (1972) 'Opinion publique, groupes de pression et autorité constituée dans la vie de l'Eglise catholique. Contribution à une théorie de la légitimité religieuse', *Social Compass* 19.2: 155–84.

Rey, Terry (1996) 'Classes of Mary in the Haitian Religious Field: A Theoretical Analysis of the Effects of Socio-Economic Class on the Perception and Uses of a Religious Symbol', PhD dissertation, Temple University.

——(1998) 'The Virgin Mary and Revolution in Saint-Domingue: The Charisma of Romaine-la-Prophétesse', *Journal of Historical Sociology* 11.3: 341–69.

——(1999) *Our Lady of Class Struggle: The Cult of the Virgin Mary in Haiti*. Trenton, NJ and Asmara, Ethiopia: Africa World Press.

——(2004) 'Marketing the Goods of Salvation: Bourdieu on Religion', *Religion* 34.4: 331–43.

——(2005) 'Habitus et Hybridité: Une interprétation du syncrétisme dans la religion afro-catholique d'après Bourdieu', *Social Compass* 52.4: 453–62.

Ricouer, Paul (1970) *Freud and Philosophy: An Essay on Interpretation*. New Haven, CT: Yale University Press.

Riding, Alan (2002) 'Pierre Bourdieu, 71, French Thinker and Social Critic', *The New York Times*, January 25.

Robbins, Derek (1991) *The Work of Pierre Bourdieu*. Boulder, CO: Westview Press.

Robertson, Roland (1992) 'The Economization of Religion? Reflections on the Promise and Limitations of the Economic Approach', *Social Compass* 39.1: 147–57.

Roof, Wade Clark (1993) *A Generation of Seekers: The Spiritual Journeys of the Baby Boom Generation*. San Francisco, CA: Harper San Francisco.

——(1999) *Spiritual Marketplace: Baby Boomers and the Remaking of America Religion*. Princeton, NJ: Princeton University Press.

Sapiro, Gisèle (2004) 'Une liberté contrainte: La formation de la théorie de l'habitus', in Louis Pinto, Gisèle Sapiro and Patrick Champagne (eds.), *Pierre Bourdieu, sociologue*. Paris: Fayard, 49–78.

Sartre, Jean-Paul (1984) *Being and Nothingness*. Trans. Hazel E. Barnes. New York: Washington Square Press.

Schäfer, Heinrich (2004) *Praxis – Theologie – Religion: Grundlinien einer Theologie- und Religionstheorie im Anschluss an Pierre Bourdieu*. Frankfurt am Main: Verlag Otto Lembeck.

Schultheis, Franz (forthcoming) 'Salvation Goods and Domination: Pierre Bourdieu's Sociology of the Religious Field', in Jörg Stoltz (ed.), *Salvation Goods and Religious Markets: Theory and Applications*. Bern: Peter Lang.

Schusterman, Richard (2005) 'Pierre Bourdieu: raison et passion', in Gérard Mauger (ed.), *Rencontres avec Pierre Bourdieu*. Paris: Éditions du Croquant, 477–81.

Scott, James. C. (1990) *Domination and the Arts of Resistance: Hidden Transcripts*. New Haven, CT: Yale University Press.

Silverman, David (2005) *Faith and Boundaries: Colonists, Christianity, and Community among the Wampanoag Indians of Martha's Vineyard, 1600–1871*. New York: Cambridge University Press.

Smith, Ted A. (2004) 'Redeeming Critique: Resignations to the Cultural Turn in Christian Theology', *Journal of the Society of Christian Ethics* 24.2: 89–113.

Stoltz, Jörg (2006a) 'Introduction', *Social Compass* 53.1: 5–11.

——(ed.) (2006b) 'Salvation Goods and Religious Markets: Integrating Rational Choice and Weberian Perspectives', *Social Compass* 53.1: 13–32.

Stone, Lora (2001) ''Misrecognition of the Limits': Bourdieu's Religious Capital and Social Transformation', *Journal for Cultural and Religious Theory* 3.1: 1–37.

Svendsen, Gunnar, Lind Haase and Gert Tingaard Svendsen (2003) 'On the Wealth of Nations: Bourdieuconomics and Social Capital', *Theory and Society* 32.5/6: 607–631.

Swartz, David (1996) 'Bridging the Study of Culture and Religion: Pierre Bourdieu's Political Economy of Power', *Sociology of Religion* 57.1: 71–85.

——(1997) *Culture and Power: The Sociology of Pierre Bourdieu*. Chicago and London: University of Chicago Press.

——(2004) 'From Critical Sociology to Public Intellectual: Pierre Bourdieu and Politics', in David L. Swartz and Vera L. Zolberg (eds.), *After Bourdieu: Influence, Critique, Elaboration*. Dordrecht, The Netherlands: Kluwer Academic Press, 333–64.

Swartz, David and Vera L. Zolberg (2004) 'Introduction: Drawing Inspiration from Bourdieu', in David L. Swartz and Vera L. Zolberg (eds), *After Bourdieu: Influence, Critique, Elaboration*. Dordrecht, The Netherlands: Kluwer Academic Press, 1–13.

Sweet, James H. (1996) 'Male Homosexuality and Spiritism in the African Diaspora: The Legacies of a Link', *Journal of the History of Sexuality* 7.21: 184–202.

——(2005) 'The Idea of Race: Its Changing Meanings and Constructions', in James H. Sweet (ed.), *The Idea of Race: Its Changing Meanings and Constructions*. Ann Arbor, MI: Pro Quest.

Tanner, Kathryn (2005) *Economy of Grace*. Minneapolis, MN: Fortress Press.

—— (2006–2007) 'Grace and Global Capitalism', *Criterion* 45.2: 14–23, 29.

Terray, Emmanuel (2003) 'Propos sur la violence symbolique', in Pierre Encrevé and Rose-Marie Lagrave (eds.), *Travailler avec Bourdieu*. Paris: Éditions Flammarion, 299–304.

Thomas, Linda E. (1998) 'Womanist Theology, Epistemology, and a New Anthropological Paradigm', *Cross Currents* 48: 4.

Thompson, John B. (1991) 'Editor's Introduction', in Pierre Bourdieu, *Language and Symbolic Power*. Cambridge, MA: Harvard University Press, 1–31.

Thornton, John K. (1993) '"I am the Subject of the King of Congo": African Political Ideology and the Haitian Revolution', *Journal of World History* 3: 181–214.

——(1997) *The Kongolese Saint Anthony: Dona Beatriz Kimpa Vita and the Antonian Movement, 1684–1706*. New York: Cambridge University Press.

Turner, Stephen (1994) *The Social Theory of Practices: Tradition, Tacit Knowledge, and Presuppositions*. Chicago: University of Chicago Press.

Urban, Hugh B. (2003) 'Sacred Capital: Pierre Bourdieu and the Study of Religion', *Method and Theory in the Study of Religion* 15: 354–89.

——(2005) 'Spiritual Capital, Academic Capital and the Politics of Scholarship: A Response to Bradford Verter', *Method and Theory in Religion* 17.2: 166–75.

Van Campenhoudt, Luc (2005) 'Professeur de sociologie "catho"', in Gérard Mauger (ed.), *Rencontres avec Pierre Bourdieu*. Paris: Éditions du Croquant, 403–18.

Verdès-Leroux, Jeannine (2001) *Deconstructing Pierre Bourdieu: Against Sociological Terrorism from the Left*. New York: Algora Publishing.

Verter, Bradford (2003) 'Spiritual Capital: Theorizing Religion with Bourdieu against Bourdieu', *Sociological Theory* 21.2: 150–74.

——(2004) 'Bourdieu and the Bāuls Reconsidered', *Method and Theory in the Study of Religion* 16.2: 182–92.

Victoria, Brian (1998) *Zen at War*. New York: Weatherhill Press.

Vidal-Naquet, Pierre (2003) 'Souvenirs à bâtons rompus', in Pierre Encrevé and Rose-Marie Lagrave (eds.), *Travailler avec Bourdieu*. Paris: Éditions Flammarion, 91–96.

Ville, Gérard (2005) 'L'Excellence s'enseigne-t-elle?', in Gérard Mauger (ed.), *Rencontres avec Pierre Bourdieu*. Paris: Éditions du Croquant, 31–34.

Vincent, Gilbert (1985) 'Le sujet de la croyance langage, croyance et institution', *Revue d'histoire et de philosophie religieuses* 65.3: 271–95.

Wacquant, Loïc J.D. (1989) 'Towards a Reflexive Sociology: A Workshop with Pierre Bourdieu', *Sociological Theory* 7.1: 26–63.

——(1992) 'Toward a Social Praxeology: The Structure and Logic of Bourdieu's Sociology', in Pierre Bourdieu and Loïc J.D. Wacquant, *An Invitation to Reflexive Sociology*. Chicago: University of Chicago Press, 1–59.

——(1993) 'Bourdieu in America: Notes on the Transatlantic Importation of Social Theory', in Craig Calhoun, Edward LiPuma and Moishe Postone (eds.), *Bourdieu: Critical Perspectives*. Chicago: University of Chicago Press, 235–62.

——(2005a) 'Introduction: Symbolic Power and Democratic Practice', in Loïc Wacquant (ed.), *Pierre Bourdieu and Democratic Politics*. Cambridge, UK and Malden, MA: Polity Press, 1–9.

——(2005b) 'Pointers on Pierre Bourdieu and Democratic Politics', in Loïc Wacquant (ed.), *Pierre Bourdieu and Democratic Politics*. Cambridge, UK and Malden, MA: Polity Press, 10–28.

Warde, Alan (2004) 'Practice and Field: Revising Bourdieusian Concepts', CRIC Discussion Paper No. 65, Center for Research on Innovation and Competition, University of Manchester.

Warner, R. Stephen (1993) 'Work in Progress Toward a New Paradigm for the Sociological Study of Religion in the United States', *American Journal of Sociology* 98.5: 1044–1093.

——(2002) 'More Progress on the New Paradigm', in Ted G. Jelen (ed.), *Sacred Markets, Sacred Canopies: Essays on Religious Markets and Religious Pluralism*. Lanham, MD: Rowan & Littlefield, 1–29.

Weber, Max (1946) 'Science as a Vocation', in H.H. Gerth and C. Wright Mills (eds. and trans.), *From Max Weber: Essays in Sociology*. New York: Oxford University Press, 129–56.

—— (1963) *The Sociology of Religion*. Trans. Talcott Parsons. Boston: Beacon Press.

——(1976) *The Protestant Ethic and the Spirit of Capitalism*. Trans. Talcott Parsons. New York: Scribner's.

——(1978) *Economy and Society*. Ed. Guenther Roth and Claus Wittich. 2 vols. Berkeley and Los Angeles: University of California Press.

Weiler, Antonius Geradus (1983) 'Theories about the Causes of Religious Indifference', in Jean-Pierre Jossua and Claude Geffré (eds.), *Indifference to Religion*. Edinburgh: T. & T. Clark; New York: The Seabury Press (Concilium).

Woolf, Virginia (1966) *Three Guineas*. San Diego, New York, and London: Harcourt Brace.

Worsley, Peter (1957) *The Trumpet Shall Sound: A Study of 'Cargo' Cults in Melanesia*. London: MacGibbon and Kee.

Wuthnow, Robert (1998) *After Heaven: Spirituality in America since the 1950s*. Berkeley, CA: University of California Press.

Yadgar, Yaacov (2003) 'SHAS as a Struggle to Create a New Field: A Bourdieuan Perspective of an Israeli Phenomenon', *Sociology of Religion* 64.2: 223–46.

Yasine, Tassadit (2003) 'L'Algérie: Matrice d'un œuvre', in Pierre Encrevé and Rose-Marie Lagrave (eds.), *Travailler avec Bourdieu*. Paris: Éditions Flammarion, 333–45.

Index

Printed in the United Kingdom
by Lightning Source UK Ltd.
124538UK00002B/259-270/A

types of violence:

1. horozontal
2. vertical or structural
3. symbolic
   (disguising & euphemizing
   #1 & #2)

who are the "masters of euphamizing"?

- teachers
- preachers
- psychologists
- judges

The Bible became the Bible not when
it was written but when it was read and
heard in public worship — The way
to study the Bible is thro'
performance theory.